The War of 1812

The War of 1812

DAVID S. HEIDLER AND JEANNE T. HEIDLER

Greenwood Guides to Historic Events, 1500–1900
Linda S. Frey and Marsha L. Frey, Series Editors

GREENWOOD PRESS
Westport, Connecticut • London

Library of Congress Cataloging-in-Publication Data

Heidler, David Stephen, 1955–
    The War of 1812 / David S. Heidler and Jeanne T. Heidler.
        p.   cm.—(Greenwood guides to historic events, 1500–1900, ISSN 1538–442X)
    Includes bibliographical references and index.
    ISBN 0–313–31687–2 (alk. paper)
        1. United States—History—War of 1812.   I. Heidler, Jeanne T.   II. Title.
    III. Series.
E354.H47   2002
973.5′2—dc21   2001050102

British Library Cataloguing in Publication Data is available.

Library of Congress Catalog Card Number: 2001050102
ISBN: 0–313–31687–2
ISSN: 1538–442X

First published in 2002

Greenwood Press, 88 Post Road West, Westport, CT 06881
An imprint of Greenwood Publishing Group, Inc.
www.greenwood.com

Printed in the United States of America

The paper used in this book complies with the
Permanent Paper Standard issued by the National
Information Standards Organization (Z39.48–1984).

10 9 8 7 6 5 4 3 2 1

CONTENTS

Photo essay follows page 138.

SERIES FOREWORD

American statesman Adlai Stevenson stated that "We can chart our future clearly and wisely only when we know the path which has led to the present." This series, Greenwood Guides to Historic Events, 1500–1900, is designed to illuminate that path by focusing on events from 1500 to 1900 that have shaped the world. The years 1500 to 1900 include what historians call the Early Modern Period (1500 to 1789, the onset of the French Revolution) and part of the modern period (1789 to 1900).

In 1500, an acceleration of key trends marked the beginnings of an interdependent world and the posing of seminal questions that changed the nature and terms of intellectual debate. The series closes with 1900, the inauguration of the twentieth century. This period witnessed profound economic, social, political, cultural, religious, and military changes. An industrial and technological revolution transformed the modes of production, marked the transition from a rural to an urban economy, and ultimately raised the standard of living. Social classes and distinctions shifted. The emergence of the territorial and later the national state altered man's relations with and view of political authority. The shattering of the religious unity of the Roman Catholic world in Europe marked the rise of a new pluralism. Military revolutions changed the nature of warfare. The books in this series emphasize the complexity and diversity of the human tapestry and include political, economic, social, intellectual, military, and cultural topics. Some of the authors focus on events in U.S. history such as the Salem Witchcraft Trials, the American Revolution, the abolitionist movement, and the Civil War. Others analyze European topics, such as the Reformation and Counter Reformation and the French Revolution. Still others bridge cultures and continents by examining the voyages of discovery, the Atlantic slave trade, and the Age of Imperialism. Some focus on intellectual questions that have shaped the modern world, such as Darwin's *Origin of Species* or on turning points such as the Age of Romanticism. Others examine defining economic, religious, or legal events or issues such as the building of the railroads, the Second Great Awakening, and abolitionism. Heroes (e.g., Lewis and Clark), scientists (e.g., Darwin), military leaders (e.g., Napoleon), poets (e.g., Byron), stride across its pages. Many of these events were seminal in that they marked profound changes or turning points. The Scientific Revolution, for example, changed the way individuals viewed themselves and their world.

The authors, acknowledged experts in their fields, synthesize key events, set developments within the larger historical context, and, most important, present a well-balanced, well-written account that integrates the most recent scholarship in the field.

The topics were chosen by an advisory board composed of historians, high school history teachers, and school librarians to support the curriculum and meet student research needs. The volumes are designed to serve as resources for student research and to provide clearly written interpretations of topics central to the secondary school and lower-level undergraduate history curriculum. Each author outlines a basic chronology to guide the reader through often confusing events and a historical overview to set those events within a narrative framework. Three to five topical chapters underscore critical aspects of the event. In the final chapter the author examines the impact and consequences of the event. Biographical sketches furnish background on the lives and contributions of the players who strut across this stage. Ten to fifteen primary documents ranging from letters to diary entries, song lyrics, proclamations, and posters, cast light on the event, provide material for student essays, and stimulate a critical engagement with the sources. Introductions identify the authors of the documents and the main issues. In some cases a glossary of selected terms is provided as a guide to the reader. Each work contains an annotated bibliography of recommended books, articles, CD-ROMs, Internet sites, videos, and films that set the materials within the historical debate.

These works will lead to a more sophisticated understanding of the events and debates that have shaped the modern world and will stimulate a more active engagement with the issues that still affect us. It has been a particularly enriching experience to work closely with such dedicated professionals. We have come to know and value even more highly the authors in this series and our editors at Greenwood, particularly Barbara Rader and Kevin Ohe. In many cases they have become more than colleagues; they have become friends. To them and to future historians we dedicate this series.

Linda S. Frey
University of Montana

Marsha L. Frey
Kansas State University

PREFACE

During the nineteenth century, the United States fought four wars. Students will readily recall the Civil War (1861–1865), but they may be less familiar with the Mexican American War (1846–1848) and even less likely to know about the Spanish American War (1898). The first American war of the nineteenth century, the War of 1812, is most shrouded in obscurity. One historian has aptly described the War of 1812 as "a forgotten conflict."[1] Yet, the war was profoundly important in the way it changed the United States domestically and the way it altered the new republic's standing internationally. Understanding the war's origins and its consequences will help the student grasp the deeper meaning of the American experience in the United States' crucial formative years.

The War of 1812 is a difficult event to comprehend. Complex diplomatic controversies about free trade seem to veil its real causes, which some have claimed had more to do with territorial expansionism. Once the war got under way, both America and Great Britain waged it in great confusion and finally concluded it inconclusively. Meanwhile, the war deeply divided American sentiment, possibly more than any other war, including Vietnam. It so fractured the political structure that it destroyed one major political party and significantly changed the philosophy of the other. This book will serve as an introduction to these events, both to provide a clear understanding of them and to supply the student with the major historical interpretations of the war's causes, progress, and consequences.

The book is organized into a chronology and eight chapters. The chronology begins in 1803 with the Peace of Amiens, the end of which marked the onset of tensions between the United States and Europe over issues of free trade and neutral rights. Important diplomatic, political, and military events are included for each year through 1815, when ratification of the Treaty of Ghent concluded the conflict.

The eight chapters illuminate general and specific aspects of the war. The first chapter provides an overview of the war's causes and a summary of the conflict from its declaration in the summer of 1812 to its conclusion in early 1815. Why the United States declared war on Great Britain in 1812 remains a question of enduring historical debate. The government's stated reason for going to war—to protect American neutrality and sailors' rights—is weighed against the claim that the conflict was merely a way to expand American territory at the expense of British Canada, Spanish Florida, and Indians.

Chapter 2 explains how President Thomas Jefferson envisioned economic sanctions as a way to show the world how a virtuous people could sacrifice the comforts of commerce to preserve their independence and honor. This chapter describes the events that prompted the embargo, Jefferson and James Madison's rationale for commercial restrictions, and the reasons they proved so ineffective. The chapter also describes subsequent efforts to resolve Anglo-American frictions through negotiation, and includes a general analysis of the period's diplomacy.

Chapter 3 examines how the United States confronted a multitude of difficulties in fighting the war, paying for it, and inspiring popular support for it. The executive and legislature are evaluated for their effectiveness in dealing with issues such as raising troops, levying taxes, reviving embargoes, borrowing money, and coordinating the military and political aspects of the conflict. This chapter also examines the war's social, political, and economic impact and describes the dire sectional divisions that eroded support for the conflict even before it had started. An analysis of Federalist discontent, especially in New England, shows how the Hartford Convention subsequently ruined the Federalist Party.

Chapter 4 explains why the United States relied almost exclusively on a militia for national defense at the time of the War of 1812. This chapter describes the early campaigns against Canada to show how bad leadership and marginal soldiers frequently proved unsatisfactory and sometimes resulted in unmitigated military disaster. This chapter also details the remarkable performance of the American navy during the war, relating the significant American naval achievement during the first year of the war and analyzing the long-term realities posed by overwhelming British naval power.

Chapter 5 describes the gradual improvement in American military skill and planning, especially the formulation of a coherent design to establish control of the Great Lakes as key to victory. Oliver Hazard Perry's triumph on Lake Erie and the reestablishment of American dominion over the Northwest are balanced by the failures of campaigns on the Niagara and St. Lawrence rivers.

Chapter 6 depicts the unsettled American frontier in the Old Northwest (the Great Lakes region) and the Old Southwest (now Alabama and Mississippi) to define United States–Indian relations before the war that forced many Indians into the British camp. The chapter concludes with an evaluation of how the war generally smashed any chance for Indian resurgence east of the Mississippi and set the stage for the tragic policy of Indian removal that arose in the 1820s and 1830s.

Chapter 7 analyzes the altered situation brought about by Napoleon's defeat in Europe and how the United States met the new offensive challenges consequently mounted by the British. The three major crises that concluded the war—the invasion of upstate New York, the Chesapeake Bay Campaign, and the New Orleans Campaign—are placed into the larger context of the war as a whole, and the chapter concludes with a general analysis of the military failures and accomplishments of each side.

Chapter 8 makes clear that the War of 1812 was a collision that neither government wanted and that efforts to resolve it diplomatically were under way even before the opening guns had sounded. Ending the war would not prove so easy, however, and not until Christmas Eve of 1814 did American and British envoys sign a preliminary peace. This chapter complements the earlier article on prewar diplomacy with an overview of wartime diplomacy.

The remainder of the book includes brief biographies of nineteen people who were important during the war as well as primary documents with explanations supplying their historical background. A glossary of selected terms lists military, political, and social usage made cryptic because of its arcane nature or its peculiarity to the period. And finally there is a thorough bibliography subdivided into categories covering General Histories, Causes of the War, Biographies, Military Histories, Diplomacy, Native Americans, African Americans, the Naval War, Diaries and Letters,

Political Histories (i.e., studies of Federalism and Republicanism), Reference Works, and Films / Electronic Media. An index for easy reference to specific items in the text concludes the book.

We are grateful to Professor Dennis Showalter for introducing us to the pleasant people at Greenwood Press, among them Barbara Rader and Kevin Ohe. Series editors Linda and Marsha Frey were always ready with advice and encouragement, and we thank them for the chance to participate in this important project. Finally, we are especially indebted to the many fine scholars of the War of 1812 for their invaluable work in the period.

Note

1. Donald R. Hickey, *The War of 1812: A Forgotten Conflict* (Urbana and Chicago: University of Illinois Press, 1989).

CHRONOLOGY OF EVENTS

1803

May 18   Peace of Amiens breaks down and war recommences between France and Great Britain

1804

December 5   Electoral College reelects Thomas Jefferson to the presidency

1805

May 22   In the *Essex* Decision, a British Admiralty Court rules that enemy cargoes can no longer be neutralized by stopping at a neutral port

October 21   Battle of Trafalgar

December 2   Battle of Austerlitz

1806

May   Britain blockades a section of the European coast

November 21   Napoleon issues the Berlin Decree that purports to blockade the British Isles

December 31   Monroe-Pinkney Treaty signed with Britain that grants the United States trade concessions but does not repudiate impressment

1807

January 7   British Order in Council prohibits trade with French-controlled ports

June 22	*Chesapeake-Leopard* Incident ends with four American sailors impressed into the Royal Navy, throwing the United States into an uproar
November 11	British Order in Council requires neutral ships to stop at British ports
December 17	Milan Decree by Napoleon declares vessels submitting to British regulations are subject to seizure
December 22	U.S. Embargo Act ends all exports in attempt to compel respect for American neutral rights

1808

December 7	Electoral College elects James Madison fourth president of the United States

1809

March 1	Embargo Act repealed and Non-Intercourse Act passed
March 4	Madison inaugurated as president
April 19	British minister David Erskine fashions an agreement with Madison administration
May 30	British foreign office recalls Erskine
July 21	Britain repudiates the Erskine Agreement
August 9	Madison reestablishes non-intercourse against Great Britain

1810

March 23	Rambouillet Decree by Napoleon orders the seizure of U.S. merchant ships
May 1	Macon's Bill No. 2 reestablishes U.S. trade with Britain and France
August 5	Cadore Letter promises revocation of French commercial restrictions, but Napoleon's Trianon Decree condemns all U.S. ships in French custody
November 2	Madison applies non-importation terms against Britain

1811

May 16	USS *President* disables HMS *Little Belt*
July 24	Madison summons 12th Congress into session
November 4	12th Congress convenes its 1st session
November 7	Battle of Tippecanoe

1812

April 4	U.S. institutes a ninety-day embargo against Britain
June 1	Madison sends war message to Congress
June 4	U.S. House of Representatives votes 79–49 for war with Great Britain
June 16	Britain rescinds the Orders in Council
June 18	United States declares war on Great Britain with a Senate vote of 19–13
June 22	Baltimore riots
July 6	12th Congress adjourns
July 12	Brig. Gen. William Hull invades Canada
July 17	Fort Michilimackinac surrenders to British forces
August 8	Hull ends his invasion of Canada and retreats to Detroit
August 10	Dearborn-Prevost Armistice temporarily ends fighting in the Northeast in the hope that Anglo-American reconciliation is imminent
August 16	Hull surrenders Detroit to the British
August 19	USS *Constitution* defeats HMS *Guerrière* 600 miles east of Boston
September 4	Dearborn-Prevost Armistice is suspended
September 17	William Henry Harrison takes command of all military forces in the Northwest
September 21	Tsar Alexander I of Russia offers to mediate the Anglo-American War
October 13	Battle of Queenston
October 18	USS *Wasp* defeats HMS *Frolic* while en route to the

West Indies, but the *Wasp* is captured by the British ship of the line *Poictiers*

October 25	USS *United States* defeats HMS *Macedonian* several hundred miles off the West African coast
December 2	Madison reelected to the presidency
December 29	USS *Constitution* defeats HMS *Java* off the coast of Brazil

1813

January 22	Battle of Frenchtown
January 23	River Raisin Massacre
February 22	British regulars and Canadian militia attack Ogdensburg, New York
February 24	USS *Hornet* defeats HMS *Peacock* off the coast of Brazil
April 15	U.S. forces occupy Mobile
April 27	U.S. forces capture York
May 1	British besiege Fort Meigs
May 3	British pillage Havre de Grace, Maryland
May 15	U.S. forces capture Fort George (Niagara Campaign)
May 27	Battle of Sacket's Harbor
June 1	HMS *Shannon* defeats USS *Chesapeake* off Boston
June 6	Battle of Stoney Creek (Niagara Campaign)
June 22	British attack on Craney Island near Norfolk, Virginia
June 24	Battle of Beaver Dams (Niagara Campaign)
June 25	British plunder Hampton, Virginia, for two days
July 11	British attack on Black Rock, New York
July 27	Battle of Burnt Corn Creek (Creek War)
August 2	British unsuccessfully attack Fort Stephenson
August 14	HMS *Pelican* defeats USS *Argus* off the southern coast of Ireland
August 30	Fort Mims Massacre

September 5	USS *Enterprise* defeats HMS *Boxer* off the coast of Maine
September 10	Battle of Lake Erie
October 5	Battle of the Thames
October 26	Battle of Châteauguay (Montreal Campaign)
November 1	Battle of French Creek (Montreal Campaign)
November 3	Battle of Tallushatchee (Creek War)
November 11	Battle of Crysler's Farm (Montreal Campaign)
November 29	Battle of Autosse (Creek War)
December 10	U.S. forces destroy Newark, Upper Canada
December 18	British capture Fort Niagara and sack Lewiston, New York
December 23	Battle of Econochaca (Creek War)
December 30	British burn Black Rock and Buffalo, New York

1814

January 22	Battle of Emuckfau Creek (Creek War)
January 24	Battle of Enitachopco Creek (Creek War)
January 27	Battle of Calabee (Creek War)
March 27	Battle of Horseshoe Bend (or Tohopeka) (Creek War)
March 28	HMS *Phoebe* and HMS *Cherub* defeat USS *Essex* off Valparaiso, Chile
March 30	Battle of La Colle Mill
April 6	Napoleon abdicates the French throne
April 29	USS *Peacock* defeats HMS *Epervier* in the Bahamas
May 6	British raid on Oswego, New York
May 15	U.S. forces burn Port Dover
May 30	British raid thwarted on Big Sandy Creek
June 28	USS *Wasp*, the second so named sloop in the war, defeats HMS *Reindeer* in the North Atlantic
July 3	Battle of Fort Erie (Niagara Campaign)
July 5	Battle of Chippewa (Niagara Campaign)
July 25	The Battle of Lundy's Lane (Niagara Campaign)

August 3	Battle of Conjocta Creek
August 8	American and British delegates begin meeting in Ghent
August 9	Treaty of Fort Jackson
August 15	British fail to retake Fort Erie (Niagara Campaign)
August 24	Battle of Bladensburg
	British burn Washington, D.C.
September 1	British forces begin the occupation of the Maine District
	USS *Wasp* defeats HMS *Avon* shortly after being re-fitted in L'Orient, France
September 11	Battle of Plattsburgh Bay
September 12	British army and navy assail Baltimore, Maryland
September 15	Attack on Fort Bowyer at Mobile
October 19	Battle of Cook's Mills
November 7	Andrew Jackson occupies Spanish Pensacola
December 15	Battle of Lake Borgne (New Orleans Campaign)
	Disaffected New England Federalists meet in a convention at Hartford, Connecticut
December 23	Battle of Villeré Plantation (New Orleans Campaign)
December 24	Treaty of Ghent signed

1815

January 5	Hartford Convention adjourns
January 8	Battle of New Orleans
January 15	HMS *Endymion,* HMS *Tenados*, and HMS *Pamone* defeat USS *President* off the New York coast
February 8	British capture Fort Bowyer at Mobile
February 16	U.S. Senate ratifies Treaty of Ghent
February 17	War officially ends as Britain and United States exchange ratifications
February 20	USS *Constitution* defeats HMS *Cyane* and *Levant* off the coast of Tangier, North Africa

March 23	USS *Hornet* defeats HMS *Penguin* near Tristan da Cunha in the South Atlantic
April 15	Americans held in abysmal conditions at Dartmoor Prison grow impatient with delays for their release and riot; British guards kill 7 and wound 31 in what British foreign secretary Lord Castlereagh calls an "unfortunate incident"
June 30	USS *Peacock* captures HMS *Nautilus* in the Straits of Sunda; informed that the war is over, the *Peacock* releases the *Nautilus*

Map 1.   Northern Theater of Operations. © Arcadia Editions Limited.

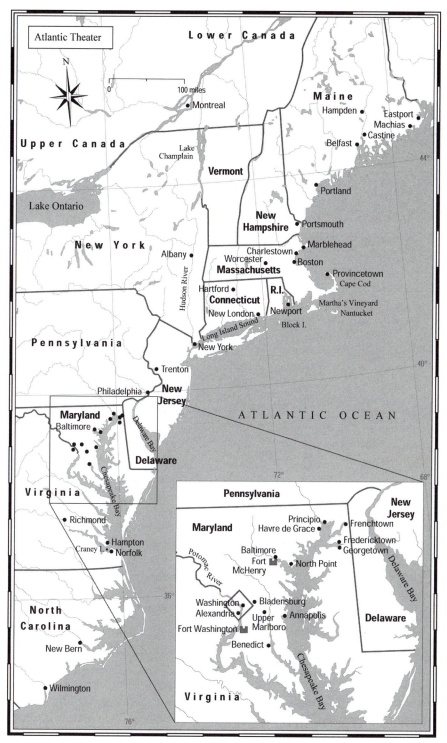

Map 2.   Atlantic Theater of Operations. © Arcadia Editions Limited.

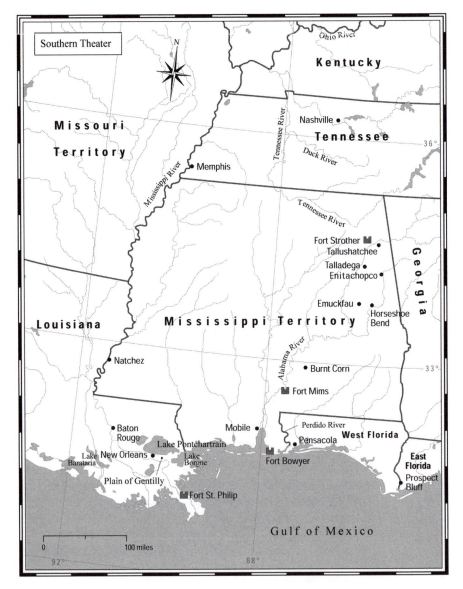

Map 3.   Southern Theater of Operations. © Arcadia Editions Limited.

CHAPTER 1

HISTORICAL OVERVIEW

Fought in the shadow of a great European war that had been going on for almost two decades, the War of 1812 was a relatively small conflict between the United States and Great Britain that lasted from the summer of 1812 to early 1815. Its causes, however, developed specifically because of the conflagration in Europe, especially when its two main antagonists—Great Britain and France—pursued war policies that threatened the economic health of the United States. Those policies and the way Americans tried to cope with them framed the starting point for one of the most confused and misunderstood episodes in American history.

Origins of the War

Neutral Rights and Impressment

Since 1793, when Europe had first plunged into war with revolutionary France, the United States had been the world's primary neutral shipper. In 1803, the war's renewal enhanced America's commercial position and noticeably boosted her trade. Yet, this favorable situation proved temporary. In 1805, a stunning British victory at sea and an equally dramatic French victory on land produced a puzzling stalemate. The British fleet could not assault the French army any more than French soldiers could attack the ships of the Royal Navy. Consequently, the enemies resorted to commercial warfare through a succession of retaliatory measures. The British issued rules called the Orders in Council that barred foreign shipping from entering European ports under French control, and the French emperor announced a series of decrees blockading Britain and targeting for seizure any ships that obeyed the Orders in Council.

This new and unpleasant development in the European war greatly affected American shipping interests even as it wounded American pride. Although American trade enjoyed significant profits operating under the perils of these commercial restrictions—only the intrepid would face such risks, and they were duly rewarded—spiraling insurance rates and constrained markets took their toll.

In addition to the obnoxious Orders in Council, the British renewed with some vigor their traditional policy of impressment to supply sailors to the Royal Navy. Impressment was essentially a rude form of conscription. All naval powers during the modern period had resorted to it at one time or another. By the early nineteenth century, Americans were not alone in regarding the practice odious, however, and even the British government saw the need to restrain the more provocative practices of the tradition. Only British subjects in British territory or harbors or on commercial vessels at sea were liable for impressment. In this last category, however, many American citizens, indistinguishable from British subjects in both appearance and speech, fell prey to the policy. Estimates vary, but it is probable that about six thousand American citizens were impressed into the Royal Navy between 1808 and 1811.[1] When confronted with such a statistic, the British responded that they were simply reclaiming deserters who had abandoned king and country.

The Chesapeake Incident and the Restrictive System

United States efforts to reach a diplomatic solution to the problem of neutral rights foundered on the issue of impressment, and a serious incident in 1807 nearly hurled the two countries into war. When HMS *Leopard* stopped the U.S. naval frigate *Chesapeake* off the Virginia coast with the aim of capturing four "deserters," three British broadsides killed three Americans and wounded eighteen others. The United States erupted into a unanimous scream for vengeance and vindication, and President Thomas Jefferson could easily have obtained a congressional declaration of war. Yet, the president's lone and lonely voice for peace was the one that counted.

Circumstance as much as principle dictated Jefferson's prudence. Economies enacted during Jefferson's first term had left the American navy weak and the army weaker. Jefferson, necessarily seeking an alternative to war, devised a plan to take advantage of war-torn Europe's reliance on the United States for resources and food. The president believed that if

America declined to export goods to Europe, both Britain and France would be compelled to reopen trade on American terms, especially those respecting neutral rights. Utilizing his considerable persuasion and power, Jefferson late in 1807 convinced Congress to pass the Embargo Act. The law prohibited exports from the United States in both American and foreign carriers.

Yet, the embargo only hurt U.S. commerce. Americans increasingly ignored the law, and the government's harsh enforcement measures made the embargo even more despicable. Anger in New England reached a pitch that threatened not just government agents, but the Union itself. Congress repealed the embargo on 1 March 1809, three days before Jefferson was to leave the presidency to his successor James Madison. Congress promptly passed the Non-Intercourse Act reopening trade with everyone except England and France. Such a course of action in one shape or another formed the main thrust of American foreign policy until 1812 when diplomacy finally gave way to war.

The War Hawks

When the Twelfth Congress convened in late 1811, its membership reflected a growing frustration with this vexing international situation. A group of young firebrands soon dubbed the War Hawks became dominant in the House of Representatives.[2] They hailed mainly from the South and the West, and one of their number effortlessly won the speakership. Henry Clay of Kentucky, already a master politician and parliamentarian without peer, was only thirty-four years old. His leadership from the speaker's chair would shape that post along its modern contours and make Clay, at this crucial point and in contrast to the reserved Madison, the most powerful man in Washington.

Native Americans on the Frontier

Clay's state of Kentucky had been filling with white settlers, causing Indians in the region anxiety over both a receding border and a vanishing wilderness. Finally, the white influx led to the emergence of two extraordinary Indian leaders. From the Shawnee of the Great Lakes region, Tecumseh and his brother Tenskwatawa (also known as the Prophet) were charismatic leaders who envisioned a sweeping league of all tribes from the Niagara River to Mobile Bay. Tecumseh's initiative coincided with a spontaneous spiritual rebirth among Indian tribes, and though both their religious fervor and their political enterprises were completely indigenous products, frontier settlers firmly believed that they were the work of British operatives in Canada fomenting discontent and upheaval. When Indian attacks increased on the western frontier in 1811, American general William Henry Harrison led an army in what is now Indiana to Prophet's Town, Tecumseh's headquarters at the meeting of Tippecanoe Creek and the Wabash River. On 7 November, Tenskwatawa ordered an attack on the American force before it reached the village. After the Indians retreated, Harrison burned deserted Prophet's Town, but he captured neither Tenskwatawa (who escaped) nor Tecumseh (who was absent).[3]

The Indian menace for white settlers on the western frontier was real, but Americans incorrectly perceived the British as the cause of that menace. Although their advocacy of maritime rights was always foremost, War Hawks were attentive to western voices that called for the eradication of the Indian threat. By implication, eliminating the British presence in Canada could best accomplish that goal. In addition, acquiring Canada would satisfy America's expansionist desires. The country's southern frontier bordered by Spanish Florida beckoned to expansionists as well who also were able to point to an Indian threat in their region and convince themselves that the authors of that threat were European agitators.[4]

The Declaration of War

An enduring debate concerns whether western and southern expansionism played a more important role in causing the War of 1812 than American concern about protecting neutral maritime rights. The War Hawks took as their motto "Free Trade and Sailors' Rights," but some observers at the time doubted that frontier and agrarian regions would want to go to war for New England shipping interests. Some historians have since echoed those suspicions.[5]

We should note, however, that agricultural interests were not immune to the economic rigors caused by the British Orders in Council when such restrictions kept their harvests from overseas markets. On a more abstract level, insults to national honor were a powerful stimulant for the proud citizens of young America. The picture of Royal Marines abducting American sailors under the color of impressment infuriated the West and South as well as the rest of the country. The rhetoric of War Hawks insisting that American honor was at stake on the high seas should not be dismissed as empty bluster, for the people of that time regarded the reputations of persons and communities as important signs of their worth and weight. An America that would meekly submit to the abuse of its neutral rights would prove itself to the rest of the world as worthless and weak. These square-jawed pioneers were not weak. They would kill to prove they were not worthless.

Madison bowed to the inevitable and sent a war message to Congress on 1 June 1812, and the War Hawks gathered enough support to pass a declaration of war against Great Britain on 18 June 1812. Yet close votes in the House (79–49) and the Senate (19–13) exposed a disturbing lack of backing for this dangerous endeavor.[6] Shipping and business interests in New England and the Mid-Atlantic states had habitually inclined to Britain for the rich markets it offered, and they were at most lukewarm about the war. Generally, they were against it. Ironically, it was the pioneer and agrarian interests of the West and South who promoted the war to secure the right to sail the seas and sell things abroad.

The War of 1812

A Splintered Republic Goes to War

At the outbreak of the War of 1812, attitudes toward the hostilities divided the United States, and no unifying purpose promised to mend the fracture. The War Hawk initiative, despite some noisy acclamation, represented only a scant congressional majority led by a fervent few. New England opposition to the war would verge on the subversive.

The United States also faced tangible obstacles to prosecuting the war. Almost five years of self-imposed commercial restriction had weakened the economy, and congressional opposition to the Bank of the United States had prevented that institution's recharter in 1811. The absence of the national bank left rudderless an already leaky financial system.[7]

Finally, America's military shortcomings posed a preposterous problem for a nation about to go to war. A woefully insufficient regular army reflected Republican thrift and the republic's suspicion of standing military forces. Reliance on poorly trained state militia proved uniformly disastrous early in the war, especially when some New England states refused to make their forces available to the national war effort. And in the early stages of the conflict, many senior officers were nothing more than relics with only a dim memory of the American Revolution.[8]

The 1812 Campaigns for Canada

Canada was the main objective for American land forces at the start of the war, and not only because it held such a tempting allure for expansionists. As one historian has aptly pointed out, the United States had declared war on Britain, and Canada was, after all, where the British were.[9]

Canada proved to be more a tough nut than a ripe plum, however. The United States squandered any advantage that would have resulted from a massed and concentrated assault. Instead, one invasion effort in 1812 started from Detroit, another crossed the Niagara River, and still another moved up Lake Champlain. Each of these three uncoordinated operations failed miserably, barely managing to penetrate Canadian soil before suffering repulse at the hands of energetic and well-commanded British and Canadian forces.

The U.S. Navy

Oddly enough, the only sterling accomplishments for the United States in the first year of the war would come at sea. This was peculiar because the disparity between American and British naval forces was vastly weighted in Britain's favor. The Royal Navy in 1812 possessed a staggering inventory of some 1,000 men-of-war, including 219 ships of the line each mounting 74 guns and 296 frigates mounting an average of 44 guns each. The U.S. Navy—all 16 ships of it—had only a few frigates, whose principal asset was that they were larger than their British counterparts. Another American advantage was the European war with Napoleon, which was always foremost for London's military planners and thus occupied the labors of the Royal Navy's largest ships.

The first year of the war at sea left the British acutely embarrassed. If London consoled itself that the best of the British fleet was fighting Napoleon, it was at best small and cold comfort. Late in the war, when European distractions eased, the British navy's preponderant weight of numbers and experience reversed fortunes on the high seas. The Royal Navy was able to establish a tight blockade of the American coast, and by war's end, the British stranglehold on American commerce was nearly complete. The blue water (oceangoing) U.S. Navy was simply not up to the task of opposing such overwhelming power.

Meanwhile, naval contests waged on the inland seas of Lake Erie and Lake Champlain were of immediate military importance, and on those waters, the U.S. Navy would again prove itself indomitable.

Privateering

Another aspect of the war at sea was the less spectacular but more vital work of American privateers that fought a *course de guerre* (war of commerce). Privately financed as their name implies, these small, swift vessels engaged in what amounted to state-sponsored piracy officially sanctioned by letters of marque issued by the U.S. government. A privateer's crew and investors could collect considerable wealth from the capture and condemnation of enemy merchant shipping, so the promise of lucrative profits spurred their activity.

About five hundred American privateers combed the sea during the War of 1812. British warships and privateers also preyed upon American merchant ships, but American devastation of British commercial shipping inflicted considerable injury on His Majesty's war effort. About 1,350 British merchantmen fell to American privateers, sometimes with the assistance of swift U.S. Navy sloops. This facet of the war increasingly injured British commerce until business interests brought considerable pressure for peace on both Crown and Parliament.

The Pivotal Battle for Lake Erie

Because control of Lake Erie was essential to success in Upper Canada, American naval officer Oliver Hazard Perry overcame considerable impediments to build a fleet of ships there. On 10 September 1813, Perry fought a fierce battle that left his British foe thoroughly defeated. Perry's report of the battle contained the succinct and soon celebrated line: "We have met the enemy and they are ours."[10]

Perry's victory on Lake Erie was a crucial turning point for American strategic fortunes in the region. The British immediately withdrew from Detroit and Fort Malden for fear that the Americans would trap them in these now worthless bastions. When the British tried to make a stand at the Thames River in October 1813, troops under William Henry Harrison defeated them and their Indian allies. Tecumseh was reportedly killed during the fight, and his dream of an Indian league died with him.

The Battle of Plattsburgh

Success eluded Americans attacking Lower Canada, however, as another hapless campaign broke down under jealous generals and inferior execution. Then, in 1814, the startling prospect of a British invasion of upstate New York loomed. The end of the European war made this offensive possible. In the spring of 1814, Napoleon admitted defeat and abdicated the French throne. Now free from the distraction of Bonaparte, the whole might of Britain's massive military establishment began to wheel toward the American conflict.

Consequently, the United States faced three grave military crises in 1814, one of which was the British invasion of New York. About ten thousand veterans of the Napoleonic Wars were ferried to Canada and soon moved down the shore of Lake Champlain to deliver a crushing blow. United States naval officer Thomas Macdonough blocked the British advance with a brittle American flotilla near Plattsburgh. The battle in Plattsburgh Bay had become an unexpectedly desperate affair when Macdonough pivoted his flagship on its anchor cables to bring fresh guns into the fight. The devastating salvo so stunned the bloodied British that they quit the action and withdrew.

Fought on 11 September 1814, this epic naval clash was as crucial an event as Perry's victory on Lake Erie the year before. Without naval support, the British army retreated from New York. The victory, coming in an otherwise dark year and reversing the failed fortunes of American military ventures in the region, temporarily muted New England dissidents. Macdonough's feat was also cheerful news for the American delegation discussing peace terms with British envoys in Europe.

The Chesapeake Campaign

The second crisis for the United States developed even before the incredible repulse of the British invasion of New York. In the summer of 1814, another redoubtable British force enlarged the scope of raids begun in 1813 on the shores of Chesapeake Bay. In August, the British army landed in Maryland and began a rapid march on the U.S. capital, brushing aside token opposition from the American militia, and setting fire to Washington's public buildings.

The British fleet then sailed up Chesapeake Bay to Baltimore, but that city's defenders were of sterner stuff than the militia outside of Washington. Enduring a terrible and extended bombardment, the stubborn garrison at Fort McHenry held and thus prevented the British fleet from breaching Baltimore's inner harbor. Deprived of crucial naval support, the British army sullenly boarded their ships, and the entire task force sailed south and out of the bay.

The summer and fall campaign on Chesapeake Bay, though appearing in part a success, ultimately proved as costly for the British as their failed New York invasion. The capture of Washington yielded little strategic advantage, and the operation's senseless vandalism diminished whatever propaganda benefit it might have produced, even among some British observers.[11] The attack on Baltimore, while more sensible from both a military and economic vantage, nonetheless failed and gave American morale a much-needed boost. An American attorney named Francis Scott Key had watched the bombardment of Fort McHenry from a British ship where he was being detained, and the episode moved him to write a poem that would be entitled "The Star-Spangled Banner." Immediately after the British departure, hastily printed copies appeared on the streets of Baltimore, and soon singers had set the verse to the melody of a well-known English tavern song. Americans everywhere would embrace it as an unofficial anthem.[12]

Victory at New Orleans

The third and final military crisis occurred in the American South on the banks of the Mississippi River.

For much of the war, the American focus on British Canada spared the South from the strain of the conflict. The United States' European neighbor in the South was Spanish Florida, a weakly garrisoned outpost of an enfeebled and crumbling empire. Although Spain had allied with Britain for the European fight against Napoleon, authorities in Spanish Florida cautiously preserved their neutrality when war broke out between the United States and Great Britain.

Yet, the South was not immune to war. Tecumseh had brought his idea of Indian union to southern tribes in 1811, and that message took hold among certain factions of the southern Indians who were already in the midst of a spiritual revival.[13] In 1813, a faction of Creek Indians called the Red Sticks massacred about 250 whites, blacks, and mixed bloods at Fort Mims just north of Mobile.[14] The event terrified the white countryside and brought out the militia of adjoining Georgia and Tennessee, the latter force led by Andrew Jackson. American forces fought a series of bloody but indecisive engagements against the Red Sticks until the spring of 1814, when Andrew Jackson crushed them at the Battle of Horseshoe Bend on 27 March. He then compelled all Creeks to sign the Treaty of Fort Jackson that imposed a massive land cession on the entire Creek nation.

The Creek War did not have any connection to the War of 1812 until Jackson's final victory in it. Refugees from Horseshoe Bend and other splinters of Creek resistance fled to Spanish Florida. A small British presence had appeared in the Gulf of Mexico to encourage Indian uprisings and attempt the capture of American Mobile. Yet, the Indians were too devastated to be of much help, and the British presence was too slight to accomplish anything other than a failed assault on Mobile's Fort Bowyer. Andrew Jackson punished the breach of Spanish neutrality by driving the British from Pensacola and establishing his headquarters at Mobile, where he expected the British to invade with a major force.

This third British blow of 1814 did not fall on Mobile, however. It was aimed at New Orleans. Jackson raced to protect the city and assembled a jumbled mix of sailors, regular soldiers, buccaneers, Creoles, and free black volunteers there to supplement the Louisiana, Kentucky, and Tennessee militia. More important than this growing number of defenders, however, was the gift of time that the British gave Jackson by prolonging their preparations for a final assault. The Americans were thus able to build what turned out to be impregnable fortifications. When the main British attack came on 8 January 1815, it suffered a shattering defeat. The British commander Sir Edward Pakenham fell mortally wounded during the attack. The victor Andrew Jackson instantly became the most celebrated American of the war, a prelude to his becoming the most revered American of his time.

Neither side knew that two weeks earlier envoys had signed a peace treaty in Europe. That the peace accord preceded the battle has caused some to describe American victory at New Orleans as an irrelevancy. Yet, this was not the case. Had the British taken possession of the city, London might have been tempted to abandon the terms of the preliminary peace to negotiate better arrangements from a position of unparalleled strength.

In addition, the psychological effect of New Orleans on the American people was incalculable. The news of the victory reached Washington in early February 1815, arriving just two weeks before the peace treaty. Jubilant citizens confused the chronology to presume that Jackson had beaten the British and forced them to the peace table. In short, New Orleans convinced Americans erroneously that despite their many military fiascos, setbacks, and abject defeats, they had won the war.

The Treaty of Ghent

Even before the guns had started to shoot, initiatives to end the War of 1812 were under way, and they continued throughout the conflict. The French invasion of Russia in 1812 made Tsar Alexander I especially eager to mediate an end to the Anglo-American conflict so that it would not divert British help. Britain rebuffed the tsar's overture, but the United States was sufficiently interested to appoint a peace delegation. Although the Russian effort proved fruitless, it did have the effect of putting a talented American team of negotiators in Europe and thus inaugurated a peace process within the first year of the war. By the summer of 1814, this five-man American delegation had settled into tiring and protracted discussions with their British counterparts in the city of Ghent. John Quincy Adams, son of former president John Adams and lately the American minister to Russia, led the gifted group that included the War Hawk Henry Clay. The British delegation, on the other hand, consisted mainly of second-rate men because in London's view the truly important peace negotiations were taking place in Vienna to sort out the aftermath of Napoleonic disarray.

Although a mediocre lot, Britain's envoys had the advantage of bargaining from virtually complete military success, and they consequently listed extensive demands that deadlocked negotiations for many weeks. Reports of British losses at Plattsburgh and Baltimore, however, altered the mood in Ghent. Moreover, the British public was tired of war, having fought the French for a quarter-century and not much wanting to fight the Americans any longer. Suddenly the foreign office in London was agreeable to concessions. The result was the rapid consummation of the Treaty of Ghent, signed on Christmas Eve in 1814.

The treaty was a testament to the fatigue of the combatants rather than a definite resolution of the disagreements that had caused the war. The United States and Great Britain merely arranged to stop shooting at one another and to restore all territory as held before hostilities. Nonetheless, the United States greeted news of the treaty with great celebrations because of what it did not contain—no cessions of territory, for example—rather than for what it did. The Senate quickly and unanimously ratified the agreement, and the United States immediately embarked on a journey of surging patriotism and national pride, comforted in the belief that they had won a "Second War of Independence," something that was partly untrue. It was hardly a war fought for independence from England except in the diplomatic sense, and the best that could be said was that the United States had not lost it.

The Hartford Convention

Federalist discontent, especially in New England, had posed a problem throughout the war, and, in 1814, some New England radicals began talking about seceding from the Union and independently negotiating peace with England. Such talk was the work of a tiny minority, but it stained all Federalists in the eyes of the country. In late 1814, as New Orleans faced capture, Massachusetts called for a convention to meet at Hartford, Connecticut. The meeting's purpose was unclear, but it was certainly not patriotic. When it finally adjourned and published the product of its labors, the Hartford Convention revealed that it was really less militant than rumored. Moderation prevailed in the convention's final report, which primarily called for constitutional amendments that would revive Federalist power.

As meek as these declarations were, they came at the worst possible time for the Federalist Party. News of Jackson's victory at New Orleans and of the peace accord from Ghent prompted the press and public to paint the convention as treacherous and foolish. In the 1816 presidential election, the Federalists would put forward their final presidential candidate—he would be overwhelmingly defeated by the Republican nominee James Monroe—and would see their congressional numbers dwindle to insignificance. Only a few years after the war, the Federalists ceased to exist as a viable political party.

The Legacy of the War

The reasons for and results of the War of 1812 kindled lively arguments among contemporaries and continue to do so among historians. At the center of the debate over causes is the question of whether the expansionism of western and southern War Hawks was more important than were British violations of American neutral rights. Interpretations based on the most reliable evidence, however, put emphasis on a sincere American desire to protect maritime rights.[15] Historians espousing this view take into consideration the new nation's hypersensitivity about its place in the world and conclude that Americans could not abide Great Britain's insults. Beyond an impulsive desire to defend the country's violated honor, Republicans gravitated to war because they sincerely held that British policy was testing the unique American experiment in self-rule. The country could not prosper if it surrendered its commercial privileges abroad; it would have no right to survive if it did not fight for its status among the sovereign nations of the world. Such an attitude helps to explain the surging national pride that came at the close of the war.

Although the Treaty of Ghent included no official acknowledgment of American maritime rights, it would be a mistake to suggest that the war did not change British and other foreign attitudes. Before the war, Britain smugly disparaged the commercial pretensions of Yankee upstarts. The American willingness to fight, however, not only surprised the British foreign office, it subtly altered the opinions of the British merchant class who began to see American skippers as rivals rather than rogues. The Royal Navy certainly developed a grudging respect for the U.S. Navy, and nations all over the world accorded U.S. envoys a greater deference than they had ever enjoyed before the war.

If war had nurtured a reluctant British respect for Americans, it did not endear the two nations to one another. In the United States, it simply revitalized and deepened animosity toward Great Britain. Americans considered the burning of Washington alone an unforgivable act. The passionate hatred the war inspired naturally gave way in time, but it was replaced only gradually by a distrust that then lingered for decades. Most Americans, in fact, thought that the War of 1812's conclusion was merely a truce that Britain would soon break when it had recovered from the fatigue of fighting Napoleon.

After Napoleon's final defeat at Waterloo in 1815, however, European energy was devoted to restoring order, legitimacy, and a balance of power within the continental framework. Britain's role in this endeavor was increasingly limited to protecting its own far-flung empire. United States–Canadian relations were an indication of this trend. Canadians themselves felt that the Treaty of Ghent had neglected their best interests, especially when London abandoned the idea of an Indian buffer state and refused to insist on British dominion over the Great Lakes. Just as Americans predicted that the British were only pausing before renewing hostilities, Canadians conversely expected the United States to recommence expansionism at their expense. For a couple of years after the war, these mutual fears even encouraged a naval arms race on the Great Lakes. Yet, in 1817, the Rush-Bagot Agreement neutralized the lakes and paved the way for additional negotiations that over the years removed fortifications along the entire U.S.–Canadian border.[16] By the 1870s, the United States and

Canada shared a 5,527-mile undefended boundary that still ranks as the longest unfortified border in the world. In fact, as the years passed, the British and Americans would more often than not find themselves in the same camp when confronting world events. The two peoples would never draw daggers at one another again. They would become partners in the twentieth century to oppose tyranny and promote a sweeping agenda for human freedom, including some of the same ideals that the United States had fought for in the War of 1812.

For the United States, the century that followed the war was one of unparalleled expansion. Andrew Jackson's crushing victory over the Red Stick Creeks in the South and William Henry Harrison's scattering of Tecumseh's allies in the North marked a prelude to Indian removal and sequestration. Denied any real protection by their erstwhile British allies, Native Americans were at the mercy of the U.S. government. A series of treaties compelled them to hand over vast areas of rich forests both north of the Ohio River and in the lush Southeast. Within thirty years of the close of the War of 1812, most Indians had been exiled west of the Mississippi River.

Meanwhile, the age of manufacturing, ironically encouraged by almost ten years of British and American commercial restrictions, flowered in the American republic. As the American people became less dependent on European production, they became less affected by European events. The United States did not face inward in turning away from the Old World. The American people instead looked toward the measureless reaches of their own continent, doggedly to march westward, testing their courage, their character, and their irresistible will.

Notes

1. James F. Zimmerman, *Impressment of American Seamen* (New York: Columbia University Press, 1966), 266–67.

2. Harry Fritz, "The War Hawks of 1812," *Capitol Studies* 5 (spring 1977): 25–42.

3. John K. Mahon, *The War of 1812* (Gainesville: University of Florida Press, 1972), 20–27.

4. David S. Heidler and Jeanne T. Heidler, *Old Hickory's War: Andrew Jackson and the Quest for Empire* (Mechanicsville, PA: Stackpole Books, 1996), Chapter 2.

5. Howard T. Lewis, "A Re-analysis of the Causes of the War of 1812," *Americana* 6 (1911): 506–16, 577–85; Louis M. Hacker, "Western Land Hunger

and the War of 1812," *Mississippi Valley Historical Review* 10 (March 1924): 365–95; Julius Pratt, *Expansionists of 1812* (New York: Macmillan, 1925, reprint ed., Gloucester, MA: Peter Smith, 1957).

6. See David S. Heidler and Jeanne T. Heidler, eds., *Encyclopedia of the War of 1812* (Santa Barbara and Denver: ABC-Clio, 1997), 571–74, for a detailed tabulation of the war vote in both houses.

7. Bray Hammond, *Banks and Politics in America from the Revolution to the Civil War* (Princeton: Princeton University Press, 1957), 229–30.

8. Hickey, *War of 1812*, 75–80.

9. Reginald Horsman, *The Causes of the War of 1812* (New York: A.S. Barnes & Company, Inc., 1962), 171.

10. David Curtis Skaggs and Gerard T. Altoff, *A Signal Victory: The Lake Erie Campaign, 1812–1813* (Annapolis: Naval Institute Press, 1997), 148.

11. *Niles' Register* 7 (31 December 1814), 275.

12. Walter Lord, *The Dawn's Early Light* (New York: W.W. Norton & Company, Inc., 1972), 295–97.

13. Heidler and Heidler, *Old Hickory's War*, 10–11.

14. Frank L. Owsley, Jr., "The Fort Mims Massacre," *Alabama Review* 24 (July 1971): 192–204.

15. Hickey, *War of 1812*, 72; Horsman, *Causes of the War of 1812*, Chapter 9; also see A. L. Burt, *The United States, Great Britain, and British North America from the Revolution to the Establishment of Peace after the War of 1812* (New Haven: Yale University Press, 1940), 210–55.

16. Samuel Flagg Bemis, *John Quincy Adams and the Foundations of American Foreign Policy* (New York: Alfred A. Knopf, 1949), 278–98.

CHAPTER 2

THOMAS JEFFERSON'S GRAND EXPERIMENT:
THE RESTRICTIVE SYSTEM AND THE FAILURE OF DIPLOMACY

The United States and Europe to 1803

The United States enjoyed a great luxury in its early years. European wars helped Americans win their independence from Great Britain in 1783, and they provided the United States time to revise her government and secure her sovereignty. Americans were largely untouched by the titanic war that broke out in 1793 between France and Europe. President George Washington and his successor John Adams kept the United States clear of this quarrel while negotiating advantageous territorial settlements and commercial agreements with Spain and Great Britain.

Washington and Adams did not enjoy a trouble-free time, however. Domestic disputes over the government's proper relation to the European war disturbed both men's administrations and contributed to the creation of America's first political parties. Reflecting Secretary of the Treasury Alexander Hamilton's attitude, the Federalist Party of Washington and Adams felt that Britain's markets were more valuable to American national security than French idealism was. Thomas Jefferson as secretary of state (1790–1794) argued vehemently for the United States to honor its treaty obligations to the beleaguered French republic. Jefferson and James Madison would found the Republican Party in part to oppose Federalist foreign policy.

The French alliance of 1778 had been crucial in helping Americans gain their independence, but, by the 1790s, it was seriously complicating American neutrality. After 1793, France was at war with much of Europe, and French leaders called on their American allies for help. Washington and Adams maintained steadfast neutrality, though. In 1800, a Franco-American agreement ended the Quasi-War (a brief, undeclared conflict with France); replaced the 1778 alliance, and regularized relations between the two countries.

When Thomas Jefferson became president in March 1801, he inherited more than this reasonably secure diplomatic state of affairs. Britain and France, the latter now under the rule of Napoleon Bonaparte, signed a peace agreement at Amiens in 1802, making Jefferson the first American president in more than ten years to have a world at peace. As the Republican Party worked to reverse Hamilton's Federalist policies of governmental growth and centralization, Jefferson scored his greatest triumph by obtaining the North American heartland from Napoleon with the Louisiana Purchase in 1803. The previously pro-French Jefferson even contemplated an Anglo-American alliance if Napoleon refused to sell New Orleans. "From that moment," he observed, "we must marry ourselves to the British fleet and nation."[1] Now with the Mississippi River and much of the great western expanse beyond it in American possession, using that peculiar option was no longer necessary.

Napoleon was intent on breaking the Peace of Amiens, however, and he sold Louisiana to the United States to help finance this new round of hostilities. In May 1803, less than two weeks after the signing of the Louisiana Purchase, the fragile Amiens truce broke down. This time, the United States would not be able to remain aloof.

The Problem of Neutral Commerce

The Rule of 1756

When war again broke out in 1803, Britain's Royal Navy was the only obstacle to Napoleon's plan of global domination. Although by diplomacy and conquest, Napoleon augmented the French navy with the Spanish fleet and Dutch ships, Britain proved invincible on the seas. Off the coast of Spain at Trafalgar, Lord Horatio Nelson destroyed the combined French and Spanish fleets on 21 October 1805. France would never again challenge British sea power during the remaining ten years of the Napoleonic Wars.

The French had lost at Trafalgar, but they had not lost the war. Instead, Napoleon won a titanic victory only a few weeks after Trafalgar. By crushing the Austrians and Russians at Austerlitz, Napoleon could claim mastery over Europe. The war continued, with England alone opposing French power.

For more than two years, the United States sat apart from these events and even prospered because of them. Ordinarily the closed nature of co-lonial commercial systems excluded American shippers from participat-ing in the direct trade between European countries and their West Indies possessions. Yet, the completeness of British victory at Trafalgar made it necessary for France and Spain to open that trade to neutral carriers, pri-marily the United States. Great Britain understandably objected to this arrangement for strategic and economic reasons.

When neutral ships claimed immunity from British interference, London's strategists asked what good it did to control the seas if they could not restrain French trade. It was not a new problem. The same quandary had existed fifty years earlier when England and France had grappled for global empire. In 1756, the Royal Navy had justified the interruption of neutral trade by establishing the principle that trade not allowed in peace would not be allowed in war. In other words, if a colonial system ordi-narily excluded foreign shipping, it could not change its rules during wartime to nullify British naval supremacy.

During the first round of the revolutionary wars with France in the 1790s, Britain had invoked this so-called Rule of 1756, but its applica-tion had not affected American neutral commerce. Technically, the restric-tion of 1756 applied to direct trade between a mother country and her colonies. Because it was not necessarily restricted in peacetime, trade be-tween the United States and the West Indies could not be restricted in wartime under the Rule of 1756. American merchant captains could bring French West Indian goods to a U.S. port, unload them, and pay the ap-plicable tariffs. The cumbersome process—called a "broken" voyage—had the key effect of transforming French or Spanish West Indian cargoes into American (or neutral) goods. The shipper could then re-export the "Ameri-canized" cargo to Europe, including France, free from British interference unless it was clearly contraband. Although the United States did not al-ways agree with Britain on the definition of contraband, everyone agreed that materiel that could directly aid the French war effort was liable for seizure.

Under these arrangements, the European war actually caused Ameri-can trade to flourish. Yet, there were problems. American efficiency tended to eliminate a key step of the broken voyage by having a ship merely visit a U.S. port without physically offloading its foreign cargo. Furthermore, friendly customs officials frequently reimbursed tariffs with "drawbacks" when the goods left port. Such practices only simulated the broken voyage. The re-export trade thus became nothing more than a way to circumvent the Rule of 1756, and British strategists plausibly found the practice unacceptable.

The Essex Decision

The American re-export trade also injured British economic interests. British shippers complained that London's lax application of the Rule of 1756 gave American mariners an unfair trade advantage. These complaints soon appeared in a pamphlet entitled *War in Disguise, or the Frauds of Neutral Flags* written by the influential English publicist James D. Stephen. According to Stephen, the British, not neutral nations, should profit from British victories. He recommended that neutral ships carrying enemy goods should be required to visit a British port to pay duties and purchase licenses before proceeding to enemy ports. Under such a plan, Britain could regulate the maritime commerce of all nations to advance her economic as well as strategic aims.

Attractive to British strategists and shippers alike, this reasoning guided relations with the United States for the next seven years. Immediately, it found expression in the *Essex* Decision of 1805. The American merchant vessel *Essex* was transporting a cargo from Barcelona, Spain, to Havana, Cuba, by way of Salem, Massachusetts, when she was seized and hauled into a British prize court. The court dismissed the Salem stop as a meaningless subterfuge and condemned the *Essex* for violating the Rule of 1756. This blunt ruling outlawed the profitable American re-export trade and unleashed the Royal Navy to prey upon American shipping directly off the United States coast.

American shippers wanted the United States government to take action. When HMS *Leander* accosted a merchant sloop off New York and fired a warning shot that miscarried, killing a crewmember on another American ship, Jefferson expelled the *Leander* and her support vessels from American waters. Yet, clearly the situation required something more forceful in light of what Jefferson described as "an atrocious violation of our territorial rights."[2]

The Non-Importation Act of 1806

The Republican Party's military and naval reductions made war with powerful Britain simply impossible, but the surrender of American neutral rights, even if cloaked in sharp diplomatic protests, would have been politically unacceptable and philosophically repugnant to the president. Jefferson instead envisioned a policy of economic coercion—a middling response somewhere between submission and belligerence—that would use the carrot of American commerce to secure neutral rights bloodlessly. It was an appealing notion for an unarmed man who nonetheless needed to fight.

The idea for such a restrictive system had its origins in the period before the American Revolution when colonists had tried to make Britain abandon intrusive imperial policies by refusing to purchase British goods. Such devices exerted only a minor influence on British colonial policy, but at the time, trade restrictions had seemed more effective than they were. Recalling this prerevolutionary struggle, Thomas Jefferson and his secretary of state James Madison believed that withholding American trade would again work, this time to win greater respect for neutral rights.

Economic coercion appealed to Congress as well, but its initial expression in the Non-Importation Act of 1806 was so timid the British never took it seriously. Enacted on 23 April 1806, the Non-Importation Act gave the British until November to adjust their policy regarding American commerce. If that date passed with no change, the United States would cease importing specified British products.

The British Admiralty saw the futility of this American ploy supported by nothing other than customs agents, a ramshackle coastal navy, and idealistic resolve. Moreover, the United States would not begin enforcing the act until 14 December 1807, a full fifty-eight weeks later than it had threatened. The delay was caused by the hope that a special diplomatic initiative undertaken by the Jefferson administration would solve the neutral rights problem and make unnecessary even the mild restrictions of non-importation.

The Monroe-Pinkney Treaty

As early as 1804, Jefferson had planned to replace Jay's Treaty, an agreement with Great Britain formed during the Washington administration that was due to expire. In 1806, he sent to London special envoy William Pinkney, a Maryland Federalist, to join James Monroe, the American minister to the British government. Their instructions were to resolve the problems created by the *Essex* Decision, especially as it had led to the Royal Navy's virtually blockading U.S. ports. Most important, however, Monroe and Pinkney were to persuade the British to repudiate their policy of impressment, and it was on that spiky point that the otherwise successful negotiations would ultimately snag.

The talks did produce a treaty, though, and a surprisingly good one, thanks to a lucky coincidence. Just before the American emissaries began their negotiations, the unfriendly Tory government led by William Pitt the Younger disintegrated when Pitt suddenly died, and the Whig Party took over the reins of the British government. The Whigs, always more sympathetic to Americans than the Tories, formed a cabinet that included Charles James Fox as foreign secretary. Fox was responsive to American complaints and considerate of American dignity.

In fact, Fox unofficially abandoned the Rule of 1756 as construed by the *Essex* Decision when he announced a partial blockade of the European coast 16 May 1806. Although it seemed to be another restrictive measure, it really was not. Neutral ships sailing from a neutral port could trade in noncontraband goods with an extensive part of the coast, but Americans did not perceive the cleverly cloaked benefit it accorded them. Instead, they condemned the measure as a "paper" blockade and kept the Non-Importation Act in place, though still in postponement. It was among the last of many disappointments that plagued Fox, and even before he had begun negotiating with Monroe and Pinkney, he became ill and after weeks of declining health, died in September 1806.

The Whig government, however, kept the spirit of Fox's intentions in the treaty signed on 31 December 1806. The document essentially satisfied almost all American demands by restoring the concept of the broken voyage. Although, the British later might have twisted some of the treaty's wording to lessen this concession, in good faith it amounted to their abandoning the Rule of 1756. The treaty profoundly disappointed Jefferson and Madison, however, because it contained no disavowal of impressment. "I am persuaded," the British minister to the United States informed London, "that no cordiality can be expected from this country whilst it is deemed necessary by His Majesty to enforce that right."[3] Consequently, Jefferson did not even submit the Monroe-Pinkney Treaty to the Senate for ratification. What might have been the best chance for a conciliatory settlement of maritime differences between the United States and Britain thus came to nothing and was unlikely to come again. The Tories returned to power in 1807.

The Problem of Impressment

Surpassing even Britain's violations of neutral rights, the most volatile issue between Great Britain and the United States was impressment. It was a long-standing and unvarying source of Anglo-American friction, and became the one permanent obstruction to Anglo-American conciliation. In fact, Great Britain never officially abandoned impressment. The end of the Napoleonic Wars in 1815 would see impressment halted as a practice because there was no longer a need for it, but it remained a policy, albeit a dormant one, long after both Napoleon's defeat and the end of the War of 1812.[4]

The British Rationale and the American Complaint

Necessity dictated Britain's obstinacy about impressment. Service in the Royal Navy was a horrid ordeal, and the Royal Navy faced a chronic shortage of manpower. The Admiralty relied on press-gangs that technically kidnapped able-bodied men from England's seaports and merchant ships. They deserted by the thousands and frequently secured employment on American merchant ships or United States naval vessels. The American merchant marine certainly did not discourage British deserters who filled labor shortages caused for one thing by the swelling re-export trade. The numbers were significant—Lord Nelson estimated that 42,000 sailors deserted during the first phase of the French Revolutionary Wars alone—and threw the Royal Navy into crisis. The British Admiralty took to searching neutral ships in British harbors and on the high seas to reclaim deserters.

Beginning in 1796, the United States furnished mariners with official certificates confirming their citizenship, but at little cost, a British deserter could purchase such papers at any American waterfront. Moreover, the British government regarded such certificates as immaterial because the Crown insisted on a principle of incontrovertible allegiance that held a Briton was always a Briton, regardless of his residence. The United States, foremost a nation of immigrants, maintained that the right to renounce citizenship in one place to take it up in another was fundamental.

The United States was unique for doing so at that time, but Americans had gotten used to being unique.

The British never maintained that they had a right to impress American citizens, but undoubtedly they did. A British "press captain," inspecting an American crew's credentials and listening to its accents, was both initial examiner and final judge in the matter, and there was no appeal of his decision. The U.S. State Department might be able to prove, after years of exertion, that an impressed seaman was really an American citizen, and usually he was then released, though without compensation. More often, the American sailor dragged off his merchant ship simply disappeared into the belly of the British navy forever.

Here then was an enormous and irreconcilable point of conflict. Great Britain could not man its indispensable navy without resorting to impressment. Yet, it attacked U.S. sovereignty and, by depriving her citizens of their liberty, leveled a grave insult at American honor.

The Chesapeake Affair

In 1807, deserters from Royal Navy ships standing off Chesapeake Bay had escaped to Norfolk, Virginia, where some of them had enlisted for service on U.S. Navy ships, including the 38-gun frigate *Chesapeake*. When the U.S. government refused to return these deserters, exasperated British authorities in Nova Scotia impetuously altered their policy regarding searches at sea to include U.S. naval vessels. The British government had never claimed such a right and, in fact, would not do so now, but this new order was the one in force 22 June 1807 when the *Chesapeake* sailed from Hampton Roads.

As the *Chesapeake* put out to open water, the 50-gun HMS *Leopard* approached her. The *Leopard's* captain hailed that he had dispatches, thus creating the impression that he wanted the *Chesapeake* to carry his mail to Europe, a common practice of ships at sea. When the *Chesapeake's* captain, Commodore James Barron, allowed a British lieutenant to board, however, he discovered that the British intended to search his ship for deserters. Barron insisted he had no deserters on board, but he also correctly asserted that the British had no right to search a U.S. naval vessel. The frustrated lieutenant returned to the *Leopard*, which promptly opened fire.

The *Chesapeake*, fitted for a long voyage to the Mediterranean, was completely unprepared for battle. Her crew managed to fire only one symbolic shot while the *Leopard* hurled three broadsides into her, killing three Americans and wounding eighteen others, including Barron. The American vessel, broken and bleeding, had to strike its colors (surrender). The British captain would not accept the *Chesapeake*'s surrender. Instead, he ordered the American crew scrutinized and authorized the seizure of four men identified as deserters.[5] The *Leopard* sailed away. The badly damaged *Chesapeake* limped back to Norfolk.

It cannot be overly emphasized how serious this incident was. Without provocation, the British Royal Navy had fired on the U.S. Navy. This was much more serious than waylaying or even shooting at merchant vessels. Furthermore, the Royal Navy essentially had taken prisoner four U.S. Navy seamen. Technically and actually, the *Leopard*'s conduct amounted to an act of war, and what happened to the *Chesapeake* certainly warranted a warlike response from the United States.

American citizens certainly thought so. Hearing about the *Chesapeake*, they flew into a rage. Norfolk rioted, and states mustered their militia. The U.S. Navy even put additional gunboats into service, and, in July, the president ordered British warships from U.S. waters. Yet, Jefferson did not want a war with Britain in 1807, in part for the same reason that he could not resort to war earlier—the United States was not prepared to fight such a powerful enemy.

London realized the incident was an unpardonable mistake, but the British would not stop impressment, even though Jefferson insisted that Americans would be satisfied with nothing less. Negotiations tried to settle the incident for the next five years, but the erratic talks did nothing more than keep alive official bitterness. Americans also celebrated as retribution for the *Chesapeake* the May 1811 thrashing of a small British sloop when the USS *President* fired on HMS *Little Belt*, and the return of two of the kidnapped sailors in 1812 actually revived American anger. The Royal Navy remained firm on employing impressment, and American submission to it was an encouragement of British condescension and contempt.

France and Britain Conduct Economic Warfare

The Berlin Decree

While Americans were preoccupied with the implications of the *Essex* Decision and smoldering over the insults of impressment, new difficulties loomed because of a sweeping decree issued by Napoleon, purportedly in retaliation against Fox's Blockade.

Napoleon Bonaparte's early military exploits in this war were simply astounding. He moved irresistibly across central Europe scoring brilliant triumphs against the Third Coalition, the alliance that Britain had forged against him in 1805. By extending his control militarily and diplomatically over most of Europe, he was able to withhold European trade to counter Britain's naval supremacy. On 21 November 1806 in Berlin, Napoleon announced the first of the decrees that would frame his Continental System, a scheme designed to close off all Europe to British commerce.

Napoleon had no navy to speak of, so his blockade was truly a paper one, meaning it only existed on the documents proclaiming it. French privateers did begin seizing neutral ships at sea, though these numbers were relatively slight. Napoleon's control of European ports, however, gave him more than adequate means to enforce the object of the decree. Napoleon could not really keep neutral goods out of Britain, but he expected to defeat the nation he mockingly referred to as one of shopkeepers by collapsing her commerce.

The Orders in Council

Great Britain also began imposing commercial restrictions on neutrals, claiming that Napoleon's tactic compelled retaliation. Yet London also believed that Britain's control of the seas should result in her commercial as well as strategic advantage. It is likely that even in the absence of Napoleon's Berlin Decree, the Tory government would have adopted a policy similar to the one it did. As it happened, Napoleon's behavior gave Britain a convenient justification for her own disregard of international law.

The British system of controlling neutral trade with the enemy consisted of only one part that was a valid object of war: blocking contraband that Napoleon could use in military actions. Otherwise, the guiding principle behind the Orders in Council was to diminish the competition of neutral carriers, allowing British shippers to take over their routes and boost British profits. At the same time, London would license neutral shipping to break the French blockade of European ports.

Claiming it was responding to the Berlin Decree, the London government announced this complex scheme in a 7 January 1807 Order in Council. By barring neutral trade between all enemy ports, even those in

Europe, the order clearly violated even the Rule of 1756, because such trade had existed during peacetime. Although this sweeping pronouncement considerably tightened the terms of commercial restriction, Britain had cause to reassess the policy in only a few months, because it was not working. On 11 November 1807, the British government released another set of Orders in Council, refining the January version to place all enemy countries, their colonies, and anywhere else that excluded the British flag under strict blockade.

Under the November order, Britain could tax American cargoes with tariffs, charge American ships for licenses, and thereby control while pilfering American maritime profits. The policy was, in the words of John Quincy Adams, such a "momentous stride of encroachment" that there is no wonder it led to war.[6] It is only surprising that it took so long to do so.

The Milan Decree

Only a month after the November Orders in Council, Napoleon angrily announced the Milan Decree on 17 December 1807. By then, he had capped his spectacular round of military victories with an equally surprising diplomatic feat. He not only coerced Russia's Tsar Alexander I to accept a dictated peace, he also apparently mesmerized the tsar to become a willing member of the Continental System. The Milan Decree reflected the towering dominion Napoleon now exerted from the shores of the Atlantic to the peaks of the Caucasus. He announced that all vessels of any nation submitting to the Orders in Council were thereby denationalized and devoid of any security afforded by their nation's flag. They would, in fact, be considered as British property and liable for seizure in port and at sea. Assuming a mood of righteous indignation, Napoleon declared that his decrees would remain in operation until Great Britain revoked her unlawful policies.

The Consequences for the United States

Taken in sum, Napoleon's Berlin and Milan Decrees and the British Orders in Council theoretically barred the American flag from almost every port in the Western world, for to obey one set of restrictions was to run the perils of the other. We should note for precision, though, that the commercial screens erected by both France and Britain were relatively porous if one were willing to pay the fees. As mentioned, Britain's orders allowed for trade through expensive licenses. Napoleon too issued permits for exports and imports under steep tariff schedules. Nonetheless, Americans were understandably unhappy about complying with these externally imposed and costly rules.

It might also seem that the United States would have found the French decrees equally as obnoxious as the British orders, but this was not the case. Napoleon's rhetoric was far more impressive than his reach. American ships continued to visit British ports after the announcement of the Milan Decree, and Napoleon was incapable of doing anything about it unless they then sailed into a European port under his power. Already bitter about impressment, Americans had more cause to resent the British orders.

In addition, Napoleon's Continental System proved too far-flung to monitor and too fragile to maintain. Spain and Russia disobeyed Napoleon's orders with increasing regularity. In 1807, when the Spanish people revolted against Joseph Bonaparte (Napoleon arrogantly had put his brother on the Spanish throne), they opened a European foothold for the British army, and Spain's colonies became open for trade. Soon Russia and Scandinavia openly defied the Continental System as well. In fact, the tsar's disobedience impelled Napoleon to embark upon his catastrophic invasion of Russia in 1812, a campaign that would begin his ruin.

By then, the United States had exhausted all diplomatic alternatives—not to mention her patience—trying to cope with the inflexible and intrusive British orders. The American response to the French and British policies before that breaking point of 1812 reveals the desperation and futility that Jeffersonian idealism produced when confronted by the realities of the European conflict.

The United States' Restrictive System

By the summer of 1807, the Jefferson administration had a dire international crisis on its hands. The only tangible American response had been Jefferson's banishment of British vessels from U.S. territorial waters and the toothless Non-Importation Act of 1806. In December 1807, Jefferson not only applied the provisions of the Non-Importation Act, he also sought a more thorough level of economic coercion that would force the European powers to respect American rights.

The Embargo

Jefferson's plan for a system of trade restrictions featured the Embargo Act (22 December 1807). The embargo prohibited all vessels in U.S. harbors from departing for foreign ports. Foreign ships could leave, but only if they carried no cargoes. Jefferson hoped that cutting off Europe entirely from American commerce would force the belligerents to adjust their illegal decrees and specifically compel Great Britain to discontinue impressment. His belief that the embargo would work was likely bolstered by communications he received from American observers abroad. One wrote that "we have only to *Shut* our ports & *remain firm*—the *People* of *England* would do the rest."[7]

The embargo, however, was essentially an American self-blockade that was to injure U.S. shipping interests even more than the British and French decrees did. It would consequently require a remarkable level of popular support and participation to succeed. Simply put, the people of England might do the rest, but the people of America would have to do their part first. It remained uncertain if they would.

The embargo also invited criticism from those interested in preserving true American neutrality. Although technically aimed at both Britain and France, the embargo really only stopped trade with Great Britain because her license system and the Royal Navy's dominance already monitored American trade to France and her allies. Jefferson's self-blockade of American maritime commerce was essentially a reverse blockade on Britain—especially on her Caribbean islands—and made the United States an unwitting part of Napoleon's Continental System.

Americans suffered more than anyone else under the embargo, and they ultimately refused to do their part and stand firm. New England ports had thrived even under Britain's infuriating control of neutral American commerce, but in 1808, under Jefferson's noble experiment, they wallowed in poverty, unemployment, and crime. As an increasing number of Americans chose to break the embargo, it became increasingly difficult to enforce. Gradually intensified enforcement provisions seriously encroached on American civil liberties, but overland smugglers still transported goods across the Canadian border, and intrepid mariners either risked encounters with Jefferson's coastal gunboats or used trickery to avoid the embargo's restrictions. When a modification of the embargo allowed bonded American ships in ballast (empty of cargo) to retrieve American property abroad, countless vessels departed with valuable goods masquerading as cobblestone ballast and returned with equally valuable goods that never had been American property.

For his part, Napoleon characteristically gave in to his first rapacious impulse. Instead of encouraging this unexpected support of his Continental System, he issued the Bayonne Decree on 17 April 1808 that authorized the seizure of American ships in French harbors. Napoleon smugly concluded that since Jefferson had prohibited Americans vessels from leaving their ports, these "American" ships were actually Britons in disguise.

Jefferson watched all this with growing dismay and finally sad resignation. His noble experiment only bred lawlessness and cynicism at home. Abroad, it emboldened adversaries to greater provocations. The political consequences were rapid and potentially devastating, threatening to undo all gains the Republicans had made in the previous seven years. New Englanders talked of disunion, Federalist opponents gained seats in Congress, and Secretary of State James Madison nearly lost his bid for the presidency because of challenges mounted within his own Republican Party. Madison's victory in 1808 was more the result of Federalist uncertainty than national or even unified Republican support.

Three days before Jefferson left office and Madison became president, Congress repealed the embargo for all countries except Great Britain and France. The system of trade restrictions had proved futile and harrowing in the grand scale of the embargo, so Americans would try something less disruptive to them and, they hoped, more troublesome to their adversaries.

Non-Intercourse and the Erskine Agreement

On 1 March 1809, Congress replaced the Embargo Act with the Non-Intercourse Act, a measure calculated to help American commerce while maintaining economic pressure on France and Britain. A long and complicated piece of legislation, it immediately excluded British and French naval vessels from American waters and after 20 May 1810 all vessels sailing under their flags. Moreover, it banned the importation of goods from those countries, but with the following proviso: if either Great Britain or France stopped disturbing American commerce, the president could restore trade with that nation. Non-intercourse thus attempted to pit Britain and France against one another for American advantage.

A signal that this ploy would bring about favorable results buoyed President Madison. The British minister to the United States since 1806 was David M. Erskine. Charles James Fox had sent Erskine to America as part of his plan to restore harmony with the United States. To that object, Erskine was an excellent choice. He was good-natured and affable with Americans, even to the point of having married one. When the Tories replaced the Whigs in 1807, Secretary of State Madison despaired that a hardliner would replace Erskine, but the friendly diplomat remained in his post, though he did so more because of the British foreign office's indifference than its desire to continue cordial relations with the United States.

Erskine's new superior in London was Foreign Secretary George Canning, whose tendency to taint his official correspondence with irritating sarcasm alloyed his considerable talent. During 1808, Canning negotiated with U.S. minister William Pinkney to end American commercial restrictions, but Canning's unbending positions doomed the talks from the outset. Now with passage of the Non-Intercourse Act and the advent of the Madison administration, he instructed Erskine to offer to exempt the United States from the Orders in Council if the United States would: (a) remove all restrictions on Britain, (b) apply the Non-Intercourse Act against France and allow the Royal Navy to enforce it, and (c) accept the Rule of 1756 as a valid regulation of neutral commerce.

The second and third propositions were obviously unacceptable, the second because the United States could not allow the Royal Navy such latitude, and the third because it would relinquish the fundamental concept of "free ships make free goods," the foundation of the American argument for neutral maritime rights. Eager for an agreement, Erskine unwisely toned down Canning's instructions during talks with Secretary of State Robert Smith. Specifically, he did not mention that London expected the British navy to enforce the Non-Intercourse Act against France. Smith also convinced Erskine that non-intercourse with France would amount to a practical application of the Rule of 1756, so there was no need for the United States to endorse it in principle. On these terms, Smith and Erskine signed an accord.

James Madison had been in office only six weeks when the Erskine Agreement evidently accomplished what Jefferson's entire second term had failed to. On 19 April 1809, the president proclaimed that on 10 June— the date slated for the withdrawal of the Orders in Council—the United States would open trade with Britain. Jubilant shippers eagerly awaited the day, their vessels straining under the weight of stout cargoes for British customers. Starting on 10 June, about 600 ships pounded heavily out of American ports under the fluttering Stars and Stripes.

Then the humiliating disappointments began. George Canning summoned Erskine home at the end of May, and, in July, Canning repudiated both Erskine and his agreement. Instead of resolving Anglo-American difficulties, the episode's aftermath so poisoned relations between the countries that they never recovered before the war.[8] Madison gloomily revived non-intercourse against Britain, but he did so mindful of its power being blunted by all those American ships, released under the promises of David Erskine, off-loading cargoes on British wharves.

The Non-Intercourse Act also gave Napoleon another excuse to impound American ships, again using the roguish logic that official non-intercourse with France meant that all American vessels appearing in French harbors must actually be British. Under the Vienna Decree of 4 August 1809, he ordered such American ships seized and sold.

Macon's Bill No. 2

Like the embargo, the Non-Intercourse Act failed to sway Britain and France and hurt American commerce the most. With non-intercourse due to expire, Congress now surveyed its narrowing alternatives. Long and tedious debates finally produced a substitute for the expiring Non-Intercourse Act. The bill passed the House on 29 January 1810, but Senate amendments essentially killed it. When the House again referred this bill to committee, caustic Virginian John Randolph had heard enough. He bluntly opposed the entire restrictive system, disparaging it as "a toy, a rattle."[9]

North Carolina representative Nathaniel Macon, who chaired the House's select committee on foreign relations, placed a revision of the original bill before Congress on 7 April. Although Macon did not support the measure, during the three-week debate that followed, the proposal would informally bear the designation Macon's Bill No. 2 to distinguish it from its earlier version. On 1 May 1810, Congress passed this latest modification of the American restrictive system.

Macon's Bill No. 2 kept the ban on British and French armed vessels in American waters, but that was the only coercive feature in this otherwise depressing surrender of American neutral rights. Repealing the Non-Intercourse Act, the measure renewed trade with Britain and France, but if either Great Britain or France revoked its intolerable policies before 3 March 1811, the president would put the other nation on notice that, unless it followed suit within three months, non-intercourse would go into effect against it. In other words, Macon's Bill No. 2 sought to coerce Britain and France to respect American rights by applying no coercion, but threatening to revive it, even though it had not previously worked. This preposterous scheme had only the marginal benefit of according Britain and France uniform treatment, something absent from both the embargo and non-intercourse. Under Macon's Bill No. 2, the United States was at least no longer an implicit member of Napoleon's Continental System. Yet, even that merit would prove fleeting.

Final Steps to War

As soon as he knew about Macon's Bill, Napoleon turned it to his benefit. With remarkable ease, he was able to convince the United States that he was revoking the French decrees affecting American commerce. On 5 August 1810, the French foreign minister Duc de Cadore wrote to U.S. minister to France John Armstrong that since Congress had canceled non-intercourse against France, the emperor was correspondingly canceling the Berlin and Milan Decrees as they affected the United States, effective 1 November. The letter ambiguously insisted that Britain must withdraw the Orders in Council or the United States must force her to do so.

Of course, the Cadore letter did not actually cancel anything. Napoleon only wanted to make it appear that the decrees were repealed. The French government continued to act on them, and Napoleon even issued (but did not publish) another decree from Trianon in August that reemphasized the French assault on American shipping.[10] Yet, Madison chose to take the French emperor at his word. He publicly proclaimed that nonimportation would go into effect against Great Britain, and Congress confirmed the gesture with the Non-Importation Act against Great Britain on 1 March 1811.

Why did President Madison readily accept Napoleon's obvious subterfuge? Possibly the president was so eager for a diplomatic success that he leapt at even a fictitious one. A more charitable gauge suggests that Madison was acting out of necessity. Both France and Great Britain were violating American neutrality, but it was barely feasible for the United States to fight one of these great powers; it was impossible to challenge them both. Napoleon's actions, false as they were, gave Madison the excuse to single out Great Britain, already unpopular for its impressment policy. Such behavior on Madison's part suggests that by the middle of 1810 he had concluded that only war would resolve the United States' graceless predicament.[11] Whether that was the case or not, his and Congress's move against Britain at this pivotal moment almost amounted to an act of war.

Naturally, the British cried foul. To offset such protests and evidently believing he could trick everyone indefinitely, Napoleon produced yet another pronouncement, this one allegedly rendered at St. Cloud on 28 April 1811 and inexplicably kept secret until May 1812. The "secret" St. Cloud Decree stated that the Berlin and Milan Decrees would not apply to American commerce after 1 November 1810, but the document was so obviously false that its abrupt appearance insulted everyone's intelligence. That Americans did not dismiss it as a clumsy forgery indicates how far toward war Britain had pushed them. That some members of the British Parliament also accepted the bogus St. Cloud Decree as grounds to revoke the Orders in Council reveals that the British suddenly, if belatedly, realized they had pushed the United States too far.

The Orders Repealed and the Declaration of War

The United States focused her anger on Britain, and the War Hawk faction in the new Twelfth Congress beat more steadily the drums of war. Meanwhile, for the first time since the appearance of American trade restrictions, Britain found herself especially hurt by them. The most telling injury was in the West Indies, a part of the empire with growing political influence. British manufacturers had felt the lash of American restrictions from the start, but they had always been second in rank to shipping interests until 1812. In that year, their influence finally assumed a leading role in shaping policy. While the British government continued to protest that Napoleon had not repealed his decrees, signs foretelling a potential economic collapse demanded a change in London's tactics. By the spring of 1812, only the stubbornness of Prime Minister Spencer Perceval's Tory cabinet stood in the way of a major adjustment with the United States.

Then on 11 May 1812, a crazed assassin killed Perceval over a private matter. A new government under Lord Liverpool finally freed itself from unwavering allegiance to pamphleteer James Stephen's ideas and moved to repeal the Orders in Council as they affected American commerce. That announcement on 16 June 1812 was nevertheless too late.

Unaware of Parliament's actions, the United States on 18 June 1812 declared war on Great Britain, citing, in part, impressment and the injurious Orders in Council.

Conclusion

Between 1806 and 1812, the United States tried to force Great Britain and France to respect American neutral rights by variously restricting American trade. Born of the belief that withholding American commerce could sway European behavior, this restrictive system required fine-tuning as the United States grappled with its ineffectiveness. The partial Non-Importation Act in 1806 excluded certain British manufactures, the general Embargo Act in 1807 locked all American ships and goods in U.S. ports, and the Non-Intercourse Act in 1809 prohibited trade with the British and French empires. Under the terms of another adjustment in Macon's Bill No. 2, an additional Non-Importation Act in 1811 excluded British ships and goods from American ports. None of these restrictions extracted concessions from Britain and France. Instead, those powers continued to plunder American shipping until Britain repealed the Orders in Council in 1812, too late to prevent the war.

During the embargo, Thomas Jefferson had quietly observed, "If nations go to war for every degree of injury, there would never be peace on earth."[12] The sentiment reflected both the nobility of Jefferson's vision and the futility of the restrictive system that vision had produced. Commercial restriction tried to preserve peace by waging a war with America's economic arsenal. The system's collapse left the United States no alternative but to intensify coercion with war. Even after the declaration of war, Madison and fellow Republicans persisted in the belief that a restrictive system could weaken Britain's war effort by damaging her markets. Thus, economic coercion strangely became a part of the war it had so strenuously sought to avoid. By folding its diplomacy into its war making, the United States ultimately revealed that the restrictive system had always been more a prelude to conflict than a way to avert it.

Notes

1. Quoted in Dumas Malone, *Jefferson the President, First Term, 1801–1805*, Vol. 4 in *Jefferson and His Time*, 6 vols. (Boston: Little, Brown and Co., 1970), 256.

2. Jefferson to Jacob Crowninshield, 13 May 1806, in Paul Leicester Ford, ed., *The Writings of Thomas Jefferson*, 10 vols. (New York: G. P. Putnam, 1892–1899), 8:451–53.

3. Quoted in Malone, *Jefferson the President, Second Term, 1805–1809*, Vol. 5 in *Jefferson and His Time*, 6 vols. (Boston: Little, Brown and Co., 1974), 705.

4. The British never again resorted to impressment after 1815, however. In the 1870 Treaty of Washington, Britain and the United States agreed to recognize naturalization as a legitimate process, which had the effect of ending Britain's doctrine of forcible repatriation and thus eliminating the primary justification for impressment.

5. One of the four, Jenkin Radford, was an actual British deserter, and the British hanged him for mutiny and desertion before the summer was over. The other three were American citizens who had not deserted but had merely fled a British warship after being impressed. The British sentenced them to receive 500 lashes each but canceled that punishment and imprisoned them instead. One died in captivity, but the British eventually returned the other two—after five years.

6. Adams to Harrison Gray Otis, 31 March 1808, in Worthington C. Ford, ed., *Writings of John Quincy Adams*, 7 vols. (New York: Macmillan, 1913–17), 3: 201.

7. Quoted in Lewis Martin Sears, *Jefferson and the Embargo* (Durham: Duke University Press, 1927; reprint ed., New York: Octagon Books, 1966), 55.

8. Canning did not help matters by replacing Erskine with Francis James Jackson, known as "Copenhagen" Jackson because he had been involved—nefariously, some claimed—in the Royal Navy's 1807 destruction of the Danish fleet while it lay at anchor in Copenhagen harbor. His embassy was so annoying that Madison stopped talking to him, and he left after a year. Only a British *chargé d'affaires* remained in Washington during the crucial ensuing two years, and only just before the war did another minister, Augustus J. Foster, appear.

9. *Annals of Congress*, 11th Cong., 2nd sess., 1702.

10. Though the Trianon Decree was a secret pronouncement, particulars of the policy it established were known to Armstrong, who did not communicate them to Madison in a timely fashion. The actual decree, however, was not discovered until eleven years later when Albert Gallatin was serving as minister to France. See Brant, *Madison*, 5: 218–20.

11. Madison informed France that if England continued to assail American shipping, it would "necessarily lead to war." See ibid., 221.

12. Quoted in Reginald C. Stuart, *The Half-War Pacifist: Thomas Jefferson's View of War* (Toronto, Buffalo, London: University of Toronto Press, 1978), 36.

CHAPTER 3

MR. MADISON'S WAR:
COUNTRY, CONGRESS, AND THE PRESIDENCY IN AMERICA'S FIRST DECLARED WAR

Before 1812, the United States had never declared war on another sovereign power. Yet, those Americans who wanted to fight Britain in 1812 were not apparently apprehensive about their ability to challenge the most powerful empire on earth. Anxiety mainly focused on the government's unproven ability to summon the country's potentially vast resources of manpower, money, and materiel and to direct them in a coherent war effort. The undertaking required politicians to work within the constitutional framework of Congress and the presidency, supervising a host of specific and broad concerns. Moreover, it required a willingness among the people to sacrifice individual comforts and occasionally their safety for what political leaders were defining as the greater good. As with any endeavor in a democratic republic, success in this war would depend on the durability and constancy of the public mood.

The People and the War

Opposition among the people to the War of 1812 matched that toward any war in American history, even U.S. involvement in Vietnam. Some opposed the war for economic reasons. Merchants in the Northeast were anxious about the potential for commercial ruin by making war on the British Empire, the most bountiful international marketplace in the world. Almost to a man, Federalists objected on political grounds. Republican policies, they insisted, made the United States an unwitting ally of the despot Napoleon. As for Republicans, older and more traditional

elements of the party were at most unenthusiastic about the war, predict-
ing that the venture would lead to high expenditures and additional taxes.

Yet, the war obviously enjoyed some measure of popular support.
Foremost champions were from the South and the West, while the Mid-
Atlantic states were divided and New England was almost uniformly
opposed.

The West and South

The region stretching beyond the Allegheny and Appalachian moun-
tains was the West of the early republic. Here the War of 1812 enjoyed
its most unqualified support, even though sometimes that support did not
translate into fervent participation. The Shawnee Tecumseh had awakened
a nativist movement among a number of Indians north of the Ohio River,
but most westerners believed that the British were responsible for all Indian
unrest. They welcomed an opportunity to make war on Britain, both to
end the redcoat riling of the Indians and to acquire Canada as a way to
extract concessions from London.

Similarly in the South, anxiety over Indians stimulated demands for
war and targeted Britain's European allies, the Spanish in West Florida.
Watercourses such as the Escambia, Alabama, and Chattahoochee rivers
flowed through rich lands inaccessible to eager white farmers because of
their Indian inhabitants. The rivers emptied into the Gulf of Mexico
through Spanish Florida and thus offered a tempting avenue from the
American interior to the wider oceans of the world. Possessing the mouths
of these rivers and farming the dark soil they watered could significantly
expand the American empire of liberty.

It would be a mistake, however, to suppose that western and southern support for the war arose exclusively or even primarily from expansionist aims. British violations of maritime rights offended westerners even
though the region was physically remote from them. Like much of the rest
of the country, these regions were outraged over the *Chesapeake–Leopard*
Affair in 1807, and many southerners and westerners came to believe that
the British Orders in Council intended to subjugate the United States commercially to restore what practically amounted to an imperial relationship.

The Mid-Atlantic

The Mid-Atlantic states of Maryland, New Jersey, New York, and
Pennsylvania greeted the war with ambivalence. Although torn by politi-

cal divisions within the Republican Party, Pennsylvania furnished valuable and tangible assistance to the American war effort. New York did so as well, despite significant opposition to the Madison administration mounted by DeWitt Clinton, who ran against Madison in 1812. New York's northern frontier saw a brisk and illegal trade in livestock, produce, and other goods into British Canada.

No other state in the Mid-Atlantic region felt the war as acutely as Maryland. That state would be the site of the worst incidents of rioting early in the war and later would suffer under repeated raids on the shores of its Chesapeake Bay. Baltimore's Federalist minority loudly protested the move to war, especially through their newspaper the *Federal Republican*, edited by Alexander Hanson. Immediately after the declaration of war, on 22–23 June 1812, a Republican mob destroyed the paper's press and ran Hanson out of town. He returned to Baltimore in July with the intention of publishing his paper from his home. Prominent Federalists, including the Revolutionary War hero Henry "Light Horse Harry" Lee, vowed to protect Hanson's operation, but their doing so only further enraged the Baltimore mob, which set upon the Hanson residence after dark on 27 July. Fearing for their lives, Hanson and his defenders accepted the Maryland militia's offer of protection and consented to confinement in the comparatively safe city jail. The large rabble pushed aside indifferent militia guards, stormed the jail, and mercilessly assaulted its "prisoners." The mob killed the aged Revolutionary War veteran General James M. Lingan and so injured Hanson and Lee that they would never fully recover their health.

Maryland voters, however, recoiled from this wanton and gruesome violence. That fall, they gave Federalists a majority in the state legislature and Alexander Hanson a seat in Congress. Later, during the British raids of 1813 and 1814, southern Maryland frequently showed only a token resistance.

Baltimore mobs assailed local Federalists, but the city's merchants financed an extensive assault on British commerce by investing in privateers. More than 100 such Maryland-based ships accounted for a third of the almost 1,350 British captures of the war. This reputation for privateering and the vulnerability of Maryland's Chesapeake Bay shoreline attracted British raids on the bay beginning in 1813, a prelude to the massive combined operations in Chesapeake Bay during the summer of 1814.

New England

The strongest opposition to the war arose in New England. Federalists were the majority party in most New England states, and Federalist philosophy exerted an almost thorough cultural and economic influence there. Clergymen, captains of commerce, and political leaders all denounced the war with equal vehemence as "a license given by a Virginia vassal of the French emperor to the English authorizing them in legal form to destroy the prosperity of New England."[1] Many New England governors would not call out their states' militias, and, from the outset, there was muted (and sometimes not so muted) talk of disunion. Finally, Federalists in New England lost patience and held a convention at Hartford, Connecticut, to plan a strategy for protecting their political and commercial interests. They did not realize that their meeting would occur in the final weeks of a war they blindly saw as endless and hopeless. They had no way of knowing that this war—the very thing they detested—would not destroy their country, but would, in prompting their unceasing complaint and impetuous reaction, destroy them.

It is thus tempting to describe all parts of New England as cut from the same political cloth, but in truth, the region was not wholly Federalist nor was it temperamentally toneless. Subtleties in politics and varying shades of opinion could occasionally appear in states as diverse as Vermont, New Hampshire, Connecticut, Rhode Island, and Massachusetts.

Vermont and New Hampshire, for instance, were unique for their ample number of Republicans who prevented their states from completely opposing the war. More typically, Federalists almost completely controlled Massachusetts, Rhode Island, and Connecticut, and these states opposed the war from the start. They consistently refused the national government's request for militia, claiming that the Constitution gave them exclusive command over their state militias. Federal law, they said, restricted the national use of state militias to fighting an actual invasion of the United States. Rhode Islanders traded with the British off the New England coast, and late in the war, inhabitants of Massachusetts's Nantucket Island made similar arrangements with the Royal Navy. The rest of the nation regarded as even worse the alleged behavior of some Connecticut citizens in December 1813. Someone—it was never revealed who—supposedly used blue lanterns to alert British blockading ships that Stephen Decatur was planning to bring his squadron out of New London into open water. That these so-called "Blue Light Federalists" had not only comforted the enemy but also aided him would enter American lore as the prime example of Federalist treachery during the war.[2]

Despite all this uproar and opposition, the war left much of New England virtually untouched except for the northern counties of Massachusetts—the Maine District—that bordered British Canada. The British claimed northern Maine belonged to them, citing long-standing confusions over the boundary. A more practical motive for the British claim was that the district obstructed land communications between Halifax, Nova Scotia, and Quebec. By 1814, the British government made the cession of this area a condition for peace, and, to back up that demand, launched a military campaign to occupy northern Maine and put a hundred-mile stretch of Massachusetts' coast under British control.

This conquest caused considerable dismay for the Madison administration. In the first place, the inhabitants of the Maine District exhibited little anxiety about the British occupation, and fully two-thirds of them swore allegiance to the British crown. Furthermore, the British occupation of this territory made it a smuggler's paradise and seriously undermined the government's efforts to stem the tide of illegal goods flowing to the enemy in Canada. As a final blow, the administration's military plans to reconquer the region somehow wound up in New England newspapers and had to be canceled.

There matters stood when New England Federalists began planning a convention to discuss the war, New England's opposition to it, and the region's place in—or, it was feared by some, out of—the nation. An examination of this final and profoundly important gesture of New England dissent will follow an appraisal of the federal government's performance during the war, beginning with the legislature.

Congress

Two Congresses (the Twelfth and Thirteenth) would sit during the War of 1812. The Twelfth Congress, which declared war in June 1812, was the more famous of the two, but the Thirteenth Congress would bear most of the burden of funding the war and raising men to fight in it.

The Twelfth Congress convened in two sessions, the first from 4 November 1811 to 6 July 1812, and the second from 2 November 1812 to 3 March 1813. The Thirteenth Congress would sit in three sessions, the last seeing the war end in 1815. Its first session was from 24 May 1813 to 2 August 1813, the second from 6 December 1813 to 18 April 1814, and the third from 19 September 1814 to 3 March 1815.

The elections of 1810 registered public exasperation over the Eleventh Congress's failure to resolve the conflict with Britain and France. For one thing, voters increased the Republican majority in both the House and the Senate, an indication that the brief Federalist resurgence spurred by the embargo was waning. Moreover, the vocal faction of Republicans called the War Hawks assumed a leading role in shaping congressional policy. When the Twelfth Congress convened on 4 November 1811, the War Hawk leader in the House, freshman congressman Henry Clay of Kentucky, was elected Speaker. Joined by notables such as South Carolinians John C. Calhoun, William Lowndes, and Langdon Cheves and Tennesseean Felix Grundy, Clay and his War Hawks would help push a reluctant President Madison to make war on Britain.

The Twelfth Congress

Careful scholars do not overly stress the War Hawks' power within either the Republican Party or Congress. A faction of Republicans led by Virginian John Randolph opposed the War Hawks, as did New Yorker DeWitt Clinton's supporters. Clintonians, consisting of commercially oriented northerners who wanted their man in the presidency, held foreign policy views not unlike the Federalists. The "Invisibles" comprised yet another Republican faction. Led by Senator Samuel Smith of Maryland, this bloc resolutely opposed the Madison administration because they so disliked both the policies and the personality of Treasury Secretary Albert Gallatin.

Within this potentially unstable Republican mix, the Federalists had a chance to reclaim some of their former influence despite their minority status. Part of that plan was to repair their reputation for being pro-British.[3] In the opening weeks of the Congress, Federalists supported Republican measures that expanded the army, prepared the militia, and explored innovative financing should hostilities occur. Federalists could only go so far, however, and in early 1812, they opposed additional taxes to refurbish the military and new commercial sanctions against Britain. When the decision for war loomed in June, they violently opposed the declaration. As it happened, Federalists were not alone in their opposition.

The Vote for War

On 1 June 1812, the House of Representatives received James Madison's war message and after three days of occasionally harsh debate, voted for war. The vote of 79–49 was troubling, though, for it revealed bitter quarrels across both party and regional lines. One of these disputes, however, appeared more compelling that it actually was. Republican John Randolph condemned the war as a dishonest ploy by expansionists who cloaked their land hunger with neutral rights as a pretense.[4] Indeed, the regional delineation of those for the war (the South and the West) and those opposed to it (New York and New England) suggested that the motto of "Free Trade and Sailors' Rights" was a mask for the war's real purpose of territorial expansion. Yet, most historians agree that the war was chiefly about defending national honor.

What is more important is that one-quarter of House Republicans either opposed the war or abstained from the vote altogether. It was hardly the act of a unified party. In the Senate, the division was worse. The upper chamber debated for more than two weeks before endorsing a declaration of war on 17 June with a close vote of 19–13. These gloomy indications of national division at the start of the war continued during it, and an acutely divided national legislature frequently struggled, sometimes unsuccessfully, to meet the demands of waging the conflict.

The Politics of War

The 1812 congressional elections exposed the intensity of Federalist hostility to the war and the extent of Republican weakness because of it. Republicans expected to record losses in Massachusetts, but their unpopularity in the Mid-Atlantic states of New York, New Jersey, and Maryland must have surprised them. The 1814 congressional elections further reduced the Republican majority as the country staggered under the weight of financial decline and military disaster. Yet, Federalists ultimately could not exploit Republican vulnerabilities, and their chronic complaints about the war finally grated too harshly both in and out of Congress. They enjoyed a brief resurgence, but they never really recovered a vigorous political standing. The various and mostly unpleasant fortunes of war damaged Republicans, but Federalists courted a deadly fate by giving credibility to the charge that they were either faithless or foolish.

In such an environment, perpetual disagreement was the main hallmark of congressional deliberation during the War of 1812. The Senate frequently refused to support the Madison administration's foreign policy plans, as when it refused to confirm Albert Gallatin as a member of the peace delegation to Europe. Even under the skillful leadership of Henry Clay, the House of Representatives was just as bad-tempered. When Madison appointed Clay to the peace delegation in Europe, he quit the House and therefore left the speakership on 19 January 1814. Langdon Cheves, a War Hawk from South Carolina, succeeded Clay by a vote of 94–59, and had to deal with a confrontational Federalist minority during the second and third sessions of the Thirteenth Congress. Federalist Daniel Webster of New Hampshire was new to the House, but he was anything but timid as he routinely excoriated the administration for its ostensible bias toward Napoleon.[5] As heated and repetitive debate mired deliberations, accomplishing anything became a challenge.

Paying for the War

Under the Constitution, all financial appropriations originate in the House of Representatives, so Congress's foremost duty was to fund the war effort. Because powerful Republicans like Clay had opposed the renewal of the Bank of the United States' charter in 1811, the country lacked a central agency that could manage the government's finances. In this vacuum, Congress implemented new taxes—a basic activity of each session—that were only partly successful. By the last stages of the war, the bank's absence had proved so injurious that Congress considered creating another one that would have been limited to the District of Columbia. Nothing came of the idea at the time, but it is instructive to note that in the postwar period, a new national bank would be one of the Republican Party's main initiatives.

At the start of the war, Congress authorized $5 million in treasury notes to cover the underperformance of an $11 million bond issue the previous March. These measures were not sufficient to the demands of the moment, but Congress adjourned on 6 July 1812 under the illusion that money matters were well in hand. As the war continued beyond the optimistic timetable predicted by the Twelfth Congress, Madison's treasury department coped with mounting costs by floating additional bond issues and using private financiers to promote and underwrite government loans. Debt expanded alarmingly, and the government's credit correspondingly declined. In a report to the third session of the Thirteenth Congress, Secretary of the Treasury Alexander Dallas described such a grim financial situation that Congress voted to issue new paper money and raise new taxes.

Republican hostility to taxes in general, even when necessitated by the emergency of war, caused much grumbling about the size and scope of levies, but the government's financial troubles did not result so much from inadequate taxes as they did from military setbacks, lukewarm public support for low interest bond issues, and the absence of a national bank. By the end of the war, military expenses totaled almost $95 million, and the government had funded 85 percent of that figure with loans. In that respect, the War of 1812 demolished the Republican Party's plan for debt retirement and the dream of balanced budgets. Yet, in the final tally, the war had not ruined the American economy. Madison's treasury department and Congress managed the war's enormous financial burdens with more success than might have been expected.

Raising Armies

As relations with Britain deteriorated in the years following the *Chesapeake* incident, Congress sporadically enlarged the U.S. military establishment, but the army never reached its full strength of 10,000 men. When war loomed, the Madison administration asked Congress to fill the regular army's quota and authorize another 10,000 regulars for a three-year term of service. Various congressional maneuvers raised that supplemental number to 25,000 regulars for a five-year term. The reason for the increase lay partly in the spiteful motives of anti-administration factions in both Republican and Federalist ranks. Raising 25,000 additional men would prove formidable if not impossible, they thought, and if this fantastic host somehow materialized, sustaining it would likely stretch the government beyond its capabilities. For their part, War Hawks were more than happy to have an army of 35,000 men, if only on paper, so under such mixed and partly mischievous sponsorship, this regular force came into theoretical existence on 9 January 1812.

During the first months of the war, the expanded army was indeed theoretical. After enticing recruits with generous cash and land bounties, the army still consisted of only about 12,000 regulars in the fall of 1812. That number steadily grew, thanks in part to increased bounties, and in spring 1813, the army totaled about 30,000 men. In early 1814, a sadder but wiser Congress authorized a force of 62,500, an unthinkable figure two years before, but the war was a harsh tutor. The army grew to about

40,000 men that spring and had increased by another 5,000 toward the end of the year, but these numbers, while impressive, made up only 72 percent of the total envisioned by the 1814 expansion. Matching recruiting realities with congressional expectations simply proved impossible.

Congress also enacted measures that expanded federal authority over state militia, a move that was most unpopular among the states, especially in New England. When shortages of men continued to vex the war effort, the Madison administration tried to introduce universal conscription. Even regions that strongly supported the war—the South and the West—had serious misgivings about a draft, but so few men were willing to volunteer that Madison directed Secretary of War James Monroe to devise a way to increase the army. In November 1814, Monroe submitted to Congress a plan that would empower the federal government to conscript men from state militias if necessary. The proposal set off a firestorm. The conscription bill passed the Senate but failed in the House because Federalist opposition to it was relentless. Webster delivered one of the most effective criticisms of the bill.[6]

Congress and the Navy

The U.S. Navy never enjoyed the level of financial support afforded the army. Although initially, some congressmen hoped the war with Britain would be waged exclusively on the seas, most Republicans persisted in their belief that naval expenditures were wanton raids on the treasury. In any event, challenging the Royal Navy's supremacy seemed certain to be both unsuccessful and expensive. Instead, Congress granted privateers wide authority and sizable bounties. The U.S. naval successes on the Great Lakes in 1813 and 1814 moved Congress to approve the construction of large seventy-four-gun warships that would conceivably have challenged British ships of the line, but the war ended before these vessels could come into play.

The Restrictive System That Would Not Die

Except for the last weeks of peace in the summer of 1812, commercial sanctions had proved singularly ineffective in securing American diplomatic aims. Congress remained oddly keen on imposing them, though, even after the declaration of war. In the summer of 1812, the Twelfth Congress approved a modified restrictive system with the Enemy Trade Act, which prohibited all trade with Britain except for those forces fighting Napoleon in Spain. Such measures persisted throughout the war, culminating in an extensive embargo put in place during the war's final year. The 1814 embargo matched the one of 1807 in scope, unpopularity, and futility, promoting nothing more than disregard for the law and enthusiasm for smuggling. After about four months, Madison despondently asked Congress to repeal this embargo, and on 31 March 1814, it went the way of its predecessors.

Just a month before its final adjournment, though, the Thirteenth Congress could not resist another fling with the restrictive system. Angry that smugglers from the outset had skirted the Enemy Trade Act, Congress strengthened it in February 1815, even though members were by then aware that the war was essentially over. Federal agents supplied with broad powers surpassed earlier levels of insupportable enforcement, but smugglers continued to flout the restrictive system, just as they had in 1808.

The Presidency

In wartime, the executive branch of the federal government, headed by the president and superintended by his cabinet officers, has the responsibility for devising strategy, directing armies, conducting diplomacy, and keeping the government financially solvent during the undertaking. Moreover, the president is constitutionally the commander in chief of all armed forces as well as the nation's chief executive, and on his shoulders rest the heaviest burdens and the greatest accountability. When the United States declared war on Britain in 1812, it commenced a thirty-one-month odyssey filled with military misfortunes and political disputes. Early military setbacks bred despair and banished the hope that the war would end quickly and require little sacrifice. James Madison would be the first president to face such a crisis. He soon learned that in addition to his functional role as the chief engineer of a sprawling political and military machine, he would also be required to lead the people in this war by inspiring them to take up a popular cause. Madison's scholarly disposition made the engineer's tasks a challenge; his retiring personality made him wholly unsuited for the role of inspirational leader.

The Education of a President

Madison hoped that the vote for war would convince the British that at last Americans were serious about protecting their rights and genuine negotiations would ensue. When that did not happen and Madison had to assert himself as commander in chief, it should have surprised nobody that he was not very good at it.

Madison was knowledgeable about many things, but he was ignorant about the tangibles of war. Seemingly unaware that war was a miserable and nasty business that ground up men and gobbled up money, Madison instead assumed that it was merely an escalated argument in which firearms supplemented heated words. Civil rules and civilized conduct would win through, he thought. He was not alone in such illusions— many in Congress and the nation felt the same way— but those people were not the president of the United States.

When it became clear that everyone had vastly overrated the country's ability to defeat the British in Canada, Madison had to deal with a military emergency just as he was coping with a political one posed by the 1812 election. That contest exposed the president's alarming political frailty. Anti-war Republicans and Federalists united to replace Madison with New York's DeWitt Clinton, and though Madison won with 128 electoral votes to Clinton's 89, it was a sobering tally for an incumbent president in the middle of a war.

The Treasury Department

Albert Gallatin, the only secretary of the treasury in Thomas Jefferson's two terms, remained in place for James Madison. When the war broke out in the summer of 1812, Gallatin was uniquely qualified to meet its financial requirements, but he was also unpopular, in part because he had so vehemently advocated the recharter of the Bank of the United States in 1811. Gallatin realized that the war would be costly, and he had already arranged before the declaration to increase government funding. His plan was to pay for the war's extraordinary expenses with loans from bond issues while funding the government's ordinary operating expenses through existing taxes. His first attempts to borrow money from the private sector, however, met with little success because lenders feared that the government without the national bank would prove a bad credit risk. Gallatin then embarked upon a groundbreaking program that included government bond issues underwritten and marketed by private interests and an operating currency of treasury notes designed to facilitate government transactions.

For a year, Gallatin supervised the government's wartime finances, but the task of working with a contrary Congress and courting private financiers exhausted him. In 1813, he requested that Madison relieve him of his post. The president reluctantly did so, appointing Gallatin to the peace delegation he was dispatching to Europe, and commencing a search for his replacement. Secretary of the Navy William Jones exercised a custodial oversight of the Treasury until Madison appointed the War Hawk senator from Tennessee, George Campbell.

Campbell had no experience with financial affairs, and he took over a Treasury Department muddled by Jones's inattention and incompetence. Campbell soon realized, however, that Gallatin had been correct in his persistent entreaties for additional taxes to a resistant Congress. Campbell found it ever more difficult to finance the war, and his health began to fail. As a final act, he drafted a hasty recommendation to Congress for internal taxes before asking Madison to let him resign from the Treasury. Madison replaced him with Pennsylvanian Alexander Dallas.

James Madison had wanted to appoint Alexander Dallas to succeed Albert Gallatin. However, Dallas was so unpopular among Republicans in his home state of Pennsylvania and so disliked by Secretary of War John Armstrong that Madison had turned to Campbell instead. By September 1814, when Campbell's poor health had forced him from the post, Armstrong had also left the cabinet and the Treasury was in such dire shape that Madison was prepared to weather even Pennsylvania's political discontent to have a qualified man as his secretary.

Dallas, confronting an urgent necessity, immediately called for extreme measures. The nation's treasury was empty, and the government risked financial ruin if it could not pay the interest on its huge debt. Dallas's broad report to Congress specified the actions essential to avoid bankruptcy: increased taxes and the formation of another national bank. Although Congress would not give Dallas the bank, it did increase taxes and did authorize him to issue a new round of treasury notes. Dallas's stern methods helped avert calamity and put the nation on the road to a sound economic footing for the postwar period.

The War Department

Madison wrestled with the problem of finding talented people for hard jobs throughout the war, and that was never truer than in the case of the secretary of war. William Eustis, a physician by trade and an administrator by no stretch of the imagination, was in the post at the start of the war, but the demands of the conflict proved him woefully inadequate, and he resigned on 3 December 1812. Madison replaced him with John Armstrong of New York. Armstrong had wide experience in military and public affairs. He was a veteran of the American Revolution, had served in the U.S. Senate, had been the U.S. minister to France, and was at the time of his appointment organizing New York City's defenses. Best of all, he was from New York, and Madison liked the idea of soothing that state's rancor after the 1812 presidential contest.

Armstrong was not universally popular, however, and James Monroe openly disliked him.[7] There were unpleasant things in his past—at the close of the Revolution, Armstrong had taken part in an abortive and half-formed anti-government movement—and he had a sharp tongue. Occasionally, he made no effort to hide his contempt for the president. Yet, Madison was long-suffering, and Armstrong remained at the War Department, benefiting from the president's support through some very dark times.

Matters had become so dismal by early 1813 that, at the start of Armstrong's tenure, there was no place for things to go but up. The new secretary immediately reorganized the officer corps. He could do little about the elderly old ruins in the topmost ranks, but his appointment of younger officers as brigadiers considerably improved the vigor of field commands in most theaters. Armstrong had his failings, but he recognized and rewarded aptitude.

He was less able at strategy and resolving personality disputes between argumentative commanders in the field and within Madison's official family. The result was a muddled plan for the conquest of Canada and chronic quarrelling among frustrated American officers. The failure of the 1813 campaign against Montreal saw Monroe openly recommending Armstrong's dismissal.

In 1814, when the British brought the war to the United States, Madison finally had no choice but to question Armstrong's competence. The secretary was convinced that the British would not threaten the capital, so he neglected Washington's defenses in the interest of economy. With the British roaming Chesapeake Bay, Madison ultimately insisted on the city's protection, but Armstrong only halfheartedly supported the initiative and wasted precious time bickering with Acting Secretary of State James Monroe over everything attendant to it. When the British easily routed the U.S. militia outside Washington on 24 August, and Madison and his cabinet had to abandon the capital, most of the blame fell on Armstrong.

There was plenty of blame to go around, and Madison did not want the appearance of administrative disarray in the wake of the Washington disaster. Yet, his efforts to soothe his increasingly irritable secretary of war proved unsuccessful. Armstrong indignantly resigned on 4 September, and his chief rival, James Monroe, offered to fill the post on 25 September. Madison reluctantly agreed, thus making Monroe the secretary of war as well as the acting secretary of state. Monroe had his hands full beyond meeting the demands of two demanding jobs, especially in trying to persuade Congress to accept novel methods of military recruitment. His plan for conscription did not pass, but Congress enacted his proposals for lowering age requirements and increasing bounties. Cheered by the news of American victories at Plattsburgh and Baltimore, Monroe still fretted over the possibility of a successful British invasion on the Gulf Coast. His trust in Andrew Jackson—though sometimes strained by the general's insubordination—paid off when news of the triumph at New Orleans reached Washington.

The Hartford Convention

In the closing months of the war, James Madison was publicly optimistic, but privately he suspected that the war would end badly, especially when circumstantial evidence made him assume that New England Federalists were plotting disunion. Monroe in the War Department likewise became sufficiently uneasy about potential New England misbehavior that he instructed military commanders in the region to exercise vigilance and put down insurgency with force if necessary.

Federalist opposition to the War of 1812 finally resulted in the Hartford Convention in late 1814. A complex set of complaints made New England Federalists snap at that particular time. Simply put, an ongoing argument with the federal government over who would control New England militias worsened when Washington's financial plight meant that the federal government could not pay for local defense measures. The burden for their own defense in a war they did not want increasingly fell to the New England states. Meanwhile, the British blockade so seriously impaired New England's financial health that the region plunged into economic depression.

In the fall of 1814, a special session of the Massachusetts legislature advocated a convention of New England delegates to articulate Federalist complaints and propose solutions to the region's political and economic difficulties. Connecticut, which would host the gathering at Hartford, appointed seven delegates. That other bastion of Federalism, Rhode Island, selected four delegates, and Massachusetts sent the largest delegation of twelve to the convention. The more moderate New Hampshire and Vermont would not participate, although two counties from each state sent delegates to bring the convention's total membership to twenty-six. It met from 15 December 1814 to 5 January 1815.

Rumors flourished during the convention's secret proceedings. From his home in Quincy, Massachusetts, former president John Adams judged the meeting as "ineffably ridiculous," but some suspected that deliberations were devising New England's secession or, at least, a separate peace with Britain.[8] Most delegates were moderates, however, and when the convention's final report appeared on 6 January 1815, it reflected the restraint of its principal author, Harrison Gray Otis.

The report was divided between New England's immediate dissatisfaction over the war—especially the problem of raising and paying for local defense forces—and long-term grievances. Those included the so-called three-fifths rule that inflated southern representation in Congress, the rising influence of the West, the hardships imposed by federal trade restrictions, the suffering caused by the war, foreign-born politicians (which was a swipe at Albert Gallatin, who was born in Switzerland), and Virginia's seemingly endless control of the presidency. The convention proposed seven constitutional amendments as a corrective for these grievances.

The most radical part of the report advocated the nullification of federal laws, and it specifically opposed disunion. At most, the convention proposed another meeting to reconsider the status of their complaints later in the year. Massachusetts and Connecticut then appointed envoys to Washington to request federal money for local defense, but news of the Treaty of Ghent made that errand pointless. Worse for the Federalists, few people would recall the convention's basic moderation. Instead, persistent Federalist complaints about the war, occasional defiance of the government, and this final deed at Hartford all seemed a pattern of persistent disloyalty and flagrant troublemaking. The rest of the country was in no mood to tolerate such behavior while celebrating the victory at New Orleans and the achievement of peace. The Federalists were doomed.

Conclusion

Madison's already shaky reputation as a war leader virtually collapsed in the wake of the British destruction of the capital in late summer of 1814. Yet, his performance after the calamity slowly earned a grudging admiration even among detractors. His last annual message of the war balanced the country's military shortcomings with its recent successes at Plattsburgh and Baltimore, but it was nonetheless frank about the difficulties still facing the nation. The unexpectedly swift breakthrough in peace negotiations in the fall of 1814 and the surprising news of Jackson's victory in early 1815 went far in remedying Madison's broken reputation. He would remain in office two years beyond the end of the war that most Americans came to believe they had won. Madison, his cabinet, and Congress enjoyed the applause triggered by that impression, but subsequent evaluations of the president, his administration, and the legislature have not always been so generous. The people have not fared so well either.

Without doubt, James Madison was a great scholar and an even greater patriot, but his talents did not tend toward the political, and his skills did not meet the fundamental requirements of successful wartime leadership. Madison's sins during the war were usually ones of omission rather than commission. He frequently let matters drift rather than try to direct them, and he tended to suffer the failings and flaws of subordinates in both his official family and the military longer than was wise. Madison was fortunate to be fighting a preoccupied foe whose attention only partially fell on the American conflict, and he was even more fortunate to have his country emerge from that conflict relatively undamaged and largely energized by it. That said, we should also note that America's first wartime president was—like Congress and the people—charting new ground in this adventure, and it is understandable that, in doing so, they all would occasionally stumble.

Notes

1. Quoted in James M. Banner, Jr., *To the Hartford Convention: The Federalists and the Origin of Party Politics in Massachusetts, 1789–1815* (New York: Alfred A. Knopf, 1970), 45.

2. Irving Brant, *James Madison*, 6 vols. (Indianapolis and New York: Bobbs-Merrill, 1941–1961), 6:233.

3. See Hickey, *War of 1812*, 32–33.

4. *Annals of Congress*, 12 Cong., 1st sess., 447–55.

5. Irving H. Bartlett, *Daniel Webster* (New York: W. W. Norton & Co., 1978), 59.

6. *The Writings of Daniel Webster, Hitherto Uncollected*, 18 vols. (Boston: Little, Brown and Co., 1903), 2:55–69.

7. Harry Ammon, *James Monroe: The Quest for National Identity* (Charlottesville and London: University Press of Virginia, 1990), 318–19.

8. Adams is quoted in Page Smith, *John Adams*, 2 vols. (Garden City, NY: Doubleday and Co., 1962), 2:1109.

CHAPTER 4

ALL WERE SURPRISED:
THE QUEST FOR CANADA AND THE WAR AT SEA

The U.S. Officer Corps

When tensions during Jefferson's second term had prompted Congress to expand the regular army in 1808, the officer corps had enjoyed a proportional increase, but staffing it became a way for the Republican Party to reward political loyalists. By 1812, the practice had rendered a wretched throng of officers that Winfield Scott described as a collection of "imbeciles and ignoramuses."[1] Aside from a handful of talented professionals, such as Scott, the army officer corps boasted only these useless dregs and a few aged remnants of the Revolution, a group almost equally useless.

The 1812 army expansion allowed the administration to add new officers, but it lacked a sensible method for choosing them. Instead, the administration tended to use political recommendations as before and, just as it had done earlier, the practice delivered up men inexperienced in command and inept in combat. Scott and his fellows were junior officers, and time and circumstance were necessary to bring them to importance. It would thus take two years of fighting before Madison would find men to lead his armies successfully, and the country's military fortunes suffered grievously in the interval.

Reliance on Militia

In addition to a regular army, in early 1812 the House of Representatives authorized a volunteer force of 50,000 men under the command of state militia officers that would be available to the president if required. The volunteer force proved an acute disappointment, especially because it failed to materialize. Inducements to volunteer were trifling and attracted only six regiments during the entire war.

The motive behind the legislation stemmed as much from American distrust of standing armies as it did from high confidence in the effectiveness of volunteer (or citizen) soldiers. Consequently, the United States relied heavily on state militias both from the necessity of covering regular army shortfalls and from the belief that citizen soldiers could best defend the republic and not yield to the age-old temptation to overthrow it.[2]

Nevertheless, such confidence in state militias was misplaced and dependence on them undesirable. Training in these state organizations varied across a range that ran from valuable to useless. Rigorous preparation could mold a relatively effective fighting force as in New England or some western states, but, more frequently, militia musters merely provided a setting for an imperfectly armed social club to drink ale and tell stories.

The American war effort suffered from the absence of any effective way to compel cooperation between militia and regular forces. In addition, brief militia enlistments made remote campaigns physically tricky, particularly when a lengthy march to a distant objective consumed the militiaman's time of service. In New England, the governors of Massachusetts, Rhode Island, Connecticut, and eventually Vermont not only refused to consent to regular officers commanding their states' forces, they insisted that the Constitution did not require a militiaman to serve outside his state unless the nation was invaded. Such scruples deprived U.S. campaigns in that region of what was arguably the best militia in the nation. Some militia from other parts of the country refused to cross the U.S. border, a stance that made invasions of Canada difficult.

Against this backdrop, militia failures became legendary, and not just in anti-war New England. In 1812, significant portions of the New York militia refused to cross the Niagara River to help Americans fighting at Queenston, Canada. In 1813, elements of the Kentucky militia mutinied, and a prairie fire scared another group home. Especially notorious were the "Bladensburg Races" of August 1814 when Maryland militia scattered and allowed the British to occupy and burn Washington.

Yet, such events do not tell the whole story. True enough, training and discipline problems plagued militia performance, but poor leadership from officers, both professionals and amateurs, often caused militia to behave disappointingly. When what proved to be some of the war's most successful officers emerged from state militias and commanded them, there could be a different tale to tell. William Henry Harrison, Andrew Jackson, and Jacob Brown effectively deployed citizen soldiers in their respective theaters of operations, proving that such men under the right circumstances could fight as well as any regular army.

The Canadian Militia

For different reasons, the British in Canada also had to rely on militia during the War of 1812. The British in 1812 and 1814 fought two different types of war in North America. In 1812 and for almost two years afterward, the European war governed Great Britain's deployment of resources. British regular soldiers in Canada at the outbreak of the war numbered about 7,000, reflecting the burden of European obligations that compelled Britain to use Canadian militia against the United States until Napoleon's surrender in 1814. In that year, large numbers of British regulars came across the Atlantic to begin a series of offensives—a development that inaugurated the second type of war. By September 1814, the British had almost doubled the number of regulars in Canada and, by the end of the year, they had transported almost 40,000 regulars across the Atlantic to press the United States in several sizeable campaigns.

Militia organizations in Canada had a rich history dating from the establishment of New France, but their status and effectiveness had deteriorated in the eighteenth century. After the American Revolution, Britain tried to reform Canada's militia so it could at least defend the U.S.–Canadian border, but the fruits of such efforts were as uncertain as they were untested, at least until 1812. Immediately preceding the war, British officers labored to organize Canadian militia units into an effective defensive force. They were most successful in regions settled by Loyalists—American refugees who had remained faithful to the Crown during the American Revolution.

In other areas, however, desertions and even defections marred Canadian militia performances, especially in the face of American invasion campaigns. The British tried to counter this problem in February 1813 by creating a Volunteer Militia Battalion to serve for the duration of the war. Such recruits would not only be more reliable, it was thought, but also better trained than short-term militiamen. The battalion fought well, but recruiting for it remained disappointingly low, so the experiment was only partially successful.

The Campaigns of 1812

Some Americans agreed with Thomas Jefferson that taking Canada would be "a mere matter of marching," and in fact, Canada did appear susceptible to invasion and conquest.[3] Divided into the four provinces of New Brunswick, Nova Scotia, Lower Canada, and Upper Canada, British possessions in North America were governed by representative assemblies and lieutenant governors. The governor in chief as well as the commander in chief of all provinces was Lower Canada's governor Lieutenant General Sir George Prevost. Prevost and Upper Canada's governor Major General Isaac Brock had a difficult task before them. The sheer vastness of Canada made it difficult to defend, especially considering its sparse settlements, some holding a vaguely uncertain allegiance to the British crown. Many of Lower Canada's inhabitants were descended from the province's original French colonists. Upper Canada's population probably did not total a hundred thousand. Aside from Indian allies and militia, the principal defense of Canada rested on about 7,000 British and Canadian regulars. In 1812, as he faced an impending invasion by American forces, Brock could muster less than 1,700 regulars in Upper Canada.

On the other hand, at the outset of the war the Madison administration had few means to attain the Canadian objective. The best strategy would have been to focus all efforts on taking Montreal or, failing that, Kingston, for to have possession of those points would have cut off the whole of Upper Canada from reinforcement and supply. Madison actually wanted to do this, but in the summer of 1812, he had neither the men nor the leaders to accomplish the goal. Instead, the administration opted for a plan that included invasions launched from Detroit and the Niagara Peninsula as well as the campaign for Montreal.

Disaster at Detroit

Before the war, Governor William Hull of Michigan Territory advised Secretary of War William Eustis that the defense of Michigan was paramount. Hull was doubtless right to declare that an army large enough to protect Michigan could also conquer Upper Canada. He also correctly concluded that control of the Great Lakes was essential for victory on the Canadian border. Yet, even Hull did not believe that he was the man to direct these ambitious operations, and the administration was inclined to agree. He was fifty-nine years of age and though a veteran of the Revolution, he did not cut a martial figure. Nevertheless, Madison had no alternatives in the spring of 1812, and he consequently made Hull a brigadier general, placing him in command of what was being styled the Northwestern Army.

Weeks before Congress declared war, Hull was marching the Northwestern Army from Urbana, Ohio, through the trackless wilderness toward Detroit.[4] When Congress declared war, Secretary Eustis chose to advise Hull by sending the information through the regular mail, and this incredible nonchalance resulted in the first mishap of the campaign. Unaware that hostilities were under way, Hull lightened his load by commissioning the schooner *Cuyahoga* to carry some of the army's baggage, including his official papers, to Detroit. As the ship crawled past Fort Malden, the British captured her and all of Hull's documents. Before Hull had even taken up positions opposite Canada, his enemy knew his army's size and location.

Decisive action might still have saved the enterprise for the Americans, but Hull arrived at Detroit on 5 July and lingered there for a week. He finally crossed the Detroit River on 12 July, issued a bombastic proclamation, and pointed his men toward Fort Malden. Hull had about twice the men the British did, and those odds improved when Malden suffered some crippling militia desertions.

As the American army approached Fort Malden, however, Hull gradually lost his nerve. He fretted about everything and wasted valuable time drilling his men and artillery. His supply line back to Detroit especially troubled him, and Tecumseh's Indian attacks on two detachments sent out to secure it paralyzed him. Word that the American garrison at Mackinac Island had surrendered caused Hull to imagine that "the Northern hive of Indians" was now free to come "swarming down in every direction."[5] On 8 August, he took everyone back to the safety of Detroit, gravely eroding the army's morale and causing his officers to question his courage and competence.

Meanwhile, the British garrison at Fort Malden received not only reinforcements but also the energetic Isaac Brock, whose inclination for offensive operations was encouraged by the obvious lack of American nerve. To alarm the jittery Americans further, Brock inflated the number of his Indian allies and later hinted that they were beyond his control in battle.

Brock moved on Detroit and lay siege to the fort where both the army and Detroit's civilians, including Hull's daughter and grandchildren, sought shelter. He then commenced a bombardment that had Hull cowering in his quarters and contemplating the carnage—especially from the "uncontrollable" Indians—should Brock choose to storm the bastion. On 16 August, without conferring with anyone or firing a shot, Hull surrendered not only the fort and its two thousand men, but also the town and a detachment of soldiers he had sent out of Detroit to meet anticipated reinforcements. The British were openly contemptuous of this contemptible deed. As they would have treated a chastised dog, they let the volunteers and militia go home with tails between their legs. The regulars, including the disgraced Hull, were shipped to Canada as prisoners of war.

Hull's surrender of Detroit did more than shatter U.S. confidence in the opening weeks of the war; it squandered one of the best opportunities for the United States to win a significant victory. The humiliating surrender left the Northwest defenseless in the face of British control and Indian violence, and the small garrison at Fort Dearborn in Chicago soon surrendered, some of them falling victim to an Indian massacre.

Hull was eventually exchanged, and in 1814 a court-martial sentenced him to death for neglect of duty and cowardice. Madison commuted the sentence on the court's recommendation for clemency, but the mercy of that gesture was perhaps sardonic for Hull. The author of one of the most discreditable episodes in American military history likely wished he was dead.

Disappointment on the Niagara Frontier

New York militia major general Stephen Van Rensselaer had no real military experience, yet he planned to launch an offensive on the Niagara frontier in October 1812. Here was some of the most picturesque yet rugged terrain in North America. The Niagara River separates the United States and Canada along a watercourse of almost thirty-seven miles flowing from Lake Erie to Lake Ontario. About seventeen miles south of Lake Ontario, the most famous of the natural wonders along the river, Niagara Falls, cascades into a great canyon. White water near the falls and stiff currents and high bluffs along other portions of the Niagara inhibited crossings. At the river's southern end, British Fort Erie sat across the river from Buffalo and Black Rock, New York, while at the northern end, Fort George and Newark sat opposite the United States' Fort Niagara.

Van Rensselaer had about 6,000 militia and regulars on the Niagara frontier, but there were problems. Irish-born Virginian Alexander Smyth, inspector general of the U.S. Army, was at Buffalo with about 1,700 of the regulars and declined to recognize Van Rensselaer's authority. In any case, hobbled by ineffective supply and lax discipline, neither regulars nor militia were very fit. Further weakening their chances, the redoubtable Isaac Brock had rushed to the Niagara from his victory over Hull at Detroit. Brock had his own problems, however. With about 1,600 men, counting both regulars and militia, and only several hundred Indian warriors, he was badly outnumbered and could expect to counter an invasion only if he concentrated his forces. Brock's best guess about where the Americans would cross was Fort George.

The Battle of Queenston

Brock guessed wrong. Rather than attacking either Fort George or Fort Erie, Van Rensselaer planned to hit Queenston across the river from Lewiston, New York, about halfway between Niagara Falls and Lake Ontario. Under the command of Stephen's nephew Solomon Van Rensselaer—a veteran who had seen his share of combat—American forces crossed the river in the pre-dawn hours of 13 October, braving batteries to scale Queenston Heights and thereby gain control of the village at the foot of the bluff. Brock was completely surprised by the attack on Queenston, and matters had spun badly for the British by the time he arrived and mounted a counterattack to recover the heights. The whole affair then turned calamitous when Brock took a bullet through his heart and died along with his assault.

Yet, the seemingly assured American victory proved fleeting. New York militiamen, refusing to cross into Canada, watched impassively from the American side of the river while Lieutenant Colonel Winfield Scott uneasily took stock of his situation on Queenston Heights, a situation made precarious by the lack of reinforcements. When Brock's successor, Major General Roger Hale Sheaffe, launched a counterattack that afternoon, he almost shoved Scott off the bluffs into the gorge, compelling him to surrender more than 1,000 Americans while bitterly noting that many of these men had hidden in nearby woods. Militia insubordination on the American side had lost the fight at Queenston as much as the final British charge had won it. The British also had to bury one of their finest leaders in Isaac Brock. Nonetheless, the Canadian fear that American numbers would prove invincible all but evaporated after the Battle of Queenston, and a new vigor marked British preparations for the defense of the border.

The Invasions That Never Happened

The defeat at Queenston prompted Stephen Van Rensselaer to resign, but the change only brought the supremely incompetent Alexander Smyth to command. Not wanting for confidence, he proclaimed to the secretary of war that with "a clear stage, men, and money . . . I will retrieve your affairs or perish."[6] Smyth believed that Van Rensselaer's crossing had failed because he had launched the army in fragments. Militiamen, standing on the American shore waiting for their turns, had too much time and latitude to decide if they would fight or not. To repair that problem, Smyth ordered the construction of boats sufficient to transport 3,000 men at one time. Meanwhile, New York and Pennsylvania militiamen deserted in droves, and disease ravaged the ranks of those soldiers remaining. Undaunted by these depressing events, Smyth reckoned by late November that he had enough means of conveyance and on the 28th another American invasion was planned to launch from Buffalo, ostensibly at Fort Erie.

It never even left shore. After spending the better part of the day loading his boats, Smyth lost heart: less than half the men were ready to embark, he said, so he called off the entire operation. The pointless exercise did not improve the confidence of the army either in itself or in Smyth. When Smyth began loading boats on 1 December only to cancel the crossing again, his exasperated soldiers lost all patience and a small riot occurred. Some fired their weapons. The incident persuaded Smyth to leave Buffalo without ceremony; the government, as exasperated as those soldiers, abolished the post of inspector general for no other reason than to terminate Smyth's relationship with the army. The 1812 campaign on the Niagara frontier was over.

Montreal Unmolested

As disappointments rolled from the west toward the east along the Canadian border, the 1812 campaign for Montreal simply never happened. Sixty-two-year-old General Henry Dearborn was to have advanced toward Montreal by way of Lake Champlain, but his operation was delayed first by an abortive armistice with George Prevost and then by obstinate New England militias. When Dearborn finally assembled a force of sorts, he had reached a point only about twenty miles north of Plattsburgh, New York, by 19 November. There the militia refused to go any farther, forcing Dearborn to return to Plattsburgh. The entire campaign for Canada had ended in dismal failure.

The War at Sea (1812–1814)

Americans distrusted a standing army, but they regarded a navy as a dangerous extravagance that invited foreign adventurism while draining public coffers. After the Revolution, the government scrapped the U.S. Navy, and it did not again exist until 1794 when anxiety about preserving American neutrality and protecting American shipping recommended its revival. When Jefferson took office in 1801, he inherited this Federalist-funded navy consisting of thirteen frigates and an additional six ships of the line under construction. Republican thrift and anti-navy prejudice stopped building on the ships of the line and dry-docked many of the frigates. Only seven of them remained seaworthy in 1812.

The Republican Party under Jefferson and Madison instead sponsored the construction of gunboats in the years before the War of 1812. About 174 of these small, narrow, shallow-draft vessels came off the ways between 1802 and 1812, and 62 were in service at the outbreak of the war. Designed for coastal defense, gunboats appealed to Republicans because they were cheap to build. Naval planners also conjectured that they would be cheap to maintain, although annual upkeep for a gunboat turned out to be about ten times that of a frigate. Furthermore, their performance during the war was largely disappointing, and many historians have criticized the reliance on gunboats as naïve. We should note, however, that neither the political establishment nor the public would have supported an expensive "blue water" navy in the years before the war. Indeed, Congress shied away from creating one even as the war began. When South Carolina War Hawk Langdon Cheves framed a bill that would have supplemented the navy with twelve new ships of the line and twenty additional frigates, Republicans rejected it.

The surviving seven frigates consequently were the backbone of the U.S. Navy as it went to war with the most powerful navy in the world. Still, as backbones go, this one was impressive, for three of these ships—the *Constitution,* the *President,* and the *United States*—were heavy frigates that boasted even more guns than their ample rating of 44 suggested. These "super frigates" were larger than European frigates. Built of live oak timbers heavy enough for a ship of the line, they could absorb enemy broadsides while answering with bigger guns that pounded opponents to pieces. Compared to British frigates, they were surprisingly nimble even for their size, and, if overmatched by a British ship of the line (twice the size and double the guns), the super frigate could run like a rabbit. Joining their large cousins were the 36-gun *Constellation, Chesapeake,* and *Congress,* the 32-gun *Essex,* and the *Adams,* whose refitting to 28 guns technically made her a corvette. Nine smaller vessels—sloops and brigs—carried 10 to 20 guns, so few that they could safely assail only merchantmen.

Such was the U.S. Navy at the outbreak of the war. Had it been only ships and guns, it would not have been enough, but the navy was more than a handful of ships. Experienced officers had seen action against the French in the Quasi-War and the Barbary Pirates in the Tripolitan War, and salt-hardened seamen were tough customers with weapons large and small. Ceaseless training honed their skills, and anything that crossed them was sorry for the experience, as several Royal Navy captains and crews were to discover.

For all its pluck, however, the American fleet was tiny when compared to the Royal Navy. The British had spent vast sums to build more than a thousand ships that patrolled the vast reaches of their world empire. The Americans did have an advantage in that the strain of touring the British Empire taxed even the Royal Navy, with the result that, in 1812, British ships were widely dispersed across all the world's oceans. On North American station, only one ship of the line, nine frigates, and assorted lesser vessels made up the British naval presence. Fearful of Napoleon's plans to reestablish a French fleet in European waters, the bulk of the Royal Navy remained there. The Royal Navy also was busy protecting shipping routes to supply British armies fighting in the Iberian Peninsula as well as West Indian and Canadian colonists. Accordingly, for the first year of the war, American waters saw only a small British naval presence.

Early Strategy

Aside from being a hopeless alcoholic who, according to some reports, never managed to see a sober afternoon, Secretary of the Navy Paul Hamilton was also incompetent. He endorsed the conventional view held by both Congress and the administration that the small U.S. Navy was too insignificant to challenge the Royal Navy. He planned to have ships remain in port where as floating batteries they would help repel invasions or, at Albert Gallatin's suggestion, perform coastal service to protect the American merchant fleet.

Several captains opposed this timid plan, including William Bainbridge and Stephen Decatur, who wanted the navy to harass Britain's commerce. Decatur's idea of sending out ships singly only differed with that of Commodore John Rodgers in that Rodgers wanted to group ships in squadrons. When Congress declared war, the administration decided to apply the idea of Rodgers's squadrons to Gallatin's idea of coastal service. Rodgers and his squadron, however, had already left port for open water to chase a richly laden British convoy sailing out of Jamaica. He pursued it all the way to England, never to catch it, yet Rodgers's cruise so alarmed the British that they spent valuable resources and time searching for him, a diversion that allowed many American merchant vessels to reach their homeports.

The Super Frigates Triumphant

The navy, especially the three super frigates, would provide the United States with the only bright pages of 1812's otherwise dark military chapter. These began with an intrepid deed by William Hull's nephew, Captain Isaac Hull, who commanded the USS *Constitution*.

Shortly after the declaration of war, Hull had left New York for open water where he had the misfortune to encounter the only British ship of the line in the hemisphere. Moreover, Hull had happened upon the Halifax squadron, for the 74-gun monster had four frigates with her. Clearly overmatched, Hull tried to run, but both the swift *Constitution* and her pursuers suddenly found themselves in a dead calm. For two days, *Constitution's* crew first towed the frigate with small boats and then resorted to kedging (pulling her through shallow water with anchors). Hull was never beyond sight of the enemy squadron, which was doing the same thing he was. When a light wind teased his canvas, Hull had the crew haul buckets of water into the rigging to wet the sails, better to catch the breeze. The faster *Constitution* finally left her pursuers behind, and when she eventually appeared in Boston Harbor, a hero's welcome awaited her officers and crew.

Greater laurels were in store for this good ship and her crew. Even before the celebrations had abated and, more important, before Hull received new orders, he put to sea again. About 600 miles out from Boston on 19 August, the *Constitution* spotted the frigate HMS *Guerrière*, commanded by Captain James R. Dacres, an officer noted for his contempt for the upstart Yankee navy. Dacres's disdain turned to dismay as the *Constitution* proceeded to smash to pieces the *Guerrière's* rigging and damage her hull in a two-hour fight that saw the two ships collide several times.[7] Adjusting his opinion regarding American seafaring abilities, Captain Dacres finally had to admit defeat. During the battle, an American naval legend was born when one of *Constitution's* crew watched cannon shot from the *Guerrière* inflict so little harm on the American frigate that he shouted: "Huzza, her sides are made of iron."[8] The *Constitution* to this day bears the nickname "Old Ironsides."

Other frigates were not idle. On the morning of 25 October, the *United States,* commanded by Stephen Decatur, demolished the British frigate *Macedonian* about 600 miles west of the Canary Islands. For ninety minutes, British captain John S. Carden watched his gun crews bested in both rate of fire and accuracy. Worse for the *Macedonian,* the *United States'* long-range firepower allowed Decatur to lay off beyond the range of Carden's guns. Unmasted and with her decks slick with blood, the British frigate surrendered at 10:30 and was claimed as a prize by Decatur and his crew, the only time a British frigate was ever subjected to such a humiliation.

The *Constitution*—this time under the command of William Bainbridge—scored another triumph off the Brazilian coast on 29 December, when she encountered the British frigate *Java* en route to India. *Java's* captain Henry Lambert was a first-rate sailor with a sound ship that was actually faster than his opponent, so he was confident of carrying the day. Lambert, in fact, closed on the *Constitution* three times to rake her with shot that beat her up badly, disabled her helm, and wounded Bainbridge twice. The perseverance and ingenuity of the *Constitution's* officers and crew, however, finally gave her the opportunity to wreck the *Java's* rigging and kill large portions of her crew, including Lambert.

The Militia of the Sea

Real injury was inflicted on British commerce during the war by a swarming group of privateers. The attraction of this type of warfare lay in its relatively high effectiveness for relatively little cost. Privateers were privately financed, and consequently small navy advocates looked upon them as performing a similar role at sea as the militia did on land. The difference was that privateers did not have to defend anything of importance; their sole reason for being was to assail and capture merchant vessels that were at best lightly armed and bring them into friendly ports for judgment. Such ports included not only those in the United States, for the French obligingly opened their ports to American privateering captures. Proceeds from captures were distributed to privateer crews and their investors, which was, some critics claimed, the main incentive for privateering in the first and last place. Critics also pointed out with some accuracy that lucrative privateering ventures drew off men needed for regular naval service.

These swift, small ships primarily stalked their quarry off the coast of Canada and in the West Indies, but some ranged to wherever they could find British shipping. By 1813, the Royal Navy countered by providing escorts to large groups of merchantmen sailing in convoy along the main shipping lanes in the Atlantic. Their effectiveness reduced, the privateers nonetheless continued to cause dismay among British shippers, for there were always stragglers from convoys and merchant vessels traveling the West Indies or near the British Isles remained easy prey.

The Tragedy of the Chesapeake

In 1813, James Lawrence took command of the *Chesapeake*, the same ship that had been involved in the impressment controversy with the *Leopard* six years earlier. By any estimation, the *Chesapeake* was an unhappy and unlucky ship whose career was marked by controversy and contention. When Lawrence took command of her, she was in Boston unable to fill out her crew because many of her disenchanted veterans had refused to reenlist. Lawrence scraped together a crew, but its members and the ship's officers had little time to train together before the *Chesapeake* went into her last fight.

In the spring of 1813, the British frigate *Shannon* was cruising off the Massachusetts coast. Captain Philip Broke had commanded the *Shannon* for seven years and had molded the ship into his own image. The ship was meticulously maintained, and her crew was incessantly drilled to meet every event with automatic precision. Broke, unique in the Royal Navy for his insistence on constant gunnery exercises, had shaped the *Shannon* into a particularly lethal machine of destruction.

Broke knew that the *Chesapeake* was in Boston Harbor, and with the audacity customary to naval captains of the time, he issued a provocative challenge to Lawrence. The *Chesapeake* was already under way, and

Lawrence did not receive the invitation, but he needed no summons to fight. The *Shannon* and the *Chesapeake* were evenly matched in rate and size, but the contrasting readiness of their crews should have been sobering for the American captain. As the commander of the *Hornet*, however, Lawrence had won several engagements against the Royal Navy, and his previous success amplified a tendency to impulsiveness.

On 1 June 1813, the *Chesapeake* came out of Boston Harbor and found the *Shannon* about eighteen miles off the coast. Lawrence stood on his quarterdeck in a dress uniform. Perhaps his inexperienced crew was the reason he did not exploit an opportunity to rake the *Shannon* as he approached her, but the two ships eventually lined up to blast one another with broadsides. The *Shannon* took a beating, but Broke's gun crews did a better job of handing out punishment. In only fifteen minutes, both the *Chesapeake* and her crew were thoroughly shattered into submission. Lawrence did not see her boarded: fatally wounded, he had been taken below to die, but he had mustered enough strength to tell his crew: "Don't give up the ship."[9] They were distressingly hopeless words under the circumstances.

The words would not die with Lawrence. The country took them up as a rallying cry. The navy adopted them as a motto. In only months, Lawrence's navy would avenge his words "Don't give up the ship" on an inland sea hundreds of miles from where they were uttered. On a banner fluttering over a U.S. Navy ship bearing his name, they would not be hopeless at all. They would be fighting words.

The Epic Voyage of the Essex

Any account of U.S. naval activity during the war must mention the fantastic exploits of the frigate *Essex* under the command of Captain David Porter. Although the ship was difficult to handle and handicapped by carrying mostly short-range guns, she made an adventurous cruise that ended only when confronted by insurmountable odds.

Departing the Delaware River in October 1812, the *Essex* sailed east to the Cape Verde Islands off the coast of Africa before heading to the south Atlantic. Porter managed to take some prizes, but the thin hunting off the Argentine coast prompted him to the audacious move of taking his ship into the South Pacific, the first American naval vessel ever to ply those waters. The *Essex* rounded Cape Horn in late 1812, enduring in the process some of the most terrifying weather and cruelest seas of any place on earth. Porter then sailed Pacific waters for more than a year during which he ravaged the British whaling fleet. Thousands of miles from any safe haven, the *Essex* lived off her enemy captures and refitted in the Marquesas Islands at the end of 1813. For two months, Porter and his crew savored the pleasures of this South Sea paradise while engaging in a series of swash-buckling adventures worthy of the most exciting fiction.

Their days of bold and carefree action, however, were numbered. In late 1813, the British gave the job of capturing the *Essex* to Captain James Hillyar, equipping him with a three-ship squadron for the task. The *Essex* departed the Marquesas in mid-December and by March 1814, had arrived at Valparaiso, Chile. It was there that two of Hillyar's ships, the *Phoebe* and the *Cherub*, caught up with her. Porter respected Chile's neutrality by in-sisting that any contest occur outside the country's territorial waters, but Hillyar was not so punctilious. The two British ships hovered just off the harbor. Porter tried to run for the open sea on 18 March 1814, but bad weather damaged his rigging, forcing him into a nearby bay. The *Phoebe* and *Cherub* bore down on him. Beyond the range of the *Essex*'s guns, the British ships inflicted terrible punishment on the disabled American frig-ate, and she had to surrender. It was hardly a creditable performance by the British—they had violated Chilean neutrality to assail a crippled opponent—but the long voyage of the *Essex* was at last over.

The Balance of Power

British naval dominance should have given her unchallenged com-mand of the seas, while greater American numbers in North America should have provided an overwhelming advantage to U.S. military opera-tions against Canada. American defeat in Canada surprised the U.S. gov-ernment, and British defeats at sea stunned the Admiralty. England's newspapers scurried to make excuses, such as claiming that the Ameri-can super frigates were actually ships of the line unfairly sailing under a false classification. Such defenses offered only hollow comfort, however. Receiving news of the *Java*'s defeat, the British Admiralty gloomily (and secretly) issued orders that henceforth British frigates should avoid indi-vidual combat with American counterparts. During the first months of the war, the balance of naval power was clearly in the United States' favor, and the consequent victories buoyed the nation stumbling under the weight of abysmal military performances on land, yet that would change because it was bound to.

Stung by criticism at home and worried about the prestige of the Royal Navy the world over, the Admiralty gradually strengthened squadrons in American waters and directed merchant vessels in the Atlantic to convoy their cargoes. The real shift in the balance of naval power occurred when Napoleon's Russian campaign unraveled and sped the decline of France's fortunes. The British developed an increasing naval presence in the American war that managed in 1813 to place ten ships of the line, thirty-eight frigates, and fifty-two support vessels on North American station. They were then able to bottle up the U.S. frigates in various ports, blockade significant stretches of the Atlantic coast, and launch amphibious raids, especially in Chesapeake Bay.

In the face of these discouraging developments, the Navy Department had to issue its own version of the British Admiralty's instructions of a year earlier: American warships that could escape the British blockade were to sail independently and devote themselves exclusively to raids on British shipping. They were not to engage in battle unless sure of victory. Although a few more high seas battles took place, by 1814 the glory days of the free-wheeling and seemingly invincible frigates were over.[10] The navy would still play an important part in the war, but it would do so on inland waters with crucial victories on Lake Erie and Lake Champlain. Those victories would come using ships that had not even been imagined when the indomitable *Constitution* claimed her first victim.

Notes

1. Quoted in Timothy D. Johnson, *Winfield Scott: The Quest for Military Glory* (Lawrence: University Press of Kansas, 1998), 15.

2. A comprehensive overview of the role of militia in U.S. history is John K. Mahon's *History of the Militia and National Guard* (New York: Macmillan, 1982).

3. Jefferson is quoted in Dumas Malone, *The Sage of Monticello*, Vol. 6 of *Jefferson and His Time*, 6 vols. (Boston: Little, Brown and Co., 1981), 109.

4. The standard account of this campaign is Alec R. Gilpin's *General William Hull and the War on Detroit in 1812* (Ann Arbor: University of Michigan, 1949).

5. Quoted in Hickey, *War of 1812*, 82.

6. Quoted in Richard V. Barbuto, *Niagara 1814: America Invades Canada* (Lawrence: University Press of Kansas, 2000), 65.

7. Traditional accounts of this fight describe it as only taking about half an hour, but the *Constitution's* foremost biographer has discovered that these rely on Hull's report, which he revised to make him appear more skilled in combat.

See Tyrone G. Martin, "Isaac Hull's Victory Revisited," *The American Neptune* 47 (winter 1987): 14–21.

    8. Quoted in Hickey, *War of 1812*, 94.

    9. Quoted in Theodore Roosevelt, *The Naval War of 1812* (New York: Putnam, 1882; reprint, New York: Da Capo Press, 1992), 182.

    10. American vessels were fighting engagements as late as 1815, though with mixed results. The *President* was forced to surrender in January 1815, but the *Constitution* continued its remarkable record by defeating the *Cyane* and the *Levant* in February 1815 after the ratification of the peace treaty. The last real naval combat of the war occurred in March 1815 when the USS *Hornet* defeated HMS *Penguin* near Tristan da Cunha in the south Atlantic.

CHAPTER 5

"WE HAVE MET THE ENEMY": THE CAMPAIGNS OF 1813

The campaigns of 1813 would see U.S. forces performing better than they had in 1812. John Armstrong had replaced William Eustis at the War Department with the result that army administration was better organized. Gifted young officers began to rise to positions of responsibility, and soldiers in the ranks showed improvement. Although many were green, when the time came, most would prove game.

In addition, in 1813, the plan to attack Canada underwent some intelligent alterations. Armstrong developed a design to assault two important naval bases at Kingston and York on the northern shore of Lake Ontario. American forces then were to capture Fort George and Fort Erie on the Niagara River. Central to this strategy was control of Lake Ontario and Lake Erie—something perceptive planners, like the dead Brock, had seen from the outset. Whoever ruled the lakes could transport men and materiel with greater ease and speed, avoiding the trackless northern frontier that had so slowed Hull's advance. Dominance on the lakes consequently meant dominion over the entire frontier.

With only twelve vessels divided evenly between Lake Ontario and Lake Erie, the British naval presence was not sizeable, but it was overwhelming in comparison to that of the United States. The Americans had only one vessel on Ontario and, after Hull's surrender, none on Erie. In September 1812, Captain Isaac Chauncey accepted the difficult job of addressing this disparity. In addition to the existing naval base at Sackets Harbor, New York, on Lake Ontario, Chauncey established another on Lake Erie at Presque Isle (present-day Erie, Pennsylvania). At these two places he commenced a building program while creating an interim American flotilla with converted merchant vessels.

These American exertions worried the British, and they tried to compete with them. In March 1813, they replaced the ineffective supervision of the Provincial Marine, which was little more than a transport service, with that of the Royal Navy when Captain Sir James Yeo took command on the lakes. Yeo managed to keep pace with Chauncey on Lake Ontario, but Lake Erie proved too remote for the British to match American shipbuilding there. Consequently, it was on Lake Erie in the fall of 1813 that Americans would finally turn the tide of the war in the Northwest.

The American Capture of York

By the spring of 1813, Chauncey was ready to increase his odds on Lake Ontario by destroying Yeo's naval bases, but Major General Henry Dearborn, commander of the Northern Army, suspected that George Prevost had too strong a defense at Kingston. The American expedition therefore struck York, the capital of Upper Canada. In late April, Chauncey's flotilla ferried about 1,700 troops across the lake from Sackets Harbor and landed them west of York on the 27th. General Zebulon Pike led the assault against General Sir Roger Hale Sheaffe, who commanded a mixture of about 800 British soldiers, Canadian militia, and Indians. Chauncey's ships kept up a bombardment as Pike moved on York and overpowered its defenders. Before he retreated toward Kingston, Sheaffe had his garrison's gunpowder magazine detonated, and the explosion accounted for most of the more than 200 American casualties. Pike was one of them, mortally wounded by flying debris.[1]

Injuries caused by the explosion infuriated the victorious Americans and they took out their anger on the village. Pike might have controlled them, but he was dead, and Dearborn was unable to stop them from looting houses, vandalizing businesses, and burning government buildings. The following year, the British would claim this violation of York warranted their sack of Washington. Yet, the American expedition against York (unlike the August 1814 British expedition against Washington) was a justifiable strategic exercise, aside from its ugly aftermath. The mission reduced a valuable British military asset. York's capture advanced American aims of equaling the British naval presence on Lake Ontario while it hindered British attempts to keep pace with American activities on Lake Erie.

The British Attack Sackets Harbor

For their part, the British sought to maintain their dominance on Lake Ontario by trying to destroy Chauncey's principal naval base. In May, Yeo's flotilla ferried 750 troops to Sackets Harbor where they launched a dawn assault under Colonel Edward Baynes on the 29th. New York militia general Jacob Brown had about 900 men, roughly divided between militia and regulars, to protect Sackets Harbor, and the place was well fortified. Brown was lucky to have those fortifications, because the militia quickly ran away, leaving only the regulars to repulse Baynes's attack. After a stiff fight—"rather a desperate business," in the words of Jacob Brown—the American regulars still held their ground, and the British had to abandon their objective and return to Yeo's ships.[2] Unhappily for the American forces, however, those with the task of guarding the base's naval stores and facilities set them on fire under the mistaken belief that the British would prevail.

The Northwestern Frontier

The surrender and consequent disintegration of American military forces in the Northwest had compounded the disastrous loss of Detroit. To reorganize shattered American military fortunes in the region, the Madison administration proposed appointing regular army officer General James Winchester to command. The idea met with little favor in the West, however, especially in Kentucky, which lobbied for William Henry Harrison. Kentucky's confidence in the victor of Tippecanoe was so high, in fact, that leaders there had made the non-Kentuckian Harrison a major general in the state's militia. Bowing to the political pressure, the War Department made Harrison the overall commander in the Northwest.

Winter delayed Harrison's plan to subdue hostile Indians and retake Detroit, but he did detach Winchester and about 850 men to the Maumee River. Winchester's foray was to prove disastrous when he was overwhelmed on the Raisin River and inebriated Indians massacred some of his men. "Remember the Raisin" was soon on the lips of every American carrying arms on the northwestern frontier.[3]

Lake Erie

In October 1812, Lieutenant Jesse Elliott staged a daring raid on two British naval vessels at Fort Erie. Sent by Chauncey to Lake Erie with orders to put together a flotilla as best he could, Elliott and about a hundred men boarded two converted merchant schooners near Buffalo early on 9 October 1812 with the aim of capturing the British ships and immediately doubling the tiny American naval presence on the lake. The mission was an invigorating success. Elliott's raiding party was only able to make off with one of the ships, the *Caledonia*—the other ran aground and under British heavy fire was finally torched by the Americans—but the deed dramatically diminished the already slim British hold on the lake.

Elliott's heroics won him a place as Chancey's second-in-command on Lake Ontario, but that required a replacement to assume command on Lake Erie. At the end of 1812, Chauncey found the man in twenty-seven-year-old Commodore Oliver Hazard Perry, who was commanding a flotilla of gunboats at Newport, Rhode Island. Arriving at Presque Isle in the spring of 1813, Perry confronted a host of problems. While struggling to complete four ships under construction at Presque Isle, he arranged the almost impossible task of bringing the *Caledonia* and four merchant ships from the Niagara River despite contrary winds that abetted the river's opposing current. After miraculously avoiding the British fleet and being refitted at Presque Isle, Perry's makeshift flotilla finally reached the deep water of the lake only after a complicated and risky process of floating the larger ships over the shallows that hemmed the harbor.

The American navy on Lake Erie was not much to look at. Perry had manned his nine ships with improvised crews drawn from Chauncey's leftovers and Harrison's army, most of whom were unrehearsed sailors at best.[4] Perry christened his 20-gun flagship the *Lawrence* in tribute to the fallen captain of the doomed *Chesapeake*. He placed the *Lawrence*'s sister ship, the 20-gun *Niagara*, under Elliott, who had returned from Lake Ontario. Such as it was, the American flotilla sallied forth to find its British counterpart at the western end of Lake Erie. Just east of Fort Malden, the ships hove to in the South Bass Islands at Put-in-Bay, their crews and captains perhaps dimly aware that they were on the verge of one of the most pivotal battles in naval history.

British Offensives in the Northwest

The Madison administration had unhappily bowed to political pressure to appoint William Henry Harrison to command in the Northwest. Holding little faith in Harrison's abilities, Secretary of War John Armstrong deliberately curbed offensive operations in the region. Consequently, while

Perry labored to expand the navy during the spring and summer of 1813, the British launched two offensives into Ohio using regulars, Canadian militia, and Indians under Tecumseh.

Although hamstrung by his War Department, Harrison established a strong bastion at Fort Meigs on the Maumee Rapids in Ohio. There with a small force he stalled General Henry Procter's offensive in the spring of 1813. Procter besieged Fort Meigs, but the Americans held firm, especially after the arrival of reinforcements under General Green Clay from Kentucky. By the second week of May, Procter saw his Indian allies melting away and his Canadian militia planning to return home for spring planting. On 9 May, he ended the siege. American losses had been heavy with 320 killed or wounded and an additional 600 falling to capture, but Fort Meigs had held, a tribute to its designer, West Pointer Eleazer Wood.

In July, Procter tried again with a larger force of about 5,000. At the suggestion of Tecumseh, Procter tried to entice the Americans out of Fort Meigs, but he was unsuccessful. He then sent a detachment to assault lightly defended Fort Stephenson on the Sandusky River. Only 160 men comprised the fort's small garrison, so Harrison ordered the twenty-one-year-old commander, Major George Croghan, to evacuate the post. Yet, Croghan was as defiant toward Harrison as he would be toward the British. When Procter attacked Fort Stephenson on 2 August with a sizeable force made up mostly of Indians, Croghan's Kentucky sharpshooters and one artillery piece cut the assault to pieces. Procter then not only abandoned the assault on Fort Stephenson, he also called off the entire campaign and returned to Canada.

This attack on Fort Stephenson was to prove unexpectedly significant. For one thing, its failure further deepened a rift between Procter and his Indian allies. In addition, it ended what would be the last British offensive in the Northwest. In only a few weeks, events on Lake Erie would change everything in the region.

The Battle of Lake Erie

Of some comfort to Oliver Hazard Perry would have been the problems of his opposite number on Lake Erie, Royal Navy captain Robert H. Barclay. A veteran of Trafalgar and therefore accustomed to polished seamanship aboard sturdy vessels, Barclay's stoicism was challenged by the frustrating shortages of everything in his Lake Erie command. Aboard his six ships he had resorted to filling out crews with army personnel and mounting guns borrowed from Fort Malden. By the fall of 1813, Barclay had also run out of time. The large number of Indians at Fort Malden had exhausted the post's provisions, so Barclay had to force a decision with Perry to reestablish supply from the eastern part of the lake.

The contest began off Put-in-Bay on 10 September 1813. Using the wind to his advantage, Perry raised a pennant on his flagship's mainmast embroidered with Lawrence's last order, "DON'T GIVE UP THE SHIP," the signal to close with the British flotilla to offset Barclay's long-range guns. Soon the *Lawrence* was under a terrific fire from the 18-gun *Queen Charlotte* and the formidable *Detroit* with its devastating 21 guns. Meanwhile, Elliott kept his place in the American line of battle with the result that he stood off at a distance, firing the *Niagara*'s long guns, but providing negligible support to the beleaguered *Lawrence*. Consequently, a two-hour slugging match left 80 percent of Perry's crew slaughtered and reduced his ship to a drifting wreck.

He would not admit defeat, however. Both the *Queen Charlotte* and *Detroit* had suffered serious damage as well, and though the *Lawrence* was spent as a fighter, the Americans still had the relatively untouched *Niagara*. At least Elliott's reluctance to break his place in the line and join the fray had preserved his ship. Perry had his flag hauled down on the *Lawrence* and rowed with several of his crew to the *Niagara* through a storm of bullets that churned the water like hailstones. For sheer brass, there was nothing like it at any other time in the war, and it paid off. Perry made the trip untouched.[5]

Aboard the *Niagara,* Perry assumed command and wasted no time in taking her in harm's way. Pointing her bow toward the center of the British flotilla, he sailed between the British ships to blast them with broadsides belching simultaneously from both sides of the *Niagara.* With two of his schooners following, Perry took only another hour to smash the *Detroit* and *Queen Charlotte* into submission. Under a black pall of smoke, blood tinted the water as the British vessels finally lowered their flags in surrender, their crews and officers, including Barclay, mangled or dead.

"We have met the enemy and they are ours," Perry hastily wrote to Harrison, taking care to detail the fruits of his victory precisely: "Two Ships, two Brigs[,] one Schooner & one Sloop."[6] Yet, there was more to it than the transient prize of a few British vessels. The real significance of the victory off Put-in-Bay was that it gave the United States control of Lake Erie and thus determined the destiny of the Northwest.

The Battle of the Thames

The first consequence of Perry's victory was Procter's decision to pull out of Fort Malden and move closer to his source of supply in the East. The retreat angered Tecumseh and all but completed the estrangement between the Indians and the British, but the two allies nevertheless accompanied each other on the trek into the interior along the Thames River.

Perry feverishly refurbished his ships to convey Harrison's army. Harrison continued recruiting for that army, especially benefiting from Kentucky governor Isaac Shelby's arrival with 3,000 militiamen from the Bluegrass state, many with horses and all eager to avenge the Raisin River massacre, taking inspiration from their governor, a sixty-three-year-old Revolutionary War veteran. Harrison's force finally totaled about 5,500 men and could have swelled larger—Ohio volunteers came crowding in with their Kentucky neighbors—but Harrison did not have sufficient provisions for a larger multitude.

Only days after Perry's victory, his ships transported parts of the army gathering at the western end of Lake Erie. American forces occupied Detroit and British-evacuated Malden before commencing a pursuit of Procter. A swift march would have put the British beyond Harrison's reach, but Procter had tried to placate Tecumseh by promising a stand somewhere in the interior. That somewhere turned out to be near Moraviantown, some fifty miles east of Detroit, where Procter placed his 800 regulars and 500 Indians in two lines anchored on one end by the Thames River and on the other by a marsh. There on 5 October, Harrison's 3,000 men, including about 1,200 of the mounted Kentuckians under Richard M. Johnson, shouted "Remember the Raisin" as they crashed through Procter's thin lines with Johnson's horsemen leading the charge. The British surrendered almost immediately, but the Indians continued fighting until dispirited by reports that Tecumseh had fallen.

Coming so soon after Perry's triumph on the lake, the Battle of the Thames was a stunning victory indeed, won at light cost of life and reclaiming the region Hull had lost the previous year. Procter eventually stood before a British inquiry that reproached him for his conduct with a public reprimand and temporary suspension from the service. Meanwhile, Harrison's quarrel with Secretary of War Armstrong did not abate after these achievements, and the general resentfully resigned from the army. Nonetheless, his political success was assured by the events before and during the War of 1812, and the memory of them in 1840 would make Harrison president.[7]

The Niagara Frontier

Fort George and Stoney Creek

As in the first campaign season of the war, activity during the second one on the Niagara River proved disappointing for the United States. In late 1813, the war would turn disastrous for the New York frontier.

In May 1813, American forces numbering about 4,500 gathered across the river from Fort George, garrisoned by 1,100 regulars and militia under General John Vincent. On 27 May, a combined operation led by Perry and Winfield Scott landed soldiers west of the fort under the cover of shelling from Isaac Chauncey's Lake Ontario flotilla. The British briefly resisted, but they unwisely abandoned the fort to fight in the open and were so outnumbered that they had to escape to the south.

It was a good start for the United States. After losing Fort George, Vincent had no choice but to abandon Fort Chippewa, Queenston, and Fort Erie to American occupation along the entire course of the Niagara River. The American commander Morgan Lewis did little more than occupy these places, however, and Vincent was able to make his way to Burlington Heights on western Lake Ontario. Lewis finally ordered Vincent pursued by brigades under William Winder and John Chandler, two generals who owed their commands to political connections rather than any military merit. Camping at Stoney Creek, some seven miles from Burlington Heights, the Americans were completely surprised by a British attack on 6 June that drove them from the field and captured Winder and Chandler.

The defeat at Stoney Creek was a major setback for the American campaign. Not only was Vincent secure at Burlington Heights, he also posed a threat to widely scattered American occupation forces. When James Yeo's Lake Ontario squadron materialized, the Americans had to regroup. Major General Henry Dearborn, who had assumed command of the operation, drew his forces back into Fort George and began sending large numbers back across the river to New York.

Beaver Dams

Dearborn nevertheless tried to expand American influence beyond Fort George. Lieutenant Colonel Charles Boerstler led an ill-fated expedition against a lightly manned British post fifteen miles away. According to Canadian tradition, a farmer's wife named Laura Secord learned of the American plan and was able to warn the British about it after a heroic twenty-mile hike. Whether Secord was responsible or not, Indians were perfectly situated to ambush Boerstler's five hundred men on 24 June at Beaver Dams. Although American forces held a sizeable numerical advantage, Lieutenant James Fitzgibbon with some meager British reinforcements managed to bluff Boerstler into surrendering. The consequences of this discreditable performance reached all the way to the top of the army, and shortly after it, congressional outrage forced the administration to relieve Henry Dearborn from command.

The Destruction of Newark

Emboldened by their success, the British began conducting raids on the American side of the Niagara River, including a particularly destructive one on a military post at Black Rock, New York, in the second week of July. New York militia general George McClure commanding American forces at Fort George grew increasingly alarmed. Most of his regulars were back in New York, and his militia had grown petulant over delays in their pay and irritable about their inadequate housing.

On 10 December 1813, McClure ordered the fort evacuated but not before he also elected to do something else. Up until now, fighting on the Niagara River had been limited to military objectives, but McClure suddenly changed all that. Under the misguided notion that destroying the nearby village of Newark would deprive British forces of a winter haven, McClure ordered the village's inhabitants out of their homes into frigid temperatures and burnt it to the ground. The appalling deed invited calumny from all quarters—the U.S. government would disavow it—but its most immediate consequence was the one predicted by McClure himself: the incensed British would mount retaliatory raids all along the Niagara border.

British Reprisals

The new British commander in the region, General Sir Gordon Drummond, angrily condemned McClure's destruction of Newark and was determined to avenge it.[8] The war on the Niagara frontier consequently took an especially ugly turn as a result. On 18 December, 550 British soldiers crossed the river from Fort George and surprised the American garrison at Fort Niagara. Overrunning the sleeping fort, the attackers made liberal use of the bayonet to exact a heavy price of eighty casualties, many knifed in their beds. The British would occupy Fort Niagara for the rest of the war.

General Phineas Riall took another raiding party into New York on 18 December to sack Lewiston and neighboring communities. Riall's Indian allies—allegedly inebriated—committed horrible atrocities on Lewiston's civilian inhabitants and left their mangled corpses strewn in the streets where they were gnawed by wandering pigs.

Stopping these British raids proved most difficult because the administration had been transferring regulars to the East for a planned campaign against Montreal. Meanwhile, whole families fled the frontier, and the New York militia could not fill its ranks. Many regarded George McClure as the real author of all the mayhem and refused to serve under him. Not until General Amos Hall replaced McClure did the militia raise enough men even to oppose the next British raid, but morale was so low that the terrible outcome was unsurprising. Near Black Rock, New York, 1,400 British regulars and their Indian allies crushed and scattered 2,000 New York militiamen. The British reduced Black Rock and Buffalo to ashes on 30 December.

Virtually unopposed in their terrible retribution, the British had put the entire Niagara frontier to flight by early 1814. Those buildings still standing were abandoned, and witnesses to the area described it as forlorn and barren. George McClure's destruction of an unoffending Canadian village had sown a terrible whirlwind of flaming devastation and violent slaughter.

The Montreal Campaign

The St. Lawrence River with Montreal as the principal objective had figured prominently in the abortive plans of 1812, but in 1813 the administration all but abandoned it as a theater for offensive operations. Secretary of War Armstrong, however, did not completely eliminate an operation against Montreal, and the result was a persistent indecisiveness that divided the attention and resources of the central and eastern forces. As already noted, the Niagara frontier suffered because of the transfer of regulars to the East for a proposed campaign there, and, in July, Armstrong finally planned an operation against Montreal. Not until October did he issue orders to launch a campaign, however. The lateness of the season—

which was a serious problem—proved to be only one of the difficulties. Even before the campaign was in progress, events on Lake Champlain diminished its chances for success. Then command troubles in the campaign itself sealed its doom.

Lake Champlain

Lake Champlain forms part of the border between New York and Vermont. At its northern end, the lake flows into the Richelieu River, a tributary of the St. Lawrence River. Because an invading army either from Canada or from the United States could use the lake for an easy passage, control of Lake Champlain provided control over the Northeast. Consequently, it was especially serious in mid-1813 when two American vessels patrolling the northern reaches of the lake ran aground near a British post on Isle-au-Noix. Compelled to surrender or face destruction by the fort's artillery, the two ships were immediately added to the British flotilla, tipping the balance of power on Lake Champlain. For the fall 1813 campaign, the lake's critical supply route would not be available to the American army.

Confusion of Command

The final nail in this campaign's coffin was driven home when Armstrong chose General James Wilkinson to replace Henry Dearborn and hence take command of the Montreal offensive. A career officer who had seen more than his share of controversy, Wilkinson was not highly regarded, especially because of rumors (which were true) that he had spied for Spain and had been involved in the Aaron Burr conspiracy from 1805 to 1807.[9] Two years after the Burr mess, Wilkinson had proved so inept as the commanding officer in the Southwest that almost 1,000 of his men had succumbed to disease or simply deserted their posts. The Madison administration named Wilkinson as Dearborn's successor more to get him out of Louisiana than to invigorate the army's fortunes on the St. Lawrence River front, and the result was predictable.

When Wilkinson assumed command, General Wade Hampton at Plattsburgh refused to recognize his authority, insisting that Wilkinson was unfit for the service and claiming that his separate force be maintained as just that—a separate force. Even the personal intervention of John Armstrong could not mend the breach between the commanders. The result was a somewhat formless plan that called for the two wings of the army to march on Montreal separately. Wilkinson's 7,000 men were to approach the city from the west via the St. Lawrence River, and Hampton's 4,000 men would march up from the south.

Hampton tarried, however, for two reasons. One, he held little belief in the plan and two, he was uncertain about the route he was to take toward Montreal. When he ultimately elected to move north along the Châteauguay River, the bulk of his militia would not leave the United States, and his regulars were so green that they inspired only anxiety in the commanding officer. Such was the state of the left wing of the American offensive when it stumbled on Lieutenant Colonel Charles de Salaberry's 1,400 French-Canadian militia in a heavily fortified position.

Battle of Châteauguay

These mismatched forces fought the Battle of Châteauguay on 26 October, a more comical than deadly affair. Hampton certainly had the advantage of numbers over his enemy, but neither he nor his men had the will to fight. The American frontal assault had only just gotten under way when the French Canadians managed to repulse it with shouting and bugle calls. Believing that de Salaberry had assembled an enormous host, Hampton contemplated abandoning the campaign. When he learned that Armstrong had authorized winter quarters back in New York, he concluded that the administration did not intend to support the invasion at all. To his thinking the matter had been decided for him, so he marched his army back to the United States. The right wing of the 1813 Montreal offensive had simply turned tail and run.

Battle of Crysler's Farm

Wilkinson did not much want to invade Canada either, and he spent most of his time planning how he was to going to assign blame for the campaign's failure. Sallying forth from Sackets Harbor, he dithered and delayed until the first week of November before commencing his movement down the St. Lawrence. Abysmal weather wracked the army with disease, including Wilkinson, who so doped himself with laudanum that even the troublesome presence of a sizeable British contingent in his rear did not overly disturb him.

Finally, at Crysler's Farm, Wilkinson resolved to turn on this enemy force, which numbered about 800 men, and destroy it. Claiming illness made him too shaky for the job (the opiates doubtless made him even shakier), Wilkinson gave it to General John P. Boyd. With about 2,000 troops, Boyd initiated the Battle of Crysler's Farm on 11 November. American assaults on British positions proved futile, but a British counterattack scattered Boyd's superior numbers with relative ease. Casualties were significant in depleting Wilkinson's army: at a cost of only 180 men lost, the British had reduced the Americans by almost 350 killed and about 1,000 captured.

Crysler's Farm would have given a resolute commander pause. Never resolute in the first place and now dizzy from dope, Wilkinson called off the enterprise, citing Hampton's retreat as his reason.[10] Rather than returning to Sackets Harbor, however, Wilkinson's army established winter quarters at French Mills near the St. Lawrence River. The winter of 1813–1814 would prove one of the coldest in memory. Badly sheltered from the subzero, wet weather and lacking the basic essentials of supplies, the army was ravaged by disease. The 1813 campaign season was over.

By the end of 1813, the preponderance of the American population and resources had turned the tide in the Upper Great Lakes region, but command failure and bad strategic planning had foiled American attempts for victory on the Niagara Peninsula and at Montreal. Moreover, the opportunity for realizing that victory was rapidly closing. The last year of the war would see the United States abandoning the idea of conquering Canada and instead facing the stark possibility of military defeat on its own soil.

Notes

1. An excellent account of the capture of York is Carl Benn's *The Battle of York* (Ontario: Milan Publishing, 1984).

2. Brown is quoted in John D. Morris, *Sword of the Republic: Major General Jacob Jennings Brown, 1775–1828* (Kent, OH: Kent State University Press, 2000), 49.

3. See Chapter 6 for the Battle of Frenchtown and the River Raisin Massacre.

4. They might have been unskilled, but Perry's crews were more than willing to challenge the British. A significant number of African Americans numbered among them.

5. After the battle, the flag would achieve the status of sacred relic. It is on display at the U.S. Naval Academy in Annapolis, Maryland.

6. Quoted in Skaggs and Altoff, *A Signal Victory*, 48.

7. Harrison's "victory" at Tippecanoe in 1811 also gave rise to one of the more absurd campaign catchphrases in American political history. In 1840, the

Whig Party ballyhooed the presidential ticket of William Henry Harrison and John Tyler with the slogan "Tippecanoe and Tyler Too!"

8. Neither Gordon Drummond nor Phineas Riall claimed that their raids on the Niagara frontier were reprisals for Newark. See Barbuto, *Niagara, 1814*, 2. Yet, the increased viciousness of these forays indicated otherwise.

9. The details of the Burr Conspiracy remain murky, but Burr possibly intended to detach the southwestern part of the United States and make himself its ruler. The standard account is Thomas Perkins Abernethy's *The Burr Conspiracy* (New York: Oxford University Press, 1954).

10. Barbuto, *Niagara, 1814*, 88.

CHAPTER 6

ENEMY OF MY ENEMY:
NATIVE AMERICANS IN THE WAR OF 1812

Long before the War of 1812, white Americans believed that the British were inciting Native Americans to make war on the U.S. frontier. The Indians, however, did not need encouragement. Increasing numbers of American settlers caused many Native Americans to seek British help before the outbreak of the War of 1812, but during much of the time between 1783 and 1812, the British had little contact and at times were even on bad terms with the Indian population.

When coalitions of native groups soundly defeated U.S. military expeditions that ventured into the Northwest in 1790 and 1791, the U.S. government responded by raising a temporary regular force that compelled many tribes to sign the Treaty of Greenville (1795). The event confirmed the Indian belief, in both the North and South, that intertribal cooperation, even unity, was the only way to prevent further U.S. expansion. Consequently, the famous spiritualism of the Shawnee Prophet Tenskwatawa that appeared in the early nineteenth century was actually a continuation of earlier movements. In the North, while maintaining contact with their southern brethren and continuing trade with British merchants out of Canada, nativist spiritual movements lauded pure traditions and religions as a way to stop white expansion.

Native Americans of the Northwest

These indigenous Indian movements occurred as white settlement in the Ohio country greatly accelerated following the Treaty of Greenville.

In the early nineteenth century, white settlement spilled into what is now Indiana and Illinois, and Indiana territorial governor William Henry Harrison began pushing the Indians to grant more land cessions. In 1809, he dictated the Treaty of Fort Wayne to Potawatomi, Delaware, and Miami headmen, a scandalous agreement because many of these Indians had no connection with the ceded land. Enraged northwestern Indians, who had embraced the nativist religious revival, talked openly of war to resist the treaty, but they could count on few allies. The unification movement of the 1780s and 1790s had faltered, and the British took little official interest in the Indians in U.S. territory. The Treaty of Fort Wayne, however, kept alive the smoldering resentment of the region's Native-American population.

Tenskwatawa and Tecumseh

Into this situation appeared a Shawnee named Lalawethika, whom many of his people had viewed as an irredeemable drunkard. In 1805, however, he had a spiritual experience so powerful that he never drank alcohol again. He took the name Tenskwatawa (known simply as the Prophet to European Americans) and became a holy man to his people. He urged a return to native ways to appease the angry Great Spirit that Tenskwatawa said was punishing Indians for their white habits and dress. Furthermore, a return to a traditional life and bravery in battle, Tenskwatawa said, would bring the restoration of Indian lands. Tenskwatawa exhorted warriors before battle that "we shall conquer if we are brave. The water will wash them away. The wind will blow them down."[1]

Tenskwatawa's older brother Tecumseh aided him in this mission. Although Tecumseh was a charismatic warrior who worked tirelessly for Indian military and political unity, stopping U.S. expansion required resources that neither Tenskwatawa nor Tecumseh possessed—at least, until 1807. In that year, the British suddenly took an interest in their former Indian allies because tensions over the Chesapeake Affair threatened a rupture in Anglo-American relations. Hobbled by their meager military resources, British Canadian officials hoped Northwestern Indians would act as a buffer between the United States and Canada. As a start, the British Indian Department in Canada opened a supply depot for Indians at Amherstburg, Upper Canada.

Nor was this all. In 1808, elderly Matthew Elliott replaced Thomas McKee as the British Indian agent at Amherstburg. Elliott, formerly the agent in the 1790s and married to a Shawnee woman, enjoyed a close relationship with many Northwestern Indians. Now, he had a delicate job. He was to cultivate his already warm association while discouraging attacks on American settlements. The British wanted the Indians as security in case of war; they did not want them to start one.

The Battle of Tippecanoe

By 1810, the British in Canada could no longer restrain Native Americans from attacking American settlements. Tecumseh met with Harrison in August 1810 and threatened a full-scale war if the terms of Fort Wayne were not modified. "I do not see how we can remain at peace with you," he plainly declared.[2] Following the meeting, attacks on outlying white settlements and farms increased, and westerners believed the British were responsible. These American pioneers became convinced that peace would only follow the removal of the British in Canada, but, in the immediate term, Tenskwatawa's following became the focus of American fears and anger. These nativists had established Prophet's Town in Indiana near the confluence of the Wabash River and Tippecanoe Creek.

The British were so worried about all this starting a war that Isaac Brock, the military commander and civil governor of Upper Canada, considered stopping all military aid to the Indians. Anglo-American discord in the summer of 1811, however, required that Brock increase military preparations in Upper Canada, so he renewed that aid. Oddly enough, Tecumseh probably was not happy about having additional weapons put into the hands of hotheaded warriors. He had been urging restraint among his followers because his efforts had not yet forged enough unity to challenge the United States. To buy time, Tenskwatawa sought to convince American emissaries to Prophet's Town of his and Tecumseh's friendship for the United States.

The continuing Indian attacks brought Governor Harrison under increasing political pressure to bring peace to the frontier. With a combined 1,000-man force of regulars and militiamen from Indiana and Kentucky, Harrison marched toward Prophet's Town in the fall of 1811. Although Harrison claimed he would only arrest those responsible for attacks on white settlements, few of the men on the expedition doubted that its real purpose was to reduce Prophet's Town and disperse its inhabitants.

Harrison's army moved into position to attack the town on 6 November, but emissaries from Tenskwatawa appeared and promised negotiations the next day to arrange the surrender of hostile Indians. The messengers even suggested a commodious place for the American soldiers to camp for the night. Tenskwatawa's real plan was to have the American army camp on ground of his choosing and then attack before dawn the next morning, hoping to have lulled the Americans into a false sense of security. He was partly successful.

The Battle of Tippecanoe began with an Indian attack at about 4:00 A.M. on 7 November that drove surprised American soldiers back into their camp or isolated them in small pockets. Both sides suffered high casualties, the Indians because Tenskwatawa had promised that whites' bullets would have no effect on the Indian warriors. Many of them recklessly exposed themselves to American fire. At first light, the American soldiers regrouped and began flanking maneuvers that finally drove the Indians away from the American camp. Fearing a concerted American counterattack, the natives fled Prophet's Town as well. The Americans burned the village and all of the Indians' winter food stores.

Initial reports of Harrison's serious casualties caused many Americans to presume the battle was an Indian victory, but Harrison was careful about cultivating his military and political reputation, so he quickly declared Tenskwatawa's and Tecumseh's confederation destroyed. The truth, however, lay somewhere in between. Harrison had suffered as many casualties as the Indians. He had held his ground and had burned Prophet's Town, but within months Indians had rebuilt it. Furthermore, rather than breaking the back of an Indian confederation, Harrison's expedition convinced many moderate Indian leaders that neither he nor the American government could be trusted. They thereafter listened more attentively to the British promises of military aid. Harrison's campaign had produced numerous (though never accurately counted) Indian deaths, and native culture required vengeance by taking an equal number of white lives. By marching on Prophet's Town, Harrison had not smashed Tenskwatawa's plans; he had provoked a new round of attacks on white settlers that would stretch through the spring of 1812.

Native Americans of the South

During Harrison's campaign, Tecumseh was traveling the South to promote the Niagara-Mobile Indian confederation. The effort was not as successful as he had hoped. Chickasaws, Choctaws, Cherokees, and Creeks greeted his message with mixed reactions; most leaders feared that his confederacy would only incite white wrath. They treated Tecumseh courteously, but they formally declined his offer to join the northern tribes. Although a small number of young Choctaw and Chickasaw warriors joined Tecumseh, many Choctaws eventually allied with the United States against the nativist Creeks. In fact, it was among the Creeks that Tecumseh would come closest to realizing his vision.

The Creek Confederation

Tecumseh enjoyed an advantage when speaking to Creeks because southern Shawnee lived in towns within the Creek nation. Both of Tecumseh's parents had been born in those towns and had migrated to the northern Shawnee after their marriage. Doubtless, Tecumseh still had relatives living among the Creeks, which is probably the origin of erroneous stories that Tecumseh's mother was a Creek. In fact, both of Tecumseh's parents were Shawnee.[3]

The Creeks, under the leadership of prophets, were undergoing a spiritual revival of their own when Tecumseh arrived in the Upper Towns, settlements removed from white influence in what is now Alabama. Like Tenskwatawa in the North, Creek prophets urged a return to native ways and religion. Creeks also resented the U.S. government's cutting a federal road through their country. Followers of Creek prophets, sometimes known as Red Sticks, were predominant in the Upper Towns, and they listened attentively to Tecumseh's pleas for Indian unity. Lower Towns in the eastern part of the nation were closer to white settlement and followed U.S. Creek Agent Benjamin Hawkins, who urged the adoption of white culture. Tecumseh spoke persuasively to the Creek National Council, the ostensible government of the entire nation, in a speech that some reported as conveying Tenskwatawa's instruction to "destroy the wheels and looms . . . and every thing used by the Americans."[4]

The Creek National Council never allied with Tecumseh or his confederation, but his eloquence inspired many Upper Creeks. Some warriors went north with him after the meeting. Within a year, a bloody

civil war would divide the Creek nation between these nativists and ac-
culturationists.

The Anglo-Indian Alliance

After meeting with the Creeks, Tecumseh returned home where attacks against white settlers had increased since the destruction of Prophet's
Town. Fearing an even larger military retaliation from the United States,
he urged caution on his followers. War with the Americans was inevitable,
he now believed, but he wanted to wait until he could strengthen his confederation and receive additional military supplies from the British.

As it happened, his desire for more help from the British coincided
with a change in British policy. Harrison's expedition against Prophet's
Town convinced Brock and other Canadian officials that the United States
planned an attack on Upper Canada. Nonetheless, the local British plan
to recruit Indian allies was complicated in early 1812 by instructions from
London to do nothing to antagonize the United States. Brock found himself in a difficult situation. Charged to protect Upper Canada, his meager
military resources meant he had to rely on Indians, so he continued to
cement his relations with them, although he did so quietly.

Indians watching American preparations for war joined Tecumseh's
growing numbers, spreading his influence throughout the Northwest as
they congregated at various points, ready for word that the war had started.
At the end of June 1812, Tecumseh was enroute to visit the British at
Amherstburg when the United States declared war on Great Britain. Brock
suddenly needed as many warriors as Tecumseh could muster to defend
Upper Canada from the expected U.S. invasion.

The Capture of Detroit

Because Upper Canada was subject to invasion from across the
Niagara River in the east and from Detroit in the west, Brock needed more
than the several hundred Wyandots, Potawatomis, Menominees, and
Winnebagos who had already gathered under British colors. When Brigadier General William Hull's 2,000-man army reached Detroit in early July,
Hull tried to secure Indian neutrality in the region and felt his efforts were
sufficient to protect his invasion of Upper Canada on 12 July 1812. As
the American army advanced on Fort Malden, however, harassing raids
by Indians unnerved the elderly Hull. News that the small American post
on Mackinac Island had fallen to a British-Indian force undid him.

Tecumseh began directing operations against Hull's greatest vulnerability—his supply lines into Ohio. The Shawnee led warriors across
the Detroit River into Michigan and in early August fought skirmishes at
Brownstown and Maguaga that prevented relief parties from opening up
those lines. In the process, Tecumseh captured a letter written by Hull to
the secretary of war relating his misgivings about the campaign and his
fear of Indian attacks. When Hull abandoned the campaign and withdrew
to Detroit, Brock aimed to use the American commander's fear of Indians
to help inferior British numbers. He arranged for a report to fall into
American hands that exaggerated the number of Indians descending on
Detroit. Brock then crossed the river and demanded Hull's surrender, in-
dicating that he could not control his Indian allies once the fighting began. Without firing a shot, Hull surrendered the fort. The mere presence
of Tecumseh and his warriors had won a bloodless battle with a terrified
old man.

Hull's surrender caused Tecumseh's numbers to soar as many isolated
Indian groups leapt at the chance to drive the Americans from the Northwest. When Captain Nathan Heald, under orders received before Hull's
surrender, sought to remove his garrison at Fort Dearborn (modern Chicago) to Fort Wayne in the Indiana Territory, Potawatomi and Winnebago
warriors fell upon the sixty-six men and twenty-seven women and children on 15 August 1812. The Indians killed fifty-two of the party and captured the rest.

Thus, Native Americans were responsible for the abandonment or
surrender of two U.S. posts in the Northwest, and they had their eyes on
others. What Tecumseh had preached for years seemed on the verge of
coming true. Acting together, Native Americans believed they could push
back American settlement, so they mounted attacks on both Fort Wayne
and Fort Harrison in the late summer. It would soon become apparent,
however, that attacking relatively strong fortifications was beyond Indian
tactics. They lacked artillery and did not have the supply network to sustain a siege, so without British cannons and supply trains, the Indians
operated best on open ground in surprise attacks on American columns.
The stubborn defense of Fort Harrison by Captain Zachary Taylor and the
relief of Fort Wayne by 2,000 men under William Henry Harrison saved
both posts.

In fact, with most American soldiers and settlers withdrawing into
forts during the fall and winter of 1812, there was little the Indians of the

Northwest could do but wait for the British to mount an offensive out of Upper Canada and Detroit.

The River Raisin Massacre

In the fall of 1812, William Henry Harrison took command of all military forces in the Northwest. Too late to launch a campaign to retake Detroit, Harrison instead burned every Indian village he could reach. The inhabitants of these towns always fled on the approach of soldiers, but they could not save their food stores. Such raids stiffened the will of many of the Indians to fight the Americans the next spring and summer.

To prepare for the 1813 campaign season, Harrison sent a column into Michigan under the command of Brigadier General James Winchester. Although instructed by Harrison to stop at the rapids of the Maumee River, Winchester on his own authority moved his approximately 900 men toward Frenchtown on the Raisin River (the modern town of Monroe, Michigan). There on 22 January 1813, a British-Indian force under Colonel Henry Procter and the Wyandot headman Roundhead attacked Winchester and forced him to surrender. Procter marched his prisoners toward Detroit, but dozens of wounded Americans were unable to travel, and the Indians massacred them. "Remember the Raisin" became the rallying cry for American soldiers fighting to avenge the deaths of the wounded at Frenchtown.[5]

Rifts in the Anglo-Indian Alliance

During the early spring of 1813, British-allied Indians of the Northwest scouted American positions to prepare for a redcoat invasion of Ohio. The invasion's major target was Fort Meigs on the Maumee River, built by Harrison's forces only a few weeks before. Colonel Henry Procter opened the siege of Fort Meigs on 1 May with about 1,000 British regulars and Canadian militia and about 1,200 Indians, some under the leadership of Tecumseh. Harrison was outnumbered, but his fortifications were strong, and he expected 1,200 reinforcements from Kentucky. When the Kentuckians appeared on 5 May, their commander, Green Clay, sent about half of them to destroy British batteries on the opposite side of the river. They drove away the British artillerymen, but their pursuit of the fleeing British soldiers ran them into a trap set by the Indians. Most either fell dead or to capture.

The scene of this carnage gave birth to an enduring legend regarding Tecumseh. Surviving prisoners would recall that after the American surrender, Tecumseh stopped Indians killing and brutalizing captives. Some remembered him scolding Colonel Procter— he reportedly exclaimed, "You are unfit to command. Go and put on petticoats!"—but there is less evidence to support this story.[6] What is indisputable was Tecumseh's growing dissatisfaction with his British allies as the siege of Fort Meigs remained stalled before Harrison's strong defensive works. Procter also paused because most of the Kentucky reinforcements had made it to the fort. Indians quickly wearied of this futile exercise and began leaving, forcing Procter to lift the siege.

Native Americans participated in other attacks on U.S. positions in Ohio during the summer of 1813, including another siege of Fort Meigs in July and a siege and attack on Fort Stephenson in July and August 1813. The failure of both caused the Indians to doubt the ability of their British allies to remove U.S. forces from the Northwest. By then, Tecumseh and the British commander Henry Procter were openly at odds.

The Battle of the Thames

These failed offenses turned into humiliating defeat in September 1813. American naval victory on Lake Erie cut crucial British supply lines with Lower Canada and forced Procter to retreat to the east. That meant evacuating Detroit, Amherstburg, and Fort Malden, a move that infuriated Tecumseh and his followers. Indian land in the United States reclaimed with a year of hard fighting would be abandoned as they moved deeper into Canada with the British army. The army moved up the Thames River in Upper Canada, but many Indians left it for their homes.

Tecumseh and his immediate followers remained, however, and fought rearguard actions to slow pursuing Americans under William Henry Harrison. On 5 October, Procter and his Indian allies finally made a stand near Moraviantown on the Thames, but Indian-British relations were at low ebb. Moreover, the regulars' morale was shattered, and the Canadian militia was irresolute. The brief battle that ensued quickly broke both British soldiers and militia, but Tecumseh and his men continued to fight in this desperate and ultimately losing cause. American numerical superiority overwhelmed the Indians, and many fell dead, including Tecumseh. According to some reports, Colonel Richard M. Johnson of the Kentucky militia fired the shot that killed Tecumseh. Perhaps he had. In any case, Johnson parlayed the claim into a successful political career that saw him elected to the vice presidency in 1836.[7]

Tecumseh's death and the British retreat from the Northwest destroyed what was left of the Indian confederacy there. What had begun as a hopeful dream among the native people of the region had been tethered by necessity to British military fortunes, and when those fortunes soured, so had the dream. It ended in the wooded Canadian interior, between a swamp and a river named for one in faraway London where planners had counted on native strength in the Northwest to win their war. After that October day, the war in that region was finished for the British, and the dream was over for the Indians.

The Creek War

While Tecumseh fought to reclaim native lands in the Northwest, the faction of Creeks known as Red Sticks fought to retrieve Creek lands and autonomy in the Southwest. Called Creeks by European Americans, this confederation of different ethnic and language groups spanned a large region in what is now western Georgia and much of modern-day Alabama (the eastern part of the Mississippi Territory during the War of 1812). In 1813, the Creek nation had commenced a violent civil war that erupted because of tensions between the Upper Towns and Lower Towns. The Lower Towns or Lower Creeks lived in the eastern part of the Creek Nation in western Georgia and the Upper Creeks to the west in central and southern Alabama. United States Creek Agent Benjamin Hawkins lived near the Lower Creeks and had spent a lifetime encouraging assimilation in white ways and the corresponding abandonment of native traditions. Lower Creeks were receptive to Hawkins' efforts, but the Upper Creeks grew to despise both him and those of their brethren they believed he had corrupted.

It would be a mistake, however, to presume that Creek tensions existed merely along a geographical division. The Creeks of mixed culture point to the complications of this society on the verge of catastrophe. Mixed-culture Creeks were usually products of marriage between Creek women and white men. Because Creek culture was matrilineal (meaning descent was traced through the mother), Creeks accepted children of these unions as wholly Creek and did not make any distinctions based on notions of ethnic "impurity." The mixed-culture Creeks moved in two worlds, frequently known by a white name in one and an Indian name in the other, sometimes acting with equal ease in white or red settings. Yet, their situation was descriptive of the cloud forming over the Creek nation. When the forces of acculturation clashed with the movement for nativism, mixed-culture Creeks would be on both sides.

The widespread Native-American spiritual revival in the early nineteenth century saw Creek prophets urging a return to native ways and the rejection of white culture, and Tecumseh's visit in 1811 seemed tangible evidence that a great spirit was melding Indians into an invincible whole. Some Upper Creeks even accompanied the Shawnee back north. Then, in 1812, nativists began attacking settlements of whites and Creeks of mixed culture. These nativists were frequently called Red Sticks, a label much misunderstood by whites then and since. The name derived from a bundle of red sticks that represented the number of days before an important event, such as war. On the way back from visiting with Tecumseh's people in the Northwest, another group of Red Sticks made war with terrible consequences when they attacked a white settlement in Tennessee, killing several people.

Civil War

Benjamin Hawkins, wishing to preempt a U.S. invasion to punish these Red Sticks, instructed the Creek National Council to resolve the matter. When the council at Hawkins's insistence sentenced their fellow Creeks to death, a group known as the law menders tracked down and executed the accused, among them the powerful Creek headman and ally of Tecumseh, Little Warrior. Relatives and friends avenged these killings, and a cycle of retaliatory attacks soon embroiled the Creeks in a civil war that coincidentally occurred while the United States waged war against Britain.

In the summer of 1813, Red Sticks besieged Tuckabatchee, the town of important headman Big Warrior. His calls for help brought even more Creeks into the conflict, and the broadening fight moved Red Stick Peter McQueen to lead a party to Pensacola in July to procure gunpowder from Spanish officials. Red Stick behavior now so alarmed Americans in surrounding territories that a detachment of Mississippi Territorial Militia ambushed McQueen and his warriors as they returned from Pensacola. On 27 July at Burnt Corn Creek, Colonel James Caller and his men initially captured the pack animals carrying the powder, but the Red Sticks regrouped and drove off the militia. This Red Stick victory possibly encouraged significant numbers to join their cause during the late summer of 1813. One of the most important new recruits for that faction was William Weatherford, also known as Red Eagle, who would find himself fighting a war that was suddenly transformed from an Indian conflict to a full-scale fight with the United States.

The Fort Mims Massacre and Its Consequences

Weatherford was the major strategist behind the next Red Stick attack. Raids on isolated farms had caused white and mixed-culture settlers in south Alabama to seek shelter in a stockade built by settler Samuel Mims north of Mobile. At Fort Mims, about 120 Mississippi Territorial Militia purportedly protected the settlers, but the monotony of uneventful days lulled everyone into complacency. The fort's main gate, for instance, went untended and remained open during daylight hours. On 30 August 1813, Weatherford led over 700 Red Sticks through that open gate. Once inside the fort, they eliminated every pocket of resistance and killed approximately 250 men, women, and children.[8] It took several hours.

The event became known as the Fort Mims Massacre, and it inflamed the white frontier. The U.S. Army as well as surrounding state and territorial militias now marched into this fray. Mississippi Territorial militia under Brigadier General Ferdinand L. Claiborne, Georgia militia under Major General John Floyd, East Tennessee militia under Major General John Cocke, and West Tennessee militia under Major General Andrew Jackson, all to be coordinated by the commander of the 6th Military District, Major General Thomas Pinckney, descended on the Creek nation in the fall of 1813. The plan was for them all to move toward the Red Stick stronghold known as the Holy Ground, but logistical problems, short militia enlistment, and poor communication prevented any meaningful coordination of the different campaigns.

Claiborne struck first against the Holy Ground on 23 December 1813. Even though he dispersed the defenders who included William Weatherford, Claiborne's militia enlistments were due to expire, and he had to retreat. General Floyd was only slightly more successful. After building forts on the Georgia line and in the Creek interior, Floyd had to wait for rations and allied Creek reinforcements before he could move against the Red Stick town of Autosse. Floyd's force destroyed the town, but most of the Red Sticks escaped, and lack of supplies forced him to retreat. When he led another foray in January 1814, Red Sticks mauled him at Calabee

Creek on 27 January. The setback and expiring militia enlistments in February convinced Floyd to give up the campaign.

Red Stick accomplishments in this opening stage of the war were impressive. The nativists held their own against armies invading from the west and the east while fending off attacks from the north out of Tennessee. This northern initiative was the combined effort of East and West Tennessee militias under John Cocke and Andrew Jackson, respectively. It began in earnest in the fall of 1813 just as the Georgia and Mississippi expeditions sputtered out. Suffering the same food shortages as had their Mississippi and Georgia counterparts, the Tennesseans proceeded slowly.

When they finally did encounter Red Stick warriors, the Tennesseans gave no quarter. On 3 November 1813, on orders from Jackson, cavalry commanded by John Coffee surrounded the Red Stick town of Tallushatchee with 900 mounted troops, killed at least 186 warriors, and captured 84 women and children. Coffee burned the village, and few Creek men escaped; many burned alive in their houses with their families. On 9 November, Jackson and his army relieved Talladega, an allied Creek town besieged by Red Sticks. Jackson saved Talladega, but his inexperienced militia failed to trap the Red Sticks.

Such victories threatened to prove fleeting. By mid-November, Jackson was running out of food. He was also running out of time because many of his militiamen were ending their terms of service. Hoping to receive reinforcements and supplies from Cocke, Jackson ordered him to join him at Jackson's supply base he had named Fort Strother. Cocke tarried, however, and detached part of his army to attack a group of villages inhabited by the Hillabee Creeks. The Hillabees had been Red Stick allies, but the destruction of Tallushatchee and Talladega convinced them to ask Jackson for peace, something Cocke did not know. Cocke's attack seemed in such bad faith that it drove surviving Hillabees back into a Red Stick alliance where they remained until the end of the war. It was a typical tragedy of warfare between whites and Indians.

Jackson desperately needed a major victory to salvage the campaign, so he staged a raid with about 800 militiamen and 200 allied Indians in January. The force arrived at a Red Stick village on Emuckfau Creek on the night of 21 January, but at dawn the following morning, 900 Red Sticks attacked Jackson's camp and almost destroyed him. Because the Americans held the field, Jackson claimed Emuckfau as a victory, but Red Sticks harassed his march back to Fort Strother, especially at Enitachopco Creek on 24 January. Jackson learned the valuable lesson that his men would have to be better trained before launching another campaign. General Pinckney also learned that these Tennesseans, especially Andrew Jackson, would not give up easily. He sent Jackson the 39th U.S. Infantry and additional supplies to renew the campaign. Jackson set out with this force on 14 March to end the Creek War at last.

Decision at Horseshoe Bend

Cherokee allies and allied Creeks under William McIntosh joined Jackson to bring his strength to an impressive 3,000 men. On 24 March, he led them toward the large Red Stick camp at Tohopeka in a bend of the Tallapoosa River known as Horseshoe Bend. On the morning of 27 March, he placed his cavalry and allied Indians on the other side of the Tallapoosa to prevent the Red Sticks from escaping across it. The bulk of the army would try to breach the sophisticated Red Stick fortifications protecting their camp. Shoulder-high breastworks spanned the open end of the horseshoe in a zigzag so the Red Sticks could place attackers in crossfire.

Jackson's efforts to reduce these defenses with his artillery did little damage, but his cavalry and Indian allies across the river stole the Red Sticks' canoes and fired into the village, drawing defenders away from the breastworks. Some allied Indians even crossed the river and attacked the rear of the Red Stick camp. As a result, Jackson's army was able to storm the defenses at about noon, forcing the Red Stick warriors back into the brush within the enclosure. What had been a carefully planned fortification now became a killing pen as militiamen and regulars flushed the warriors from hiding places and shot them down. One of the few Red Stick warriors to survive Tohopeka described his men under this onslaught "like the fall of leaves."[9] The killing lasted until dark, and, when it was over, about 800 Red Stick warriors were dead and 350 of their women and children were prisoners. The Battle of Horseshoe Bend quashed Red Stick power.

Surviving Red Sticks remained at large, but most were homeless and hungry as troops systematically destroyed Indian food stores. After Jackson ordered Fort Jackson constructed at the confluence of the Coosa and Tallapoosa rivers, starving Red Sticks began surrendering there and at surrounding camps. Among them was William Weatherford. Jackson not only accepted his surrender, he also released him. It was an uncharacteristic act of clemency for Jackson, but he probably did it in the hope that Weatherford would persuade other Red Sticks to capitulate. Many defeated nativists, however, could not bear the thought of surrender and fled instead to Spanish Florida. They hoped to forge an alliance with the British, enemy of their enemy, should the redcoats ever appear in the Gulf.

During the summer of 1814, a small British force under Major Edward Nicholls did land on Florida's Gulf Coast, hoping to take advantage of the Creek War. The British arrived too late, however, for only a small remnant of Creeks remained who were willing to ally with them against the United States. When the major British invasion on the gulf took place in December 1814, it would not have a large Indian contingent to help in the assault on New Orleans.

The Treaty of Fort Jackson

Andrew Jackson wanted to ensure that no foreign power would use southern Indians against the United States in any future war. He summoned the headmen of the Creek nation to Fort Jackson in August 1814. Creeks expected Jackson to inflict some punishment in the way of land cessions on Red Stick towns, but they were not prepared for the harsh terms Jackson imposed on the entire Creek nation, including those who had allied with the United States. On 9 August 1814, Jackson forced the assembled Creek leaders (only one of whom could be called a Red Stick) to sign the Treaty of Fort Jackson ceding about half of all Creek lands to the United States, an area comprising some twenty-three million acres.

These terms caused more Creeks to migrate to Florida to join the nativists who had preceded them. They became indistinguishable from other Florida Indians, Creek cousins called the Seminoles, who had clashed with Americans already, and now hostilities with the United States continued, provoked in part by the Treaty of Fort Jackson. Over the next half-century, three more Indian wars with the United States would scar the Florida peninsula.

The New York–Canadian Frontier

Native American participation in the fighting on the New York–Canadian border, primarily on the Niagara River frontier, was different from Indian involvement in the Northwest and Southwest. The Iroquois formed the region's primary Indian population that spanned across both sides of the international border. These once powerful people had suffered a fate similar to that of other Indian nations east of the Mississippi River as white settlement increasingly restricted the lands of the Six Nations (the Iroquois Confederacy) in New York. The famous Iroquois headman, Thayendanegea or John Brant, had allied with the British during the American Revolution and, in the years following it, he moved part of his people into Upper Canada to the Grand River. Known as the Grand River Iroquois, they maintained ties of family and friendship with the Six Nations on the other side of the Niagara River in New York. At the start of the War of 1812, the Grand River Iroquois allied with the British while the Six Nations in New York declared their neutrality. Both groups vowed not to fight each other in the coming war, but the pledge unfortunately proved impossible to keep.

The Grand River Iroquois effectively supplemented weak British forces in Upper Canada. The prospect of encountering Iroquois warriors in battle especially terrified U.S. militiamen. At Queenston Heights in October 1812, the presence of several hundred Grand River warriors under headman John Brant caused American militiamen to refuse to cross the Niagara River into Canada, costing the United States the battle. The Grand River Iroquois continued to fight alongside British regulars and Canadian militia on the Niagara frontier for the remainder of the war and occasionally mounted independent actions. In June 1813, they were instrumental in securing the surrender of an American force of almost 500 U.S. regulars under Lieutenant Colonel Charles G. Boerstler at Beaver Dams.

The truce between Grand River Iroquois and New York Iroquois ended when the British invaded the U.S. territory in July 1813 to attack Black Rock, New York. Fearful that the invasion threatened land belonging to the Seneca (one of the Six Nations), Seneca warriors under Young King allied with Black Rock's defenders. The act ended New York Iroquois neutrality. Grand River Iroquois destroyed or carried off Six Nations property in subsequent raids out of Canada. The two groups were soon fighting a civil war intensified by a blood feud as a cycle of attack and retaliation continued into 1814. The ugly rupture finally ended at the Battle of Chippewa on 5 July 1814. While British and American regulars fought on open ground, Iroquois killed each other in the surrounding woods. The experience of killing friends and family in what many viewed as a white man's fight rendered such an emotional shock that the Six Nations withdrew from the war.

Although both groups suffered destruction of property and terrible casualties, war's end left them less wronged than it did the Indians of the Northwest and Southwest. The Grand River Iroquois had served the British in Upper Canada, and on the other side, the Six Nations had for a time allied with the United States. Such assistance meant that, unlike their brethren in the Northwest and the Southwest, the Iroquois retained most of their lands at the end of the War of 1812.

Conclusion

The War of 1812 was in large part an Indian war. Native American alliances with the British and the United States proved pivotal in all theaters, and Indians suffered population losses and destruction of property. Unlike their white allies, most Indians also suffered territorial losses. The treatment of the Creeks in the South was injurious and unjustified. Many had allied with the United States in the Creek War, but that did not protect their lands from the grasping terms of the Treaty of Fort Jackson. Northwestern Indians did not fare much better, as the British abandoned the idea of sponsoring an Indian buffer state to inhibit American settlements.

This Indian buffer state in the Northwest became a major obstacle to the peace negotiations at Ghent in the fall of 1814. Both Isaac Brock and Henry Procter had promised Tecumseh and his followers an award of land carved from the modern states of Ohio, Illinois, and Indiana because the British government saw such an Indian refuge as a means of protecting Upper Canada from future American aggression. When U.S. negotiators made clear they would never agree to such terms, the British envoys compromised with Article IX of the final treaty, which stipulated that Indian allies of both sides would retain the lands they had controlled as of 1811. After the treaty was ratified, some argued that Article IX should restore Andrew Jackson's enormous land cession to the Creeks, but the United States insisted that the Creek War had not been part of the war with Great Britain. The Treaty of Fort Jackson consequently was not related to the Treaty of Ghent.

Article IX was a dead letter not only for the Creeks and the North-western tribes; all Native Americans east of the Mississippi had been so weakened by the war that securing more land cessions from them proved relatively easy during the ensuing years. Whether allied with the United States, Great Britain, or neutral in the War of 1812, Native Americans felt weakened and demoralized by the conflict. As more settlers flooded into the West, most Indians succumbed to a policy of removal that forced them across the Mississippi River during the 1830s. Among them was an aged, stooped figure who had once dreamed of an invincible Indian host reclaiming sacred birthrights from white intruders. Tenskwatawa would spend his last years in Kansas, "sunken and haggard," far from his and his dead brother's home on the Wabash.[10]

Notes

1. Quoted in Gregory Evans Dowd, *A Spirited Resistance: The North American Indian's Struggle for Unity, 1745–1815* (Baltimore: The Johns Hopkins University Press, 1992), 30.

2. Quoted in John Sugden, *Tecumseh: A Life* (New York: Henry Holt and Company, 1997), 189.

3. Ibid., 13–14.

4. Quoted in Dowd, *Spirited Resistance*, 146.

5. American propaganda tended to amplify this tragedy, but the truth was bad enough. As one historian has stated, "War propaganda aside, this [the River Raisin Massacre] was the worst example of Native misconduct while acting in concert with a British force during the war." See Sandy Antal, *A Wampun Denied: Procter's War of 1812* (Ottawa: Carleton University Press, 1997), 180.

6. Sugden, *Tecumseh*, 337.

7. Rivaling William Henry Harrison's absurd political slogan of 1840 was Richard M. Johnson's that commemorated his exploits at the Battle of the Thames with the chant: "Rimpsey, rampsey, rumpsey, dumpsey, Colonel Johnson killed Tecumsey!"

8. Alarming rumors reported casualties at Fort Mims as high as 600, but there were not that many people at the stockade. See Frank L. Owsley, Jr., *Struggle for the Gulf Borderlands: The Creek War and the Battle of New Orleans, 1812–1815* (Gainesville: University Presses of Florida, 1981), 38–39.

9. Quoted in Joel W. Martin, *Sacred Revolt: The Muskogees' Struggle for a New World* (Boston: Beacon Press, 1991), 1.

10. Quoted in Sugden, *Tecumseh*, 388.

CHAPTER 7

1814:
THE YEAR OF CRISIS

The spring of 1814 ushered in major changes on both sides of the world. Napoleon's defeat was complete by April, and his exile to the Mediterranean island of Elba signaled not only peace for Europe but the transformation of the war in North America as well. British veterans now free to wage war against the United States would bring British strength to 30,000 men in Canada alone, and a serious offensive would loom from that quarter as a result. The Royal Navy also appeared in greater strength and joint operations occurred on both the Atlantic and Gulf coasts.

Lake Erie

U.S. control of Lake Erie remained secure, but the reprisals McClure had set off the previous year at Newark continued. On 15 May, American forces under Colonel John B. Campbell crossed to Port Dover on Lake Erie's northeastern shore and razed the town in revenge for the British raid on Buffalo. Trying to stop these gruesome retaliations, the U.S. government reproached Campbell for destroying Port Dover, but the British would cite the raid as another instance of American savagery that justified their ransacking expeditions on Chesapeake Bay later that summer. Meanwhile, British fortifications on Mackinac Island held firm when American naval and land forces assailed them in late July 1814. In the aftermath, it became untenable for the United States to maintain any naval presence on Lake Huron, so the situation on the Upper Lakes had stabilized into a stalemate.

Lake Ontario

At best, Lake Ontario remained an uncertainty in the last year of the war. Chauncey and Yeo refused to engage one another, each hoping that his own building program would make victory certain in any battle. The resulting arms race on Lake Ontario put into service ships of remarkable size as British yards at Kingston and American ones at Sackets Harbor matched efforts. In late 1814, both sides laid keels for two ships of the line each, but the war ended before they were completed. In fact, Yeo and Chauncey never faced off on Lake Ontario as Barclay and Perry had on Lake Erie. Their impressively growing armadas instead became transports and provisioners for their armies.

Even the activities of those armies were indecisive, for they mainly consisted of British attempts to hinder Chauncey's naval-building program and American efforts to defend it. In May, General Gordon Drummond and 750 troops rode Yeo's ships to Oswego, New York, where a fort garrisoned by about 300 Americans guarded a supply depot for Sackets Harbor. Two assaults in as many days finally saw the British on 6 May in possession of the post, which they destroyed and abandoned, but with little long-term effect. Two weeks later, Master Commandant Melancthon Woolsey was transporting thirty-four cannon to Chauncey's ships at Sackets Harbor when the presence of a British squadron obliged him to duck into Sandy Creek some seventeen miles east of his destination. When a British force followed him, American riflemen and Oneida Indians stopped it with a stinging attack, allowing Woolsey to proceed and deliver Chauncey's ordnance.

As the war continued, the building of ships on Lake Ontario went on—and on.

The Niagara Frontier

In March 1814, James Wilkinson came out of his miserable winter quarters at French Mills to lead about 4,000 men into Lower Canada and threaten Montreal, but this campaign would be as fruitless as the ones before it. Moreover, it was the concluding chapter in Wilkinson's mottled military career. On 30 March, the British stopped him at La Colle Mill, and he retreated to the United States. Soon after his return, the administration removed him from command, replacing him with the energetic

Jacob Brown, whom Armstrong had commissioned in the regular army following his heroic defense of Sackets Harbor the previous year.

Brown's appointment was part of a pattern that saw talented officers gradually replacing the incompetent and fossilized ones of the war's first two years. Brown himself appreciated ability, especially that evidenced by Winfield Scott, a firm believer in rigorous drill. Brown invaded Canada on 3 July, leading 3,500 men across the Niagara River to recapture Fort Erie. Unlike the previous year when American forces had rested on this laurel, Brown immediately sent his army into the Niagara Peninsula to fight the large body of British soldiers that lurked there.

Battle of Chippewa

As it marched toward the Chippewa River, the American army encountered advance elements of Major General Phineas Riall's 2,000-man mixture of regulars, militia, and Indians. The bulk of Riall's force was north of the river, but he had placed Canadian militia and Mohawk Indians in a forest south of it to pester the American advance. On 5 July, Brown ordered militia and Iroquois Indians under Peter B. Porter to clear out this nest of snipers. Porter's detachment entered the woods but soon encountered British reinforcements and quickly fled in considerable disorder.

This skirmish now developed into a major engagement as Riall elected to move south of the Chippewa and launch a full attack. Ordered by Brown to break this British onslaught, Winfield Scott marched his regulars through a storm of shot and shell with such disciplined precision that Riall suddenly had a revelation: because Scott's troops were clad in gray uniforms, Riall had thought they were militia; now watching their orderly advance under heavy fire, he reportedly cried out: "Why, those are regulars!"[1] As Scott's regulars exchanged a volley with the British line, American artillery put Riall's guns out of action and forced him to scamper back across the river, leaving five hundred of his men dead or wounded on the field.

American victory in the Battle of Chippewa had come at a cost of 318 casualties, but the entire affair was a tribute to the incessant drill Scott had imposed on his brigade. Although the myth persists that the gray uniforms Scott's men wore at Chippewa became such a symbol of courage and poise under fire that the U.S. Army adopted them as cadet dress at West Point in 1816, documentary evidence indicates that cadets' gray uniforms were implemented for reasons unrelated to the Battle of Chippewa.[2]

Battle of Lundy's Lane

Brown had intended to clear the British from the Niagara region and then use Chauncey's flotilla for combined operations against British bases on Lake Ontario. Brown could not exploit the victory at Chippewa, however, because Chauncey would not bring out his ships, citing his ill health as the reason, but also venting his resentment over Brown's presuming to dictate the movements of the navy. Brown sadly concluded that he would have to withdraw to Fort Erie. While doing so, he ordered Winfield Scott to guard his rear and block possible British raids into New York.

Scott was doing just that when he became aware on 25 July of Riall's army taking positions just west of Niagara Falls on a little hill astride a roadway named Lundy's Lane. Scott was greatly outnumbered, especially when General Gordon Drummond brought in sizeable reinforcements, but he chose to attack anyway, and when Brown with the main American army marched to the sound of the guns, Lundy's Lane became the bloodiest battle of the war. During its height, the din of cannon and musketry overwhelmed the sound of Niagara Falls.

With costly frontal assaults, the Americans made modest gains against the left and center of the British line, holding these positions against repeated British counterattacks and earning the admiration of the redcoats. The contest became a lethal stalemate that raged until midnight. In the course of the battle, both Drummond and Riall were wounded, and Riall was captured. Brown had suffered a wound as well, and Scott was so severely injured that he did not serve again in the war. Although the Americans continued to hold their positions, Brown's successor in command, Eleazar Ripley, withdrew the army toward Fort Erie. Total American casualties were approximately 750, which amounted to an astonishing 35 percent of the force engaged. British losses matched the number of Americans, but were 21 percent of their larger force.

Ripley's withdrawal of the mangled American army drew criticism, but the British did not molest his retreat. Everyone had seen enough killing for a while.[3]

Conjocta Creek and Fort Erie

The battles of Chippewa and Lundy's Lane had proven the mettle of the American military, but they had accomplished little else. Nothing matching the ferocity of Lundy's Lane would occur in the Niagara Theater for the remainder of the war, but British attempts to retake Fort Erie would nonetheless result in significant casualties.

On 3 August, American sharpshooters stopped a British raid into New York at Conjocta Creek with light casualties for both sides, but the attacks on Fort Erie were more serious. Brown's wounds required that General Edmund P. Gaines take command of the 2,000 Americans who garrisoned the fort, and he had busied himself bolstering its defensive works. It was a good thing he had, for the British mounted a furious artillery bombardment on 13 August as a prelude to a pre-dawn assault two days later. Troops under Colonel Hercules Scott and Lieutenant Colonel William Drummond mounted the charge in which Scott was mortally wounded. Drummond's men gained the interior of a bastion and struggled with the American defenders there for almost two hours until a powder magazine exploded, killing Drummond as well as hundreds of others. The survivors limped back into British lines.

Despite this catastrophe, the British refused to give up, continuing their ceaseless bombardment and daily skirmishing with the American garrison. Gaines suffered a wound that brought Brown back into command, even though he had not completed his convalescence, and he dismissed suggestions that he abandon the fort. Instead, he sent out two columns to capture the British batteries late on 17 September. After a sharp fight that cost the Americans 500 men and the British 600, the Americans took two of three batteries and spiked them before returning to the fort. Matters remained in an uneasy standoff until Major General George Izard in November ordered Fort Erie evacuated and blown up. The last American invasion of Canada was over.

The British Invade New York

In 1814, additions to British troop strength allowed them to turn the tables on the United States and conduct a major offensive on the northern frontier. Under the command of Governor-General Sir George Prevost, 10,000 British regulars entered the United States at the end of August and followed the western shore of Lake Champlain toward Plattsburgh, New York. Only about 3,500 inexperienced troops defended Plattsburgh because the Madison administration, not expecting the British invasion, had stripped the town's defenses to beef up those at Sackets Harbor. The American commander, General Alexander Macomb, refused to retreat, however. Instead, he harassed the British advance as best he could. When Prevost paused north of the Saranac River to await the British flotilla on Lake Champlain, Macomb used the extra time to summon militia from other parts of New York and Vermont.

Battle of Plattsburgh Bay

The American navy on Lake Champlain had not been idle since suffering the setback the previous year. A building program similar to Chauncey's frantic pace on Lake Ontario had brought parity between the American and British squadrons. Royal Navy captain George Downie's fleet boasted the largest ship on the lake, the 37-gun *Confiance*, as well as three other large vessels and twelve gunboats. United States Lieutenant Thomas Macdonough had the 26-gun *Saratoga*, the 20-gun *Eagle*, the 17-gun *Ticonderoga*, the 7-gun *Preble*, and ten gunboats.

Although Downie held a slight advantage in long-range firepower, as the aggressor he also labored under the necessity of forcing a contest regardless of the disposition of Macdonough's forces. Macdonough accordingly tucked his ships into Plattsburgh Bay to compel Downie to conduct a close battle. In addition, by cleverly setting his anchors, Macdonough could use anchor cables to turn his ships at their moorings. Such a maneuver proved decisive during the battle.

On the morning of 11 September, Downie moved into the bay and headed directly for Macdonough's anchorage where the *Confiance* commenced a devastating punishment of the smaller *Saratoga*. The other vessels in both squadrons also slugged it out. At such close quarters, the contest was a particularly nasty fight. A loose gun carriage crushed the life out of Downie, while on the *Saratoga*, a gunner's head hurtled through the air and struck Macdonough, temporarily knocking him senseless.[4] When the *Saratoga*'s guns fell silent, it appeared that she must either surrender or collapse under the *Confiance*'s guns. It was then that Macdonough ordered the ship pivoted on her anchors and thereby exposed the *Confiance* to the *Saratoga*'s portside guns, heretofore shielded from the battle. The American flagship's fresh battery proceeded to pound the *Confiance* into submission, and her surrender prompted the other ships of the British flotilla to lower their flags as well. The British gunboats fled. It had taken two and a half hours.

Macdonough's victory message to the secretary of the navy emulated that of Perry to Harrison the year before: "The Almighty has been pleased to Grant us a Signal Victory on Lake Champlain in the Capture of one Frigate, one Brig and two sloops of war of the enemy."[5]

Battle of Plattsburgh

As the fleets fought on the bay, Prevost sent his men across the Saranac River to trounce the American militia outside of Plattsburgh. As the army prepared to attack Macomb's fortifications, however, Prevost received word of Macdonough's victory and immediately lost heart. Just that quickly control of Lake Champlain had passed to the Americans, and Prevost consequently ordered a retreat. Worse than this abject withdrawal in the face of inferior numbers, the British departure was so rapid and disorganized that it resembled more a rout than a retrograde.

The affair ruined Prevost's reputation, which he was never able to defend. When summoned to England to explain his actions, the governor-general died before the inquiry convened. As for the United States, another epic hero had emerged in the person of thirty-year-old Thomas Macdonough.

The War Ends in the North

Three years of fighting on the northern border had given birth to two American military traditions, created two American naval heroes, and secured the political careers of two westerners. Yet, the fighting had not conquered Canada, and it had only resulted in divided control of the region's lakes. The war was soon to be over, leaving matters much as they had been when it began, except for the devastated Niagara frontier, the smoldering ruins of villages on both sides of the border, and the hundreds of men dead or maimed. Little wonder that here were the seeds for the longest and most persistently peaceful border in the world.

The Atlantic Offensive

The Royal Navy was key to Atlantic coastal operations, both for the blockade that gradually extended northward to include New England and for amphibious operations in the Maine District and Chesapeake Bay.

The Maine District

Because the northern counties of Massachusetts—called the Maine District and now constituting the state of Maine—were a geographical protrusion into Canada, they impeded overland communication between Quebec and Halifax. The British hoped to resolve that problem by absorbing part of Maine. The British government ordered the operation in June 1814, instructing the governor of Nova Scotia, Sir John Sherbrooke, to occupy the pertinent part of the district.

The campaign got under way on 11 July. The Royal Navy ferried 1,000 men under Lieutenant Colonel Andrew Pilkington to Moose Island where a small garrison of eighty-five Americans at Fort Sullivan immediately surrendered. On 1 September, 2,500 men under Sherbrooke invaded Castine on the Penobscot River where the Americans blew up their fort and retreated upriver. The British quickly followed both on foot and on a small flotilla, easily taking Hampden where U.S. navy captain Charles Morris burned the USS *Adams* to prevent its capture. The British extended their influence up the Penobscot to Bangor and later occupied Machias on the coast, establishing control over 100 miles of the Maine shoreline. As they confiscated public property and compelled citizens to swear allegiance to the British Crown, they made Castine a trading center for British goods and a holiday spot for their furloughed officers.

The U.S. government watched these events with dismay. Especially disturbing was citizen indifference to the British occupation. If anything, many Maine inhabitants jumped at the profits from trade with British merchants and customers in New Brunswick and Nova Scotia. An administration plan to retake the area faltered when Massachusetts governor Caleb Strong refused to commit his militia, and the War Department finally discarded the plan when its particulars became widely known. At war's end, the British still occupied eastern Maine, though its value as a bargaining chip would not be as high as London had hoped.

Chesapeake Bay

The British had begun pillaging the shores of Chesapeake Bay in 1813, conducting especially destructive raids on Havre de Grace, Maryland (3 May 1813), and Hampton, Virginia (26 June 1813). Their greater resources in 1814 would bring about a far more extensive use of raids on the bay. The motives were also different. The British government wanted General Robert Ross to create enough havoc to draw American forces from the Canadian theater. In addition, British anger over the wanton destruction of places like York, Newark, and Port Dover stimulated a desire to exact retribution on otherwise unoffending American targets. Chesapeake Bay was a perfect setting for such a mission: the Royal Navy under Admiral Sir Alexander Cochrane could travel its waters at will, ferrying Ross's soldiers to various targets that could include Washington, D.C., and Baltimore, Maryland.

Moreover, by the summer of 1814, angry men contemptuous of the American people and eager to punish what they regarded as the United States' betrayal of Britain during the struggle with Napoleon were guiding the British war in Chesapeake Bay. Such a man was Admiral Sir George Cockburn, whose exploits in 1813 had only whetted his appetite for predatory behavior in the bay. A major influence on the 1814 Chesapeake campaign, Cockburn would urge the attack on Washington as a way to humiliate the United States.[6]

Joshua Barney's Flotilla

In 1813, the United States had tried to stop raiding in Chesapeake Bay by creating a flotilla under Captain Joshua Barney. A veteran of the American Revolution and recently a captain of a successful privateer, Barney had a little squadron consisting of only gunboats and barges, but its daring and skill had hampered British operations somewhat. When the British arrived in the bay again in the spring of 1814, however, Barney was so overmatched he had to hide in the Patuxent River. The British wanted no distractions for their upcoming operations, so Captain Robert Barrie's flotilla searched out Barney's squadron and tried to destroy him. Although the American flotilla survived the British attacks with the help of covering shore batteries, it would never sail the bay again. When the British mounted their major offensive in southern Maryland, Barney destroyed his vessels to keep their capture from augmenting Cochrane's already sizeable fleet.

The Defense of Washington

Secretary of War Armstrong committed one of the most grievous misjudgments of the war when he predicted that the British would not attack Washington because it was strategically unimportant. Armstrong was right about the lack of Washington's strategic significance, but he completely missed the mark by not taking into account the political and psychological necessity of protecting the nation's capital. In any event, Armstrong believed that the militia, rather than fortifications, could best defend any targets the British would choose and that troops did not need to be assembled until an attack was imminent. The attitude resulted in a policy that was inexpensive, but in terms of actually guarding anything, it proved disastrous.

Fearful of stepping on his touchy secretary's toes, Madison waited until July to create a special military district that included Washington, D.C., citing "the fierce aspect which British military power now had."[7] The tardiness of the decision was bad enough, but matters worsened when Madison appointed General William Winder to command the new district. Winder's only military experience had been as a prisoner after being captured following the disastrous Battle of Beaver Dams in 1813. In fact, Madison made the appointment to placate Maryland's Federalist governor Levin Winder, William's uncle. The job undid William Winder, who apparently confused activity with action. He ceaselessly inspected his district without preparing it in any meaningful way for an impending attack.

The Battle of Bladensburg

Such was the situation in mid-August 1814. Cochrane had assembled twenty warships and assorted transports in the bay, and Ross was ready to deploy his army of veterans from the Peninsular War. The navy transported 4,500 men up the Patuxent River to Benedict, Maryland, where they disembarked on 19–20 August. Two days later, they were at Upper Marlboro, Maryland. They marched toward Bladensburg, near the Eastern Branch of the Potomac northeast of Washington. Cockburn overcame Ross's misgivings about the expedition, and the march continued.

Winder did little to impede Ross's march. Meanwhile, members of the Madison administration, especially Secretary of State James Monroe, engaged in a great deal of frenetic activity, none of it particularly useful. The assembling militia was untrained and vaguely unwilling, but at least American numbers swelled to a decent size. Including regulars and Barney's crews from the destroyed flotilla, about 7,000 American soldiers stood at Bladensburg on 24 August, awaiting the British arrival. It was dreadfully hot.

About 2:00 P.M., the British came into view and crossed the river, beginning an attack in front of glazed American eyes. The hiss and whine of British Congreve rockets—an ineffective weapon with a nonetheless terrifying effect—unnerved the already edgy militia. When redcoats began flanking the American position and Winder ordered a retreat, the militia did not need to be told twice. Their withdrawal turned into a rout resembling "sheep, chased by dogs," and their disgusted fellow citizens derisively labeled it "the Bladensburg races."[8] Barney's crews remained, firing guns rescued from their doomed flotilla until exhausting their ammunition and falling to capture.

Washington's inhabitants were already in flight, mingling with the westward stream of wide-eyed soldiers stumbling back from Bladensburg. First Lady Dolley Madison directed the packing and transport of the administration's papers and, most famously, had Gilbert Stuart's portrait of George Washington cut from its frame to rescue it as well. Madison himself, with Attorney General Richard Rush and James Monroe, crossed into Virginia, fugitives from their own capital, enduring the sullen stares of dejected citizens.

The Sack of Washington

The British marched into Washington that evening. Perhaps because he believed, in European fashion, that capturing an opponent's capital meant defeating him in the war, General Ross searched for someone who could begin surrender negotiations. Possibly he wanted to give the appearance that his occupation of Washington was something other than organized vandalism. Others, like Cockburn, did not care about such appearances. The admiral helped to burgle the executive mansion before setting it on fire as "spectators stood in awful silence."[9] Down the mall, others burned the Capitol, the treasury, and the war and state departments. Only the patent office was spared, thanks to Superintendent Dr. William Thornton, who persuaded a young British lieutenant that the destruction of the records would rank with history's most grotesque deeds of barbarity. Meanwhile, across town, Captain Thomas Tingey followed procedure in burning his own navy yard, including a heavy frigate and a sloop nearing completion.

Cockburn had a grand time as the fires lit the night. He personally directed the demolition of the *National Intelligencer*'s offices, a newspaper that had condemned his 1813 raids in Chesapeake Bay. The British withdrew from Washington the next day, 25 August, and boarded Cochrane's transports five days later at Benedict. Reaction to the burning of Washington was mixed, although many Britons celebrated it as giving the

Yankees their just deserts. Any value to British objectives, however, was dubious. As has been repeatedly demonstrated in wars throughout history, deeds calculated to break an enemy's spirit frequently brace it instead, rousing from unplumbed depths otherwise inexplicable patriotism. George Cockburn laughed as Washington burned, but it would not be the last laugh.

The Attack on Baltimore

Although they consented to Cockburn's urgings about marching on Washington, Cochrane and Ross always preferred to attack Baltimore. The city was a rich and tempting target, the one because of its burgeoning commercial activities and the other because it was a base for privateers. In early September, Cochrane's fleet accordingly moved up the bay, everyone on board confident that Baltimore would prove as easy to take as Washington had been.

U.S. Senator and Maryland militia major general Samuel Smith planned otherwise. Beginning in 1813, he began coordinating efforts for the city's defense. By the time the British were bearing down on Baltimore, he had amassed almost 10,000 men and had erected an elaborate series of fortifications. Consequently, when Robert Ross landed 4,500 men at North Point on 12 September, he was in for a stiff fight. After covering half of the fourteen miles to Baltimore, the British clashed with 3,200 militiamen under General John Stricker, forcing their retreat, but at considerable cost, especially when an American sharpshooter killed Ross. His death so disheartened his army that for the remainder of the campaign against Baltimore, British troops appeared only to go through the motions.

As these events unfolded, Cochrane's fleet launched an attack against Fort McHenry that guarded Baltimore's inner harbor. Once past the fort, the British ships could cover the army's advance by bombarding American positions. Fort McHenry, however, proved obstinate. About 1,000 men under Major George Armistead huddled under the rain of constant British salvos that continued for more than twenty hours. Miraculously, the fort sustained little damage and the garrison few casualties. In the meantime, shore batteries thwarted Cochrane's attempt to launch an amphibious assault down the Patapsco River. At the close of the bombardment, the British fleet had not reduced the fort, as Francis Scott Key excitedly noted while verses began to form in his mind.

Colonel Arthur Brooke, who had assumed command of the army after Ross's death, was approaching Baltimore's main defenses when he received word that the navy would not be able to support him. He called off the campaign and ordered the return to the ships, which pulled away before dawn the next morning. Baltimore was saved, and the Chesapeake Bay campaign was ended.

The Gulf Coast Offensive

After their failure at Baltimore, the British turned their attention to the Gulf Coast, a region they thought would afford them grand opportunities. For one thing, New Orleans was at least as rich a prize as Baltimore. Situated about a hundred miles up the Mississippi River, New Orleans was the commercial center through which most western commodities passed to the rest of the world. Cochrane planned to seize the city's treasures, taking care to include cargo ships in his fleet for that purpose.

Originally, the British were motivated to attack the Gulf Coast for the same reasons they had assailed the Chesapeake: to divert American military resources from the Canadian border. Once the campaign was afoot, however, the potential to establish a British foothold in the Mississippi Valley took precedence. As a result, the ultimate assault on New Orleans would be one of the most pivotal moments of the conflict, even though it occurred after the signing of a peace treaty in Europe.

Prospect Bluff and Pensacola

To attract Indian allies for the Gulf Coast offensive, Cochrane had already sent arms to Native American refugees from the 1813–1814 Creek War.[10] They gathered at Prospect Bluff on the Apalachicola River, Spanish Florida, where British agents Colonel Edward Nicholls and Lieutenant George Woodbine busied themselves in the spring of 1814 preparing the Indians for an assault on Mobile. In August, Nicholls and Woodbine moved their headquarters to Pensacola, the capital of Spanish West Florida, whose excellent harbor could provide the Royal Navy with a shelter to land the British army. Although officially neutral during the Anglo-American war, Spanish authorities did little to discourage Nicholls's presence or plans.

Fort Bowyer

In September, Nicholls mounted his attack on Mobile. The United States had seized this port city in West Florida from Spain in 1813 under the somewhat dubious rationale that it had been included in the Louisiana Purchase and thus was illegitimately in Spain's possession. Whatever the value of that argument, the United States had taken pains to protect Mobile from seaborne attack. Fort Bowyer sat on Mobile Point, a peninsula in Mobile Bay, with a garrison of 160 regulars, Major William Lawrence in command.

The British assault on 15 September was a disaster. Nicholls's force of 225 Royal Marines and Indians could not breach the fort's works, and the two ships that were supposed to support the attack could not maneuver in shallow waters. The flagship *Hermes* even ran aground under the fort's guns and was abandoned. The affair did not impress the Indians, whose allegiance to the British was shaken.

Andrew Jackson Takes Pensacola

Lauded for his success in the Creek War, Tennessee militia general Andrew Jackson had received a major general's commission in the U.S. Army following William Henry Harrison's resignation from the service. Charged with the defense of the Gulf Coast, Jackson believed that driving the British from Pensacola should be a primary objective, but the Madison administration reminded Jackson that Spanish Pensacola was the property of a neutral power. In October 1814, Secretary of War James Monroe (who had succeeded Armstrong) told Jackson not to invade Florida, but by the time the order reached the general, he had already acted.[11]

On 7 November, Jackson attacked the Spanish capital with 4,000 regulars, militia, and Indians. Although the Spanish governor did not have enough men to mount a defense, the British managed to destroy the forts on Pensacola Bay before retreating to Prospect Bluff. Jackson hastily departed the city to move his army to Mobile, which he believed would be the site of the British invasion. After a few weeks, however, developments finally convinced him that New Orleans was the actual target, so he raced there, arriving on 1 December. Jackson was fortunate that his misperception had not cost him Louisiana, for while he was late coming to New Orleans, the British would be later still.

Preparations at New Orleans

When Jackson arrived in New Orleans, he found defeatism the prevailing mood. Sensing that his time was precious, Jackson began defense preparations with such speed that the population began to think that the appearance of the British did not necessarily call for immediate surrender. Jackson erected batteries at possible lines of attack and obstructed almost all the water approaches from the gulf. His proclamation to the people of Louisiana summoned everyone, most famously the "free people of color," to defend the city. A special corps of black troops formed by Colonel Jean Baptiste Savary responded to the call, and other troops from all over rushed to the city, some from as far away as Baton Rouge, where Jackson's friend John Coffee assembled 850 Tennessee riflemen.

Even a motley assortment called the Baratarian pirates came to New Orleans' defense. Their leader, a colorful figure named Jean Lafitte, had rejected a British alliance in favor of seeking clemency from the Americans in exchange for help in repelling the British invasion. Jackson originally paused over accepting the services of those he described as "hellish Banditti," but when Lafitte offered guns, ammunition, and men, Jackson was in no position to refuse.[12] Lafitte would receive a presidential pardon for his loyalty at New Orleans, but the pirate's life again beckoned him after the war, and in only a few years, he had taken it back up, cruising for plunder off Galveston.

Even with Jackson's heartening preparations, some Louisianans remained nervous, and when the state legislature discussed surrendering to the British, Jackson had it briefly disbanded. It was a pattern of iron-handed rule that became a habit with Jackson. He proclaimed martial law on 16 December and kept it in force until he received official word of the peace the following March, even though no tangible threat to the city existed beyond mid-January. Jackson threw into jail a legislator who had criticized him and then had federal judge Dominick Hall arrested when the judge ordered the prisoner released.

Whether military necessity compelled such draconian measures would be a source of debate forever afterward, but for the people of New Orleans during that fearful winter, there was no debate and no appeal. They were not the first, nor would they be the last, to discover the perils of crossing Andrew Jackson. Indeed, the British were about to learn this lesson as well.

The British Attack on Lake Borgne

Almost ten thousand British soldiers were gathered in Jamaica for the campaign against New Orleans. To replace the dead Ross as their commander, London dispatched Edward Pakenham, who was not only an able soldier but was also the Duke of Wellington's brother-in-law. Before Pakenham arrived, Cochrane's fleet brought the army to the Gulf Coast, arriving off Cat Island at the mouth of the Mississippi on 13 December. Surveying the options available for their approach to New Orleans, the British ultimately decided the best one was through Lake Borgne.

American forces on Lake Borgne consisted of 5 gunboats crewed by 185 men under Lieutenant Thomas ap Catesby Jones. To clear the lake, the British simply overwhelmed Jones's squadron on 15 December with a force of 45 boats and 1,200 men, though doing so proved more difficult than they had imagined. Consequently, the fight on Lake Borgne cost the British time, and time for Jackson was even more precious than Jones's gunboats.

Villeré Plantation

After clearing Lake Borgne, the British occupied Pea Island, where they suffered from wretched cold and wet winds. With Spanish and Portuguese fishermen acting as guides, the British laboriously ferried men across Lake Borgne. Landing at Bayou Bienvenu, they proceeded to Bayou Mazant and then rowed themselves along a canal to Jacques Villeré's plantation, thus bringing them to the Mississippi River about eight miles below New Orleans. It all took more time, and not until 23 December would 1,600 men be ready to seize Villeré's house and establish a headquarters there. Meanwhile, Villeré's son fled to New Orleans and raised the alarm.

The British appearance so near New Orleans was especially alarming because it was surprising. Jackson's previously effective intelligence network had let him down, and he now tried to compensate by fighting the British at Villeré Plantation before they could bring the rest of their army up. He immediately collected 1,800 men and descended on the British position. With the support of two ships in the Mississippi, the *Carolina* and the *Louisiana,* Jackson attacked that very night, surprising the British encampment with a ferocious assault. The fight was confused and ultimately indecisive, with Jackson retiring from the field, but it caused the British commander John Keane to take pause, and thus earned Jackson more time. Such was the situation when Edward Pakenham finally arrived to take command of the campaign two days later on Christmas.

The Two Sides Gird for Battle

As the British continued to move up to this forward position, Pakenham could count more than 4,000 men in his command, but he did not realize the numerical advantage he then had over Jackson. Blessed with even more time, Jackson established a defensive position line behind the Rodriguez Canal. As Pakenham augmented his numbers, American forces frantically clawed at the ground and piled up dirt only two miles from the British camp. Ultimately, the American earthworks stretched along the length of the canal from a cypress swamp on the east to the Mississippi River on the west. While Jackson's army worked, the *Carolina* and *Louisiana* pestered British activity by lofting shells into the redcoat camp. Finally, the British removed at least that annoyance by directing their guns at the ships, destroying the *Carolina* and driving the *Louisiana* out of range.

Despite restoring a relative calm, Pakenham did not at all like what he saw developing around him. Events had progressed too far to call off the campaign, however. Feeling the need to do something, on 28 December he sent two columns toward the American lines, but Jackson's force, now totaling about 4,000 men, put up such a stiff fire in combination with the *Louisiana* that Pakenham pulled everyone back before a full fight ensued. As Pakenham digested this episode, he brought up additional cannon and men, delaying the final contest and giving Jackson even more time to prepare for it.

He used the time to strengthen his fortifications further, extending his line to a full mile and bolstering it at intervals with additional artillery. Jackson even had time after all this labor to establish two additional lines behind his main one. On the western bank of the Mississippi, he ordered the *Louisiana's* cannon pulled off and mounted as a shore battery to pound Pakenham with flanking fire.

The Battle of New Orleans

Pakenham's impressive batteries commenced a bombardment of Jackson's line on New Year's Day, 1814, but the British aim was too high. When the American batteries began to answer, their better aim shattered barrels of sugar the British had unwisely substituted for sandbags around their guns. Cannon barrels hurtled from their carriages, and gun crews fell dead, all amid the sticky mess created by the scattered sugar.

Everything began to go wrong for the British. Pakenham was certain he needed every man he could muster to attack Jackson's line, so he waited for even more reinforcements to arrive at his camp. When soldiers did double duty by packing their knapsacks with cannon balls for the artillery, they courted disaster on the sometimes rough waters of Lake Borgne: when one boat capsized, the weighted soldiers struggled all the way to the bottom and drowned.

Pakenham finally massed about 6,000 men. Cochrane tried to float large boats in Villeré Canal by damming it, thus bringing more men to the Mississippi, but the experiment had proved disappointing. As it was, only 600 troops were available to cross the river and attack Jackson's flanking battery on the west bank. Under Colonel William Thornton, this force was to strike at night to seize the American guns and direct them against Jackson's main line. Closely following this bombardment, Pakenham planned to send three columns against Jackson's main line at first light. Pakenham's 5,300 men would be marching across a plain directly at the American force, now grown to 4,700 men, but if Jackson's line could be shelled along its length by the captured battery, it would probably break. Everything depended on Thornton then, for the brief British probe of Jackson's position at the end of December showed that an unassisted assault across the open ground would be suicidal.

The battle at last happened on 8 January 1815, and because Thornton was late, it was decided before the first shot. Although Thornton captured the American guns, he would never have the chance to use them. Pakenham anxiously started his assault without hearing from the batteries across the river, and without Thornton's support, Pakenham's advance was doomed.

Starting in a dense fog that shrouded the plain, British troops were nearing American lines when the mist suddenly dissipated. The redcoats at 500 yards out made fine targets for cannon and even finer ones for riflemen at 300 yards. Many of those who survived to come within 100 yards of the American line did not survive much longer, and those who did fell prone to play dead. A small column nearest the river came closest to the American line, but only briefly, finally recoiling from the storm of bullets and shell. Pakenham had a horse shot from under him as he rode to rally his men, and he had just mounted another when a hail of bullets killed him.

Surveying the hideous heaps of British dead and wounded, General John Lambert abruptly stopped the battle. It had lasted an incredible thirty minutes. Jackson consented to an armistice so that Lambert could bury the dead and prepare Pakenham's body for transport to England. As though awakening from a bad dream, Cochrane simply could not believe it had happened, and he implored Lambert to mount a new attack, but Lambert knew that it was hopeless. More than 1,500 of his men were dead or wounded, 500 more were captives, and Jackson's casualties behind those dark fortifications amounted to only 13.

In fact, the tally of British losses for the entire campaign stretching from 23 December to 8 January was a startling 2,450 to American losses of 350. Andrew Jackson had saved New Orleans and had become the United States' premier hero of the war.

Fort Bowyer: The Last Battle of the War

The British remained on the outskirts of New Orleans for ten days after the battle, and though occasional skirmishing broke out, Lambert would not fight at this gruesome place again. Cochrane persisted, however, in the belief that triumph of some sort would grace British efforts if they just kept at it. He dispatched a squadron of ships up the Mississippi to attack Fort St. Philip about a third of the way to New Orleans, but a massive bombardment could not reduce the stronghold. The failure finally convinced Cochrane, and the British withdrew from the area.

They did not altogether withdraw from the Gulf Coast, though. In early February, British ships surrounded the spit of land where Fort Bowyer sat and covered Lambert's landing of 5,000 men and artillery that soon awed William Lawrence's garrison into surrender. Winning Fort Bowyer could not have erased the British memory of that bloodied plain at New Orleans, and the small pleasure of smashing this American fly with a hammer proved fleeting. News of peace arrived before the British could take Mobile, and terms of the treaty returned the fort to the United States.

Conclusion

Nobody won the War of 1812. The United States improved its military showing in land campaigns during 1813 and 1814, but those

improvements did not render decisive results. New and energetic officers—
Winfield Scott, Jacob Brown, Alexander Macomb, and James Macdonough
in the North, Samuel Smith at Baltimore, and Andrew Jackson at New
Orleans—had finally given the United States victories. It had taken Madison two years to find these men, but at last they had emerged.

And not a moment too soon, for 1814 could have been a disastrous
year for the United States. It was at worst an indecisive one. In the last
year of the war in the northern theater, American troops won victories at
Fort Erie and Chippewa and stood their ground at Lundy's Lane, but the
significant triumph came at Plattsburgh—and that on the waters of Lake
Champlain—when Macdonough repulsed a serious invasion. Meanwhile,
the British occupied eastern Maine and burned the nation's capital, American setbacks partially offset by the successful defense of Baltimore. The
British attack on New Orleans was an unadulterated disaster, but in its
real meaning, Jackson's victory, like that of Macdonough at Plattsburgh,
stopped something bad from happening rather than causing something
good to happen.

In a way, that description—avoiding tactical defeats rather than
winning meaningful strategic victories—sums up both the American and
British military experience in the War of 1812. It was an experience that
would be reflected in the peace settlement that ended the war.

Notes

1. Quoted in Johnson, *Winfield Scott*, 50. Riall's exclamation is sometimes
reported as "Those are regulars, by God!"

2. Ibid., 63. Apparently, the war department's decision to establish cadet
gray was based on the thrift and availability of gray cloth.

3. Brown had explicitly ordered Ripley to hold his position at Lundy's
Lane. See Barbuto, *Niagara, 1814*, 227–28.

4. Roosevelt, *Naval War*, 351.

5. Quoted in Hickey, *War of 1812*, 193.

6. In 1815, Cockburn would command the ship that took Napoleon to
his final exile at St. Helena.

7. Quoted in Brant, *Madison*, 6:271.

8. Walter Lord, *The Dawn's Early Light* (New York: W. W. Norton and Co.,
1972), 140; Glyndon G. Van Deusen, *The Life of Henry Clay* (Boston: Little, Brown
and Co., 1937), 90.

9. Anthony S. Pitch, *The Burning of Washington: The British Invasion of 1814*
(Annapolis, MD: Naval Institute Press, 1998), 120.

10. The Creek War is discussed in Chapter 6.

11. Monroe in December nervously wrote to Jackson that, if he attacked Pensacola, he should withdraw immediately, explaining to the Spaniards that his invasion had been only to free the city from "British violation." See Heidler and Heidler, *Old Hickory's War*, 46.

12. Robin Reilly, *The British at the Gates: The New Orleans Campaign in the War of 1812* (New York: G. P. Putnam's Sons, 1974), 224.

CHAPTER 8

THE TREATY OF GHENT

Early Efforts at Peace

The War of 1812 had hardly begun when both belligerents extended peace feelers. The repeal of the Orders in Council four days before the American declaration of war eliminated a principal cause of conflict, and London thought that after such a generous concession, avoiding a war would only be a matter of exchanging suitable communications. Just eight days after the declaration, Secretary of State James Monroe sent a letter instructing Jonathan Russell, the U.S. *chargé d'affaires* in London, to consent to a ceasefire if Britain would withdraw the Orders in Council and end impressment. British foreign minister Lord Castlereagh emphasized the repeal of the orders, but regarding impressment, he had to decline Russell's terms. Meanwhile, on learning of the repeal, Major General Henry Dearborn and Governor General George Prevost entered into an armistice. Madison was clearly eager for peace, but only if Britain satisfied American grievances over impressment as well as neutral rights, so he repudiated the armistice. His Majesty's government simply would not abandon impressment.

The Russian Mediation Offer

Just as the United States and Britain were drawing swords, Tsar Alexander I of Russia suddenly found himself at war with Napoleon. When Alexander broke from the Continental System in 1809, he opened Baltic ports to American ships. If that was not bad enough, in 1812, he signed a peace accord with Britain and began openly trading with her. Napoleon punished the Russian defection by declaring war on 22 June 1812 and mounting an invasion that in September crushed the Russian army at Borodino and captured Moscow.[1]

Fearful in his dire hour of need that the American war would distract Britain from helping him, Alexander tried to end that faraway conflict. While Moscow fell to Napoleon, Alexander suddenly and unexpectedly offered to mediate the Anglo-American dispute. The U.S. minister in St. Petersburg, John Quincy Adams, said that President Madison would welcome the initiative, though Adams spoke from nothing more than intuition. The tsar, thus encouraged, officially tendered the offer, and the long conveyance of the message commenced, landing it in Washington the following year. As Adams astutely had foreseen, Madison accepted Alexander's offer. He promptly nominated Secretary of the Treasury Albert Gallatin and Senator James A. Bayard of Delaware to join Adams as peace commissioners. By then, it was March 1813.

Madison's acceptance did not arrive in St. Petersburg until June 1813, only just ahead of Gallatin and Bayard who were traveling through Sweden at the time. They did not know until they arrived in Russia that Britain, worried that Alexander would side with the United States on impressment and neutral rights, had rejected the tsar's offer. Alexander was nothing if not persistent, however, and he again offered to mediate on 1 September 1813. The British again courteously—but no less firmly—refused.

The Problem of Distance and Delay

The British wanted to end the distracting war with the Americans, but they wanted to end it on their terms. For that purpose, Castlereagh proposed direct talks, suggesting a neutral site in Sweden or, if agreeable, London. The American commissioners preferred steering their own negotiations as well: such talks could better avoid European political shoals sure to arise with the unpredictable Alexander at the helm. Everyone was apparently eager to start at least moving toward peace, but telling Washington about the new plan for direct negotiations and receiving Madison's approval took months. Talk of direct negotiations began in January 1814, and by the time the commissioners heard from the United States the year was half over.

Routinely slow methods of communicating over great distances always threatened to confound diplomacy, but in questions bearing on avoiding and then ending the War of 1812, delays were especially exasperating. Distance doomed the Monroe–Pinkney Treaty in 1807 and the Erskine Agreement two years later, because the diplomats, working under the pressure of limited time, felt compelled to exceed or violate their instructions.

In 1812, the lack of instant communication prevented Britain's repeal of the Orders in Council from averting the American declaration of war. Finally, an extended suspension of any actual progress toward peace occurred while the parties mulled over and ultimately abandoned the offer of Russian mediation.

The Russian offer did serve as a bridge for the British and the Americans to come together directly, but its unexpectedness was not so helpful. In the end, Alexander had only added another complication that further postponed an Anglo-American settlement while the cumbersome rituals of diplomacy and international gamesmanship were played out on a global scale at a snail's pace.

Once negotiations got under way, the American commissioners overcame the problem of distance and delay the only way they could. Just as their predecessors had, they made some crucial decisions on their own authority, hopeful that they would avoid the mistakes that had doomed the work of previous envoys, optimistic that the president and the U.S. Senate would find their work acceptable.

The Delegations

The U.S. Peace Commission

When direct negotiations with Britain became a possibility, Madison appointed two additional commissioners to join Adams, Bayard, and Gallatin. Speaker of the House Henry Clay and Jonathan Russell, the U.S. *chargé* in London and recently appointed minister to Sweden, filled out one of the most talented diplomatic missions in American history. Waiting for these new members would mean still additional delay—especially in the case of Clay, who would have to travel to Europe—but the exceptional diversity and depth of this gifted group made the pause in this case well worthwhile. With the exception of the somewhat inadequate Russell—Madison apparently named him because he expected the negotiations to take place in Göteborg, Sweden, Russell's host country—each of the other members brought a unique flair and an exceptional intelligence to the task before them.

Occasionally its members' extraordinarily strong personalities threatened the delegation's unity. The two most flamboyant American stars were of starkly different temperaments and from opposite ends of the country, a bad mix that could have been a prescription for disaster. Western War

Hawk Henry Clay and New Englander John Quincy Adams did not shrink from fierce disagreement with each other during the negotiations. Even their unusual and dissimilar routines put them at odds: Adams usually rose in the pre-dawn hours to write in his voluminous journal, just about the time Clay was returning from an all-night session of cards and whiskey. Albert Gallatin performed indispensable service as referee and peacemaker to keep Clay and Adams in public harmony, reminding them that "we must remain united or we will fail."[2] The delegation might vehemently disagree in private, but it always appeared united to the British.

His political and personal enemies in the Senate tried to keep Gallatin from serving on the delegation by initially refusing to confirm him. The rebuke cruelly embarrassed both Madison and his former secretary of the treasury, especially since Gallatin had already arrived in Europe and was on his way to Russia when the Senate acted. Madison stood by his appointment, however, and the Senate eventually confirmed him. It was good for the delegation's fortunes that Madison persevered and the Senate relented. Gallatin's first diplomatic mission revealed him as a keen student of human nature, and his absence from the delegation might have proved a grave handicap in allowing Adams and Clay to train more ire on each other than on the British. [3]

The British Delegation

The delay in starting negotiations meant that not until 8 August 1814 would these Americans begin discussions with their British counterparts. The timing was significant. Napoleon's defeat and exile to Elba earlier in the year occupied London's most gifted envoys. When negotiations opened with the Americans, the foreign office's real talent was in Austria, where a great European conference (the Congress of Vienna) was sorting out the disarray caused by two decades of warfare. Consequently, the British delegation sent to end the American conflict was at best of middling ability.

The British delegation consisted of three commissioners. Lord Gambier of the Royal Navy had commanded the British fleet that launched the sneak attack on the Danish fleet at Copenhagen in 1807, an act internationally deplored and even regarded with some embarrassment in England. Henry Goulburn, an undersecretary in the Ministry of War and Colonies, was too young to have made much of a mark and his chief duty of preserving Canadian interests in the negotiations would suffer from his inexperience. William Adams, an admiralty lawyer, could presumably lecture everyone on the minutiae of maritime regulations, but diplomats rarely welcome tutorials from either colleagues or adversaries.

It is evident that the British foreign office knew the limits of their emissaries, for Castlereagh required them to submit any important subject to him for review. In addition to Castlereagh, Lord Bathurst (secretary for War and the Colonies) and the Duke of Wellington could have weighed in if necessary. Bathurst, Goulburn's superior, was familiar with even the obscure aspects of the war in North America, having directed the conflict's overall strategy. Wellington had become England's greatest military hero, his campaigns in the Peninsular War (1808–1814) earning the kind of praise usually reserved for the dead Nelson. Yet, the intricate peace talks at the Congress of Vienna absorbed these men, and they could not have helped but regard the negotiations with the Americans as little more than a distraction. Ultimately, the British government decided that those negotiations, like the war they aimed to end, were best resolved quickly and with as little fuss as possible. That decision, however, came only after several key developments.

The Negotiations

Ghent Rather than Göteborg

The plan to meet at Göteborg had fallen through, and the Americans for obvious reasons balked at meeting in London. Instead, the negotiations took place at Ghent, in modern Belgium. Diplomats at Vienna had just placed that area under the control of the Netherlands (a servant of British interests), and Ghent itself was under British military occupation, so the American delegation might have rightly questioned how the city, except for its smaller size and fewer amenities, was any different from London for their purposes.

In addition, after Napoleon's defeat, Britain sent experienced British regulars in large numbers to fight the American war in earnest, and the peace talks that finally began in August 1814 proceeded under the shadow of military events that featured possible American disasters and probable British triumphs. For all its talent, the unhappily situated American delegation did not have a happy prospect before it.

Impressment Off the Table

The United States had insisted from the start of the war that an explicit repudiation of impressment was necessary for any peace, and that demand remained in force during the arrangements for negotiations. Secretary of State Monroe specifically advised his commissioners that they were to obtain British renunciation of impressment. Otherwise, he instructed, "all further negotiations will cease, and you will return home without delay."[4]

Albert Gallatin, however, warned that Great Britain was unlikely to surrender this point, especially since the American performance in the war had been so disappointing. Additionally, the end of the European war likely meant that impressment would end anyway, because Britain's need for it would vanish with Napoleon's exile. Weighing this development, the president suddenly changed his mind, and the secretary of state amended his instructions. "You may omit any stipulation on the subject of impressment," Monroe wrote the American delegation on 27 June 1814.[5]

This amounted to a profoundly important concession on the part of the United States. Arguments about impressment had always ruined reconciliation before the war, and American insistence about the issue would surely have killed the peace negotiations in 1814. Preserving the principle of impressment was the British delegation's only nonnegotiable position. When the United States abandoned their demand even before talks had begun, the odds for ending the war increased immeasurably.

Neutral Rights and other American Demands

No such liberality guided the American delegation on the issue of neutral rights. Indeed, Monroe's instructions were nothing short of fantastic considering the military situation when he drafted them. He wanted to require the British to repudiate paper blockades, compensate American shipping for damages under the Orders in Council, explicitly define contraband, renounce the Rule of 1756, and recognize the right of neutrals to trade with enemy colonies.

Nor was this all. Monroe wanted the British to restore slaves that they had liberated to their owners or compensate them accordingly. He wanted the British to pay damages for the undefended towns and private property they had destroyed. In an amazing instruction that would have sounded whimsical in any other setting, Monroe told the delegation to try for all of Canada. Barring the receipt of that prize, the United States at least was to make no arrangement that would impair or diminish its naval presence on the Great Lakes.

Monroe told his commissioners not to give up a single inch of American territory, including the Columbia River region that the United States uncertainly claimed in the Pacific Northwest. If the British mentioned Florida, the American delegation should solemnly claim that West Florida was a part of the Louisiana Purchase and indignantly insist that Spain's cession of East Florida to the United States was only fair, considering that Spain, like its neighbors, had occasionally preyed on American shipping.

British Demands

Aside from their instructions not to relinquish any aspect of impressment or modify any other Royal Navy policies, the British delegation had a wide degree of latitude, though its members did not seem to realize it. In fact, the British would try to extract concessions from the Americans that were just as implausible as Monroe's demands.

The foreign office wanted to establish a neutral Indian enclave as a frontier barrier between the United States and Canada. This Indian state ideally would stretch from the Missouri River eastward to Lake Champlain.

In addition, the British wanted to adjust the eastern and western ends of the U.S.–Canadian border. Britain coveted the northeastern part of the Maine District to keep Montreal and Quebec in the interior accessible to St. Johns and Halifax on the Atlantic. These places otherwise depended on American indulgence during winters that each year iced up the St. Lawrence River. As it happened, the idea was not so fanciful in 1814 because a British invasion had already occupied a portion of the Maine District that summer.

More capricious was the western scheme in which the British would move the Canadian border southward to make possible their navigation of the Mississippi River. As justification, the British cited terms in the Treaty of 1783 that called for joint use of the river. Meanwhile, they held in reserve a plan to bar New England fishermen from Nova Scotia's abundant cod fisheries—their mutual use had also been agreed to in 1783—unless the Americans could give them something equal in value. In any event, Britain planned to control the Great Lakes and dictate to the United States how far from the Canadian boundary it could place any defenses.

The Settlement

The Indian Barrier State

A misstep by Gambier, Goulburn, and William Adams at the start of the talks revealed their second-rate status in the foreign office. They were apparently under the impression that the formation of the Indian barrier state ranked as a primary condition for peace. Perhaps they had come by the notion because attempts to create an Indian barrier between the United States and Canada had been a staple of British diplomacy since 1792. In addition, Canadians were especially eager to see such a buffer created between them and their grasping American neighbors.

In the larger scheme of things in 1814, the Indian state did not much matter to the British foreign office. Preserving autonomy over its own relations with Indians, however, mattered a great deal to the U.S. government, and the American delegation would not consider any such Indian enclave in any form or size. When it became aware of the insupportable position the British delegation had assumed in the face of American resolve, London ordered the idea abandoned, and the British emissaries had the mortifying assignment of discarding as irrelevant something they had insisted was especially important. The result was an initial American diplomatic victory that, in one sense, buoyed the American team in Ghent as much as it discomfited the British one.

The final arrangement regarding Indians called for each side to make peace with any Indians it was fighting to restore the situation of 1811. Although the British could point to their belief that the situation of 1811 would negate any changes caused by the War of 1812, the fact remained that this concession not only abandoned the Indian buffer state on the Canadian border, it also effectively abandoned Britain's Indian allies in North America. This British compromise had the most acute effect in the American South, where Andrew Jackson's 1814 treaty with the Creek Indians extracted a vast 23-million acre land cession to the United States. Reflecting London's indifference to the fate of the North American Indians, the foreign office would subsequently see no reason to protest that land cession as a violation of the Treaty of Ghent when the United States argued that technically it was not.[6]

The Canadian Boundary

The British delegation asserted that a new boundary between Canada and the United States should rest on the standard of *uti possidetis*—meaning that whomever controlled territory in 1814 would keep it—with some adjustments. When the British put this claim forward, their forces held two captured American forts in the Great Lakes region. Fort Michilimackinac (pronounced Mee-shlee-mackinaw) on Mackinac Island was a distant outpost valuable for the fur trade along the western stretches of

Lake Huron, and Fort Niagara in New York controlled the northern entrance of the Niagara River from Lake Ontario. British forces had also occupied a section of the Massachusetts coast in the Maine District that extended inland to the Penobscot River.

Although the United States had abandoned Fort Erie, the British envoys in Ghent did not know that and thus included it in their calculations. American forces still occupied Fort Malden in Amherstburg, Canada, south of Detroit on the western peninsula of Ontario. To maintain British ascendancy on the Great Lakes, the British delegation wanted to hold on to Forts Michilimackinac and Niagara and reclaim Forts Erie and Malden. In exchange for these latter two sites, they would restore to the United States the Maine District's coastal villages of Castine and Machias. To acquire their land route to the Canadian interior, the British also wanted to trade the area of Maine they had captured east of the Penobscot River for the region north of the Aroostook River. Finally, to extend their influence into the continental heartland, they proposed redrawing the western Canadian border to bring navigable waters of the Mississippi River into British territory.

Even if the Americans had been agreeable to accepting *uti possidetis*, the British proposals were clearly objectionable under the principle's selective application. When the American delegation bluntly refused to modify the prewar boundary, Gambier and his associates proposed that the American delegation draft a counterproposal on all points. At that point, the British emissaries actually were supremely indifferent to anything the Americans had to say, but the ploy promised to prolong talks while British veterans completed the job they had begun with the sack of Washington. The military humiliation of the Yankee upstarts in the Champlain Valley and at Baltimore would only be a matter of time, the British delegation thought, so it set about taking as much time as needed to receive news of these cheerful events.

Status Quo Antebellum

When news of the military situation in North America reached the peace talks in Ghent, it was the Americans who had cause for celebration. The vaunted British veterans had been repulsed at Plattsburgh and at Baltimore. Clouds had gathered over the Congress of Vienna as well, especially when disagreements between the victorious allies threatened to put them at each other's throats and offered an opening for the reemergence of dangerous French militarism.

Given such European uncertainty, the Duke of Wellington was much less likely to sail to North America to direct military operations there, and Parliament suddenly balked at funding the American war when the European one might be on the verge of yet another revival. In any case, Wellington was candid in his assessment of British prospects in North America: without control of the Great Lakes and unless London was prepared to commit larger land and naval forces to the conflict, victory was doubtful. Furthermore, in his view, the existing military situation could not support the extreme demands advanced by the delegation in Ghent. He recommended that the foreign office instead draft a treaty based on the *status quo antebellum*—meaning, the reestablishment of the situation as it existed before the war.

The Treaty of Ghent

So great was the respect accorded Wellington that the British government immediately followed his advice. Prime Minister Lord Liverpool wrote to Castlereagh on 18 November 1814 that, given the worsening European situation, "it has appeared to us desirable to bring the American war, if possible, to a conclusion."[7] Such a result was more than possible. With the elimination of American demands regarding impressment and British demands for the Indian barrier state and adjustments to the Canadian border, peace became probable.

The delegates signed the Treaty of Ghent on 24 December 1814. In the main, the agreement was a simple termination of fighting based on the *status quo antebellum* with provisions to return all territory and prisoners captured during the war. Under these terms, it was obvious that the United States gained nothing in the Treaty of Ghent for which it went to war. There was no British recognition of neutral rights or any repudiation of impressment. The treaty was mute on the issue of free ships making free goods, paper blockades, or the presumably limitless reach of the Rule of 1756.

Yet, for everything it did not address, the treaty was most creditable in American eyes for what it did not contain. The American delegation at Ghent had managed to thwart the British attempt to establish an Indian barrier state, fix in Britain's favor the balance of power on the Great Lakes, and change to Britain's advantage the lengthy reaches of the Canadian border. The American delegates had held a fragile line during some dark days in 1814 when each day's mail might have brought bad news about additional and perhaps decisive American defeats. Rekindled British concern over European instability ultimately helped these forlorn envoys, but it was their stubbornness, even in the face of desolate reverses and internal divisions, that bought time for American victory to tell the tale. Britain finally accepted stalemate as the best bargain. The American delegation wisely did so as well.

Perhaps the most important aspect of the treaty in the long term was its plan for joint commissions that would sort out questions that eventually might have vexed Anglo-American relations to trigger another war. The commissions would settle issues concerning the Canadian border and confused territorial possession with conversation rather than combat. In the years to come, new commercial agreements with Britain sprouted and a grudging but meaningful cooperation ensued to demilitarize not only the Great Lakes but also the entire length of the Canadian border.

These continuing events vindicated the American peace commissioners' decision to depart from the letter of their instructions, but those men also had the satisfaction of immediate validation. When the Treaty of Ghent arrived in the United States in February 1815, President Madison and his cabinet instantly endorsed it, and the Senate unanimously ratified it on 16 February 1815. Oddly, the Senate vote and the country's grand celebrations revealed a United States more solidly unified than it had been at the war's outset. The repudiation of New England separatism and Andrew Jackson's victory at New Orleans contributed to the triumphant mood, of course, but there was more to it than that. In 1815, merely not losing to the greatest empire on earth was the equivalent of winning. American patriotism surged as in no time since the winning of independence, and Albert Gallatin commented with some contentment that "the war has renewed and reinstated the national feelings and character which the Revolution had given . . . and I hope the permanence of the Union is thereby better secured."[8]

Notes

1. Nobody knew at the time that Napoleon with this triumphant invasion had sown the seeds of his own destruction. Although Alexander was unable to make war after Borodino, he nonetheless refused to make peace, leaving Napoleon

and his army to languish in Moscow. Napoleon, unprepared for Russia's fierce winter and eventually unable to feed his 500,000 soldiers, organized a retreat across the country he had so recently conquered, now a frozen wasteland. Unraveling events finally forced him to abandon his army and rush to France, raise another army, and take the field against a new alliance of Russia, Prussia, and Austria as they again joined his constant adversary Great Britain. He had played his last winning hand, however, and the Fourth Coalition defeated him in the spring of 1814.

2. Quoted in James Gallatin, *A Great Peace Maker: The Diary of James Gallatin* (New York: Scribner, 1915), 28.

3. The Senate also had refused to confirm Jonathan Russell as minister to Sweden. The Senate eventually reconsidered and reversed this slap at the Madison administration as well.

4. Quoted in Julius W. Pratt, "James Monroe," in *The American Secretaries of State and Their Diplomacy*, edited by Samuel Flagg Bemis, 15 vol. (New York: Alfred A. Knopf, 1927–1966), 3:270.

5. Quoted in Alfred Thayer Mahan, *Sea Power in Its Relation to the War of 1812*, 2 vols. (Boston: Little, Brown and Co., 1919; reprint ed., Westport, CT: Greenwood Press, 1968), 2: 414.

6. The United States claimed that the Creek War was unrelated to the War of 1812 and hence was not subject to the stipulations that ended the latter conflict.

7. Arthur Wellesley, ed., *Supplementary Dispatches, Correspondence and Memoranda of Field Marshall Arthur Duke of Wellington K.G.*, 15 vols. (London: n.p., 1858–1872), 9:438.

8. Quoted in Robert Allen Rutland, *The Presidency of James Madison* (Lawrence: University Press of Kansas, 1990), 188.

James Madison. Photograph courtesy of the Library of Congress.

HENRY CLAY.

Henry Clay. Photograph courtesy of the Library of Congress.

USS *Constitution* vs. HMS *Guerrière*. Photograph courtesy of the Library of Congress.

TECUMSEH.

Tecumseh. Photograph courtesy of the Library of Congress.

Oliver Hazard Perry transfers his flag, Battle of Lake Erie. Photograph courtesy of the Library of Congress.

Tecumseh falls at the Battle of the Thames. Photograph courtesy of the Library of Congress.

CAPTURE AND BURNING OF WASHINGTON BY THE BRITISH, IN 1814.

The British burn Washingaton, D.C., 1814. Photograph courtesy of the Library of Congress.

Andrew Jackson. Photograph courtesy of the Library of Congress.

The Battle of New Orleans. Photograph courtesy of the Library of Congress.

The Hartford Convention lampooned. Photograph courtesy of the Library of Congress.

BIOGRAPHIES:
THE PERSONALITIES IN THE WAR OF 1812

John Quincy Adams (1767–1848)

At the beginning of the War of 1812 John Quincy Adams, though only forty-five years old, was a seasoned American diplomat who had served as U.S. minister to Russia since 1809. In 1813, Tsar Alexander I had an emissary approach Minister Adams with an offer of mediation of the war between Great Britain and the United States. Both Adams and Madison liked the idea and the president nominated Adams, James Bayard, and Albert Gallatin to the peace commission in Russia. After the other two arrived, however, the British refused to be a party to the negotiations, but suggested instead that the United States and Great Britain negotiate directly. Madison accepted and appointed the original three commissioners (including Adams) as well as Henry Clay and Jonathan Russell to treat with the British. Adams was instrumental in having the negotiations take place in a neutral location at Ghent, in modern Belgium.

On 8 August 1814, the American diplomats began negotiations with their British counterparts. Adams, by far the hardest working of the American contingent, was doubtful from the beginning that any compromise could be reached. The British negotiators presented what the Americans viewed as unreasonable demands that included the carving out of an Indian buffer state from U.S. territory, the demilitarization of the Great Lakes border, and the end of all U.S. fishing in Canadian territorial waters (an especially outrageous demand to the New Englander Adams, who knew that his section depended on those fishing revenues).

Ultimately by adopting Adams' stance that the Americans hold firm in denying the British demands, the American delegation was able to reach a very favorable compromise with the British delegation. With the end of the war in Europe, Adams noted that it was no longer necessary to insist that the British renounce impressment in the treaty, and the British abandoned their call for an Indian buffer state in return for an American promise that all Indian lands taken in the war would be returned. After over two decades of war in Europe, the British were ready for peace, and Adams sensed an opening. The final treaty, signed on Christmas Eve 1814, returned both countries to *status quo antebellum.*

Adams spent the first part of 1815 negotiating trade concerns with Great Britain, and shortly afterward was rewarded by President Madison with the appointment as minister to Great Britain. His diplomatic successes earned him appointment as secretary of state under James Monroe in 1817 and election to the presidency in 1824.

John Armstrong (1758–1843)
From 1803 to 1810, John Armstrong served as U.S. Minister to France and as a result was involved in many of the preliminaries to the United States' declaration of war against Great Britain 1812. During his tenure in France, Armstrong spent much of his time trying to persuade the government of Napoleon to curb its sanctions against neutral trade with Great Britain. Failing in this endeavor, Armstrong resigned in disgust in 1810 and lived quietly until the outbreak of war brought him back to national service.

As a veteran officer of the American Revolution, Armstrong was one of few Americans with combat leadership experience. For the first few months of the war he served as a brigadier general commanding in New York City, but his military experience brought him appointment as secretary of war in February 1813, replacing the inefficient William Eustis.

Armstrong tried to bring some order to the War Department in the hopes of turning around the disastrous military situation left from 1812. To coordinate military affairs, Armstrong divided the nation into nine military districts and ordered the creation of the "Rules and Regulations of the Army of the United States," the first comprehensive set of U.S. Army regulations.

Realizing that poorly trained militia caused many of the early losses in the war, Armstrong was determined to recruit more regulars. He found, however, that most men preferred the shorter enlistments in militia service, so he proposed conscription as the best way to raise a regular army. Political enemies in Madison's cabinet opposed him.

More than political squabbles troubled Armstrong's tenure as secretary of war. His dictatorial attitude toward the commanders of the nine military districts caused tremendous friction and many misunderstandings. Never in the nation's history had the secretary of war had so much responsibility, and despite Armstrong's best intentions, the demands of the job overwhelmed him. He sometimes violated the chain of command to issue orders to subordinates of his military commanders, and he muddled defense policy by haphazardly selecting coastal areas for increased protection. Armstrong's independent ways increasingly troubled President Madison, especially when the secretary failed to consult him on important decisions.

The British raid on Washington and the subsequent burning of the capital dashed Armstrong's chances of remaining secretary of war. Armstrong did not believe that the British would ever attempt a raid that far into the interior and thus concluded that the capital's meager defenses were adequate. He disapproved of Madison's appointment of William Winder to command Washington's defenses and consequently did not cooperate with Winder's efforts. Even worse, he did not allow Winder to call up surrounding state militia until the British were almost upon the capital. When the British routed the militia and entered Washington, Armstrong was universally blamed as most responsible for the disaster. Madison hoped that tempers would cool and that he would be able to retain Armstrong as secretary of war, but Armstrong himself exacerbated the controversy by defending his actions in the newspapers. The president accepted Armstrong's resignation.

Armstrong's tenure as secretary of war saw a mixture of successes and failures. His attempts to coordinate military activities and standardize military regulations were admirable and met with some success. However, Armstrong failed to implement smooth cooperation between military districts and frequently interfered in the routine activities of their commanders. His greatest failure was the loss of Washington, and that catastrophe meant the end of Armstrong's government service.

Isaac Brock (1769–1812)

Major General Isaac Brock of the British army had spent a decade in Canada at the outbreak of the War of 1812. He commanded all regular and militia troops in Upper Canada in 1812 as well as overseeing the civil administration of the province. Because most regular British forces were in Europe fighting Napoleon, Brock had to rely primarily on Canadian militia and Indian allies to defend both the Detroit and Niagara river frontiers. He worked hard to secure funds and supplies as well as to train his largely civilian army to meet possible U.S. invasions, all the while trying to persuade his superior in Quebec, Sir George Prevost, that Upper Canada was defensible and hence should not be abandoned.

Brock's refusal to forsake Upper Canada required bold action after the American declaration of war. He correctly assessed that no American assault was imminent on the Niagara, so he rushed the bulk of his regulars to Amherstburg on the Detroit frontier. There, at Fort Malden, he conferred with the great Shawnee headman Tecumseh about Brigadier General William Hull's invasion from Detroit. Yet by the time Brock arrived at Amherstburg, Hull had already lost his nerve and would soon be in full retreat. Brock planned to take advantage of Hull's fears.

Brock's regulars, militia, and Indian allies crossed the Detroit River on 16 August and approached the fort guarding Detroit. Even though the American post could easily have withstood an attack, Brock hoped he could bluff Hull into surrendering with claims that his Indian allies would be uncontrollable should they have to fight for the fort. The prospect so terrified Hull that he surrendered his army and the city. Brock had just that quickly ended the threat to Upper Canada from the west.

After the fall of Detroit, Brock moved to the Niagara frontier to bolster thin defenses there. He expected the Americans to attack either Fort Erie or Fort George, and their attack at Queenston on 13 October 1812 considerably surprised him. He quickly moved reinforcements to the area but, by the time he arrived, Queenston's defenders were in flight. As Brock led a gallant but reckless charge back up Queenston Heights, he was shot in the chest and died on the field. The British would later claim that their eventual victory at Queenston was inspired by Brock's bravery and singular sacrifice. The British government posthumously knighted Brock and the people of Canada conferred on him the title of "hero of Upper Canada." He was buried on Queenston Heights beneath a monument dedicated to him.

Jacob Jennings Brown (1775–1828)

At the outbreak of the War of 1812, Jacob Brown was serving as a brigadier general of the New York state militia. Brown did not see significant action until the spring of 1813, but his situation on the border between the United States and Canada required him to keep his militia on almost constant alert from the beginning of the war. In May 1813, Brown's abilities were tested when the British attempted to take the valuable port of Sackets Harbor on Lake Ontario. American forces guarding this important naval base numbered about 1,000 men, half of them regulars and half militia. When the British regulars approached, Brown's militia ran and exposed his regulars to overwhelming numbers. During the desperate fight, Brown persuaded about 300 militiamen to return by lying to them that the British were being repulsed. When these men marched to the field, the British retreated. Brown was rewarded for this victory with a brigadier general's commission in the regular army.

During the summer of 1813, Brown's brigade was part of Major General James Wilkinson's attempt to take Montreal. Although the campaign was abandoned before reaching Montreal, Brown's performance again earned him the praise of his superiors and, in early 1814, he was named commander of the Army of the North with headquarters at Sackets Harbor.

In July 1814, Brown took about 3,500 regulars and militia across the Niagara River to capture Fort Erie and move north toward Lake Ontario. He won the Battle of Chippewa only to be disappointed that the naval support he had expected on the lake would not be available. As Brown retreated toward Fort Erie, he fought a major battle near Niagara Falls at Lundy's Lane on 25 July 1814. In the severely fought battle, he was seriously wounded in the thigh.

Brown had to relinquish command and, in his absence, the British besieged the American army at Fort Erie. Although not yet recovered, at the end of August, Brown returned to his command as the British mounted a devastating artillery barrage. Brown launched an attack on the batteries on 17 September that disabled much of the British artillery and forced them to withdraw. Although this success was of limited military value, it came at a time when the United States was suffering reverses on almost every other front. Brown's defense of Fort Erie enhanced his already exceptional reputation, and, following the war, he was given one of the two major generals' slots in the regular army.

Robert Stewart, Viscount Castlereagh (1769–1822)

British Foreign Minister Viscount Castlereagh was partially responsible for the repeal of the Orders in Council by the British in June 1812.

The cabinet did not realize at the time that the United States had already declared war, but when that news arrived, Castlereagh immediately opened negotiations with the American *chargé d'affaires* Jonathan Russell to end the conflict. These talks with Russell proved fruitless when it became apparent that the United States would accept peace only if the British government also renounced impressment. While Castlereagh realized that a war with the United States would distract Great Britain from its titanic struggle with Napoleon, he also believed that the European conflict was the more imperative crisis and consequently refused to bow to any American demand that might blunt the British war effort against France.

When Tsar Alexander I offered to mediate the Anglo-American war, Castlereagh was apprehensive that the tsar would rule against British interests and refused the proposal. The United States' quick response to the Russian offer, however, convinced Castlereagh that the Americans were eager for peace, and he offered to begin direct negotiations. President James Madison accepted and appointed a talented delegation, but Castlereagh's selections were mediocrities because Napoleon's defeat required him to use his best diplomats at the European peace conference in Vienna. Just as he had regarded the American war a minor distraction, he also judged efforts to end it as secondary to the larger issues posed by Europe.

Castlereagh outlined the ideal terms his commissioners were to obtain. He wanted the United States to accept the policy of impressment, to agree to the demilitarization of the Great Lakes, to permit the establishment of an Indian buffer zone in the American Northwest, and to grant Britain navigation rights on the Mississippi River. Rather than treating these stipulations as the best possible terms, the British commissioners mistakenly regarded them as the least that their government would accept. Their stubborn insistence deadlocked the negotiations into the fall of 1814 until Castlereagh instructed them to be more flexible and maintain constant contact with London. Having set that matter straight, Castlereagh again directed his attention to European matters, traveling to Vienna and leaving subordinates to deal with the situation in Ghent. Through a combination of flexibility and indifference, Castlereagh was in part responsible for British accommodations that resulted in the Treaty of Ghent.

Henry Clay (1777–1852)

A member of the War Hawk faction in Congress and Speaker of the House at the outbreak of the War of 1812, Henry Clay of Kentucky had early advocated war with Great Britain to avenge the violation of American neutral rights and had boasted that Kentuckians alone could conquer Canada. In the months before the summer of 1812, Clay and the War Hawks not only pressured President James Madison to embrace war, they also worked to increase the country's preparedness by boosting military spending.

As Speaker of the House, Clay greatly strengthened that position's role in shaping the legislative agenda and used his superb oratorical skills to persuade the House to continue strengthening the military. He pushed President Madison to make Canada the primary military objective of the war and was influential— sometimes to the annoyance of the administration—in deciding important military matters, such as the appointment of William Henry Harrison to command American forces in the Northwest. Clay was less successful in shaming New England members of the House into supporting the war effort.

By the end of 1813, Clay lost hope that Madison's military policies would defeat British forces in Canada, so the following year, he accepted a place on the U.S. commission to negotiate peace with the British at Ghent. Clay wanted to ensure that any treaty preserved U.S. interests, especially those concerning the West. The former speaker did not always get along with his fellow American commissioners, especially John Quincy Adams, who believed that Clay's drinking and gambling jeopardized their mission. Nonetheless, Clay proved a shrewd negotiator in resisting British demands for an Indian buffer state in the Northwest and for navigation rights on the Mississippi River.

After the Treaty of Ghent was signed on 24 December 1814, Clay joined Adams, who had gained an appreciation for the Kentuckian's negotiating skills, in further talks with the British in London about trade between the two countries. Clay then returned to the House of Representatives. Over his long career he would win renown for his negotiating prowess in forging compromises that averted sectional confrontation over the issue of slavery.

Sir Alexander Cochrane (1758–1832)

At the outbreak of the War of 1812, Admiral Sir Alexander Cochrane was serving in the Caribbean as the governor of the island of Guadeloupe. Early in 1814 he was recalled to sea duty and replaced Admiral Sir John Borlase Warren as commander of the fleet off the eastern coast of North

America. One of his first actions was to promise freedom to American slaves who joined British military forces, an act for which he was roundly condemned in the United States. Another controversial measure taken by Cochrane in the summer of 1814 was his direction of coastal raids and the destruction of American towns in retaliation for American actions in Canada. These activities were especially effective against the New England coast, where inhabitants were already lukewarm about the war.

In August 1814, Cochrane commanded the British expedition up the Patuxent River that resulted in the capture of Washington, D.C. In September, his fleet ferried troops under Major General Robert Ross to Baltimore. While Ross attempted to take the city by land, Cochrane bombarded Fort McHenry, which guarded Baltimore's harbor. His failure to reduce Fort McHenry was compounded by Ross's death and the army's inability to penetrate the city's land defenses.

Cochrane's repulse at Baltimore led him to accelerate planning for an expedition against New Orleans. He had already dispatched marines to the Gulf of Mexico to gather Indian allies there, but that initiative proved disappointing. Nonetheless, Cochrane collected forces at Negril Bay in Jamaica for a major campaign that began on 14 December 1814 as British naval forces moved into Lake Borgne near New Orleans. After defeating American gunboats on the lake, Cochrane's fleet mainly supported the British army assailing New Orleans until its defeat on 8 January 1815. Abandoning the campaign, Cochrane helped the army capture Fort Bowyer guarding the entrance to Mobile Bay, but word of the peace treaty arrived before Cochrane could move on the city itself.

Although he had served in the war against the United States for less than a year, Cochrane had cut a considerable swath, directing his ships in operations that spanned from New England to the Gulf of Mexico.

George Cockburn (1772–1853)

Destined to earn an infamous reputation in the War of 1812, British rear admiral George Cockburn (pronounced Coburn) was serving in European waters at the outbreak of hostilities. Early in the war, he was transferred to the command of Admiral Sir John Borlase Warren with orders to eliminate U.S. supply sources on the shores of Chesapeake Bay. Commanding from his flagship HMS *Marlborough*, Cockburn moved throughout the bay in the late winter and spring of 1813, destroying anything of any conceivable use to American military forces.

His broad definition of military targets and an apparent penchant for ruthlessness earned him a shameful notoriety among Americans. In May 1813, Cockburn smashed much of Havre de Grace, Maryland, because he claimed an elderly militiaman had fired on his ships. He shelled unoffending towns on Maryland's Eastern Shore and joined Admiral Warren for operations against Craney Island at Norfolk, Virginia. Failing to take that strategic port, Cockburn vented his fury on nearby Hampton, Virginia, allowing his men to loot the town and indulge in rape and murder.

American condemnation of these excesses irritated Cockburn. When in the summer of 1814, Vice Admiral Sir Alexander Cochrane replaced Warren, Cockburn enthusiastically helped to plan a major campaign on the Chesapeake. He accompanied the overland march on Washington, D.C., and personally directed the destruction of the American capital, particularly of the executive mansion and the offices of a newspaper critical of his activities. In the Baltimore campaign, Cockburn again accompanied the army as it marched on the city and was present at the death of Robert Ross. Following Cochrane's departure for the New Orleans campaign, Cockburn continued to raid Chesapeake towns before moving south during the winter. January found him on the Georgia coast destroying supplies and liberating slaves to serve in his raiding parties. He was preparing a major attack against Savannah, Georgia, when he learned that the war had ended.

Cockburn was a talented officer whose reputation for viciousness was possibly exaggerated. The War of 1812 marked only a brief episode in a naval career that spanned more than thirty-five years, but his exploits in the conflict revealed a stunning contempt for American sensibilities as well as American property. The most charitable assessment would state that he did not coddle Britain's enemies. Perhaps that was the reason the British government in 1815 selected George Cockburn to command the ship that ferried Napoleon Bonaparte to his final and forlorn exile on St. Helena.

Stephen Decatur, Jr. (1779–1820)

Stephen Decatur had been an officer in the U.S. Navy for over a decade at the outbreak of the War of 1812. When war was declared, he was commanding one of two naval squadrons along the United States' east coast. Decatur operated out of Norfolk, Virginia, while the other squadron, under Decatur's senior officer Commodore John Rodgers, operated out of New York.

At the start of the war, Decatur and Rodgers disagreed about how the U.S. Navy should carry out operations. Decatur believed that American ships should sail singly or in pairs to attack British commerce, but Rodgers wanted to maintain squadrons. Rodgers's seniority won the argument, but his first raid (with Decatur along) failed to reap any significant gains. Furthermore, acclaim for Isaac Hull's defeat of the *Guerrière* encouraged other captains to try Decatur's plan. The result would be some of the most stirring ship actions in U.S. naval history, including those of Stephen Decatur.

Decatur, in command of the *United States*, departed Boston in October 1812 and on the 25th encountered the frigate HMS *Macedonian*, fighting her to surrender in a little over an hour. Furthermore, Decatur took this prize back to the United States, where he was greeted as a national hero and with good reason: the *Macedonian* was the only British frigate captured in the history of the Royal Navy.

The tightening British blockade in the spring of 1813 trapped Decatur in harbor at New London, Connecticut, with the *United States* and the *Macedonian*. He spent the next year strengthening New London's defenses but saw no sea duty. In the spring of 1814, he moved to New York to assume command of the USS *President,* but the British blockade held him at bay there as well. He had to be satisfied strengthening New York harbor's defenses. In January 1815, Decatur at last tried to run the *President* past the blockade, but she ran aground. She was so slowed by damage that, once free, Decatur was forced to surrender to three British pursuers. Word of the peace treaty arrived soon after, saving Decatur from censure for his rash and unsuccessful exploit.

After the war, Decatur received his pick of assignments and again demonstrated his élan by intimidating Algiers into recognizing American rights in the Mediterranean. The War of 1812, however, would cast a long shadow for Decatur. In 1820, he quarreled with former naval officer James Barron over Barron's behavior before the conflict. The argument ended in a duel that left Stephen Decatur dead at age forty-one.

William Henry Harrison (1773–1841)

At the outbreak of the War of 1812, William Henry Harrison had been territorial governor of Indiana for over a decade. He had negotiated land cession treaties with the various northwestern Indian tribes, acquiring vast tracts for white settlement and triggering increasing opposition from Native Americans. Particularly resistant were followers of the great Shawnee Tecumseh and his brother Tenskwatawa (the Prophet). In November 1811, while Tecumseh was visiting southern tribes to promote native unity, Harrison led a combined force of regulars and militia against Tecumseh's followers at Prophet's Town on Tippecanoe Creek. Tenskwatawa persuaded the Indians to launch a preemptive strike against Harrison's army, but the Americans were able to drive them off and destroy Prophet's Town. The campaign not only started a war between the United States and many Native Americans in the Northwest, it also drove the Indians into the arms of the British on the eve of the War of 1812.

When the United States declared war on Great Britain in June 1812, Harrison did not have a military command. His popularity with westerners, however, caused them to insist that he be given command of northwestern forces after William Hull's surrender of Detroit in August 1812. To bolster Harrison's case, Kentuckians named him major general of the Kentucky militia. Madison bowed to the pressure in the fall of 1812 and appointed Harrison commander in the Northwest.

Harrison assumed his command too late to start a major campaign, but he wanted to put in place enough troops to retake Detroit the following spring. Immediately the preparations met with disaster when British and Indians attacked one of the columns he sent forward under Brigadier General James Winchester, destroying it on the Raisin River in January 1813. In spring, Harrison consolidated his reduced force in the Northwest by building Fort Meigs on the Maumee (Miami) River near Lake Erie. It was there, in late April 1813, that the British under Colonel Henry Procter and Native Americans under Tecumseh besieged Harrison's army. The arrival of American reinforcements and a sortie from the fort that disabled British guns convinced Procter to abandon the siege.

Throughout the summer of 1813 Harrison cooperated with Oliver Hazard Perry as he prepared to challenge the British Navy's control of Lake Erie. Following Perry's stunning victory on 10 September 1813, Harrison pursued the British and Indians as they retreated into Upper Canada. When Procter and Tecumseh stopped to fight the Battle of the Thames on 5 October 1813, Harrison defeated them, and Tecumseh was killed.

Harrison's military career ended with this battle. Although he retained command of the Northwest, the removal of the British and the destruction of Tecumseh's confederation meant the end of active campaigning in the region. Such inactivity weighed heavily on Harrison, who brooded that his government had not shown sufficient gratitude for his actions in 1813. He took to quarreling with Secretary of War John Armstrong and finally resigned his commission in early 1814. It would prove a temporary interruption in his public career. His victories over the Indians and the British would enhance his political career after the war and ultimately win him election to the presidency in 1840.

Isaac Hull (1773–1843)

Captain Isaac Hull commanded the USS *Constitution* at the start of the War of 1812. Following the outbreak of war, he was ordered to take the *Constitution* from Chesapeake Bay to join other American warships at New York City. Before reaching his destination, he encountered a British squadron in calm waters off New Jersey. With wind Hull could have outrun his pursuers, but without it, he was in danger of falling to capture. For several days, he led the British on a dramatic sea chase, towing the *Constitution* with rowboats and kedging her through shallow waters. When a breeze finally allowed the *Constitution* to slip away, Hull evaded British ships off New York to make port in a jubilant Boston. Americans had a new hero.

After resupplying the *Constitution*, Hull set out in early August to seize British shipping off Canada before news of war reached merchants there. He then sailed toward British Bermuda to take additional British merchant prizes, but on 19 August 1812, he encountered the British frigate *Guerrière*. The two ships fought a four-hour slugging match that ended with the resilient *Constitution* victorious and bearing the new nickname "Old Ironsides." Seeking to improve on an already signal victory, Hull's final report of the battle claimed he had defeated the *Guerrière* in thirty-five minutes.

The victory occurred at a time when America's war fortunes were very low (Hull's uncle William Hull had surrendered Detroit on 16 August), and Isaac Hull was further hailed as a national hero. Congress authorized the striking of a gold medal to honor the victory. Content to rest on his laurels, Hull commanded U.S. naval facilities ashore for the remainder of the war.

Andrew Jackson (1767–1845)

Although he had been a major general in the Tennessee militia since 1802, Andrew Jackson had little military experience at the start of the War of 1812. Yet Jackson emerged from the war as one of the United States' most successful combat commanders and perhaps the war's most popular hero.

When the United States declared war on Great Britain in June 1812, Jackson eagerly volunteered to lead Tennessee troops into any theater of action. Early in the war, he expected to receive instructions to assume a command in the northwest where most of the fighting was taking place. Disappointed in that hope, Jackson enthusiastically accepted command of 1,500 Tennessee volunteers when the government called them up late in 1812.

Jackson led his men to Natchez, Mississippi Territory, intending to march them to New Orleans to cooperate with Major General James Wilkinson in the defense of that city. His army was to remain in Natchez, however. In early 1813 when it appeared that the threat to New Orleans had been exaggerated, the government ordered Jackson to disband his army and return to Tennessee. Unwilling to dismiss his men so far from their homes because they would have to travel in small bands through a wilderness inhabited by potentially hostile Indians, Jackson wrote a sharp letter to the War Department criticizing its indifference and then disobeyed the order to disband his force. Instead, he personally led it back to Tennessee, sharing his men's considerable hardship on the march and earning their affectionate admiration in the bargain. They gave him his most enduring nickname—Old Hickory.

Jackson remained idle for several months after returning to Tennessee, but in September 1813 the Fort Mims Massacre again summoned him to action. Supply problems and the short enlistments of his militia hampered Jackson's campaign against the Red Stick Creek Indians. He won victories at Tallushatchee and Talladega in November 1813 but had to suspend the campaign at the end of the year while awaiting reinforcements. Finally on 27 March 1814, Jackson had sufficient forces and supplies to launch a decisive attack on the main Red Stick stronghold of Horseshoe Bend (Tohopeka) on the Tallapoosa River. The Battle of Horseshoe Bend broke the back of the Red Sticks, and, in August 1814, Jackson forced the entire Creek Nation to sign the Treaty of Fort Jackson ceding over 23,000,000 acres to the United States.

By the late summer of 1814, the government had made Jackson a major general in the regular army and ordered him to defend the Gulf of Mexico coast. To prevent the British from using Spanish Pensacola as a staging area for a bigger invasion, Jackson took that city in November 1814. Shortly afterward, Jackson learned of a large British force heading from Jamaica for New Orleans and quickly marched his men to that city, arriving on 1 December 1814 just ahead of the first British landings.

In addition to the formidable task of defending a city almost surrounded by water, Jackson was undermanned and underarmed for the coming campaign. A combination of luck, skill, and British arrogance saved the day for the Americans, however. While Jackson was weakest, the British remained cautious, and only after he had received reinforcements and constructed daunting fortifications did they attack. On 8 January 1815, in a frontal assault against Jackson's heavily fortified lines, the British suffered such horrific casualties that they soon broke off their campaign. The victory at New Orleans made Jackson a national hero.

Andrew Jackson's record in the war was a mixture of success, disappointment, and controversy. Concerning this last, he developed a reputation for demanding ironclad discipline from his troops and for running roughshod over civilian rights. Nonetheless, his victories at Horseshoe Bend and New Orleans earned him enormous popularity and eventually propelled him to the presidency.

Thomas Macdonough (1783–1825)

At the beginning of the War of 1812, Lieutenant Thomas Macdonough of the U.S. Navy was considering leaving the service for a more profitable career in the foreign merchant trade. The declaration of war, however, changed his mind. When his assignment to the USS *Constellation* left him idle—the *Constellation* was not ready for sea—Macdonough requested a transfer to command gunboats off the Maine coast. He held that command only briefly and was soon placed in charge of all American naval forces on Lake Champlain, a post he held for the duration of the war.

Initially Macdonough's flotilla consisted of only five boats in bad repair, but the British could boast of few resources of their own on the northern part of the lake, so the lieutenant had time to improve his force. The situation worsened considerably in the summer of 1813 when the British captured two of his largest and most heavily armed vessels. Macdonough's redoubled efforts to acquire more vessels rendered him three sloops and two gunboats by the end of the summer. He also supervised the construction of three additional ships (the *Saratoga*, the *Ticonderoga*, and the *Eagle*). Despite these efforts, British naval forces proved superior in size and guns when combined British forces began their invasion of New York in early September 1814. Macdonough withdrew his flotilla to Plattsburgh Bay to find favorable waters for the upcoming battle.

On 11 September 1814, Macdonough maneuvered the British into a close engagement that favored his short-range guns. He also contrived to swing his flagship *Saratoga* on its anchor chain at a crucial point to disable the British flagship *Confiance*. Macdonough thus secured the surrender of all of the British vessels except their gunboats. American victory at the Battle of Plattsburgh Bay convinced the British to suspend their invasion and withdraw from American soil in that theater.

James Madison (1751–1836)

When he became president in 1809, James Madison inherited disputes with both Great Britain and France regarding American neutral rights. When negotiations with Great Britain failed, Madison reluctantly agreed to Macon's Bill No. 2, passed by Congress in 1810. This act restored trade with all nations but stipulated that if either Britain or France stopped harassing American shipping, the United States would resume nonintercourse with the other. When Napoleon indicated through intermediaries that he would revoke his edicts affecting American commerce, Madison announced that trade would be halted with Great Britain. Napoleon was lying, but Madison persisted in instituting the policy against Great Britain.

By 1811, domestic political pressures were pushing Madison toward war with Great Britain. A growing congressional faction known as War Hawks believed that the only way to remedy British violations of American neutral rights was with force. Many War Hawks were westerners who also believed that the British in Canada were inciting Indians to attack American settlers. As an increasing number of Madison's advisors urged the president to present a war message to Congress, on 1 June 1812, he finally asked Congress to declare war on Great Britain. A sharply divided Congress voted narrowly for war, unaware that the British government had decided to abandon its obnoxious policies.

Madison's administration and the War Hawks tried to increase military preparation, but the United States still entered the conflict ill prepared. For his part, Madison proved unable to provide the kind of leadership needed to prosecute the war. At the outset, he faced a vigorous challenge from Federalists and anti-war Republicans in his 1812 reelection bid. After winning a second term, Madison strengthened the War Department by replacing the ineffective William Eustis with John Armstrong as secretary of war, but neither Madison nor Armstrong were capable of bringing coordination and cooperation to the various theaters of operation. Consequently, administration plans to conquer Canada remained unrealized, and in 1814 Madison had to deal with three separate British invasions of American soil.

Politically and psychologically, the most alarming was the British raid in Chesapeake Bay and the threat to Washington, D.C. Until the summer of 1814, Madison had not questioned Armstrong's insistence that Washington would never be menaced, and when he finally insisted that some preparations be made to defend the capital, they proved tardy and ineffectual. As the British approached Washington on 24 August, Madison acted on his conviction that as commander in chief he should be present with the defenders of the capital. Accordingly, he rode out with his cabinet to Bladensburg, Maryland, to meet the British. It was a courageous gesture, but the American debacle at Bladensburg swept Madison up in the flood of retreating Americans and left his wife Dolley on her own to escape Washington as the British entered the capital.

As soon as the British departed, Madison returned to the capital to find the president's house gutted and the government in disarray. To put his cabinet in order, Madison finally had to accept Armstrong's resignation and appoint Secretary of State James Monroe in his place. Monroe's constant sniping against Armstrong had given Madison pause, but the change was to have a happy effect on the administration's war policy. Military news, in fact, improved with reports that the British invasion on Lake Champlain had been repulsed.

Politically, however, the president faced New England's increasing opposition to the war. The December 1814 meeting at Hartford, Connecticut, greatly alarmed him, especially when it was rumored that New England disunion would be its result. Yet, Andrew Jackson's victory at New Orleans and the successful peace negotiations at Ghent vindicated Madison's public optimism and discredited his enemies.

Despite this good fortune, James Madison does not merit high marks as the United States' first war president. He failed to prepare the country for the conflict and then proved ineffective in coordinating military activities. He tolerated divisions in his cabinet and allowed matters to drift to the point of possible disaster in the last year of the conflict. The emergence of talented military commanders and the timely arrival of a peace treaty saved Madison from the consequences of his shortcomings.

James Monroe (1758–1831)

James Monroe had been serving as James Madison's secretary of state for more than a year at the outbreak of the War of 1812 and consequently had wrestled with the disputes between the United States, Great Britain, and France. Since American grievances mainly focused on British impressment of American seamen and seizure of American merchant shipping, Monroe attempted to negotiate an end to these practices with the British minister to the United States. When that effort failed, Monroe encouraged President Madison to prepare for war and urged Congress to increase military spending. In early 1812, Monroe helped persuade Congress to put an embargo on all British trade, hoping that London would take it as a warning that the United States intended war if the British government did not repeal the Orders in Council. When this gesture also proved fruitless, Monroe strongly encouraged Madison to send a war message to Congress in June 1812.

Following the declaration of war, Monroe hoped that his military experience in the American Revolution would win him a field command, but Madison wanted to keep Monroe in the cabinet. After Secretary of War William Eustis was forced from office at the end of 1812, Monroe became more involved in military affairs when Madison made him acting secretary of war as well as secretary of state. Monroe drew up more aggressive military plans for an invasion of Canada that he hoped to command, but both his plans and hopes were thwarted when John Armstrong replaced him in the War Department in February 1813. Monroe disagreed with Armstrong's selection and over the next year argued for his removal.

Monroe finally succeeded when Armstrong was blamed for the British raid on Washington, D.C., in August 1814.

Meanwhile, State Department duties kept Monroe busy. Monroe and Madison accepted the Russian tsar's mediation offer and prepared a delegation to go to Russia. After his emissaries had departed, Monroe learned that the British had refused the Russian offer. The British, however, did propose direct negotiations. Sensing that Napoleon's fortunes were falling in Europe, Monroe and Madison jumped at the chance for negotiations before British troops freed from fighting in Europe could come to America. In addition to commissioners already designated for the Russian negotiations (John Quincy Adams, James Bayard, and Albert Gallatin), Monroe selected Henry Clay and Jonathan Russell to round out the American team that would gather in Ghent.

During the late summer of 1814, as the negotiators began their work in Ghent, Monroe and other members of the Madison administration waited nervously as a British army force marched on the capital. Present at Bladensburg, Maryland, when the British appeared, Monroe probably contributed to the American rout by repositioning troops on his own authority and neglecting to consult with the American commander. Following that fiasco, Monroe helped to remove important documents from Washington before the British took the city.

After the British sack of Washington, Armstrong's resignation from the War Department made way for Madison to appoint Monroe acting secretary of war. Monroe threw himself into his new job (as before, he remained the secretary of state) and was partially responsible for the quick and successful American defense of Baltimore. He devoted considerable energy to military preparation and raising additional troops. He unsuccessfully tried to persuade Congress to institute conscription and labored to move supplies and men to help Andrew Jackson defend the Gulf Coast.

At war's end, Monroe was exhausted from his strenuous labors and eagerly relinquished his duties at the War Department. He had the satisfaction of knowing that he was partially responsible for American success in the last months of the war. The country would register its appreciation by making him Madison's successor to the presidency.

Oliver Hazard Perry (1785–1819)

Oliver Hazard Perry had been an officer in the U.S. Navy for more than a decade at the outset of the War of 1812. Stationed at Newport,

Rhode Island, where he commanded gunboats for coastal defense, he requested a more active command as soon as he learned of hostilities and was assigned to the Great Lakes under Captain Isaac Chauncey in the spring of 1813.

Instructed to build a squadron that could wrest control of Lake Erie from the British, Perry began building new vessels at Presque Isle from green wood and purchasing others to arm and refit. He launched his two largest vessels, the brigs *Lawrence* and *Niagara*, that summer. By August 1813, Perry had a flotilla of seven vessels and crews filled out with soldiers from William Henry Harrison's army. He moved west on Lake Erie to find the British squadron under Captain Robert Barclay.

The Americans and British sighted each other on 9 September and began preparing for battle. The following day, Barclay tried to destroy Perry's flagship *Lawrence* with his long-range guns before the rest of Perry's ships could enter the fight. In a move that caused considerable controversy later, Jesse Elliott kept the *Niagara* in a position removed from the battle, and the *Lawrence* consequently suffered such a hard pounding that it disabled her and butchered her crew. When the *Niagara* finally moved nearer to his position, Perry lowered a rowboat from the drifting *Lawrence* and with five uninjured sailors transferred his flag to the *Niagara* on which he again took command of the battle. Sending Elliott to direct the movements of the flotilla's smaller ships, Perry steered the *Niagara* through Barclay's squadron to fire broadsides from both batteries and batter the British into surrender.

The Battle of Lake Erie was a relatively small engagement, but Perry's victory had tremendous consequences. The British losing control of Lake Erie meant that they also lost control of the northwestern frontier. Perry's operations were remarkable for that dramatic result, but his methods of achieving his success were just as notable. With dogged determination, he had built a small fleet of warships on an inland sea and had readied it for combat, even though he was hampered by shortages of everything, including men. The relationship between Perry and William Henry Harrison provided a model of extraordinary army–navy cooperation devoid of rivalry that was responsible for both Perry's Lake Erie victory and Harrison's triumphant pursuit of retreating British forces.

In the closing months of the war Perry took command of the USS *Java*, but he did not see combat again. Meanwhile, controversy regarding Jesse Elliott's mysterious behavior during the Battle of Lake Erie troubled and distracted Perry, even calling into question his claim as the author of the victory. In 1819, yellow fever killed Perry at the age of thirty-four while he was serving in South American waters.

Robert Ross (1766–1814)

At the outbreak of the War of 1812, British major general Robert Ross was fighting under the Duke of Wellington against Napoleon's forces in Spain. He served there with high distinction and earned several decorations for bravery.

By the summer of 1814, most British forces in Spain were withdrawn, and Ross was given command of a brigade slated for service against the United States. In August 1814, Ross led 4,500 men in Vice Admiral Sir Alexander Cochrane's expedition on Chesapeake Bay. On 19 August, Ross's troops went ashore on Maryland's Patuxent River and marched to Upper Marlboro where Ross elected to proceed overland against Washington, D.C. On 24 August, he scattered hastily mustered American militia at Bladensburg, Maryland, and pressed on to Washington. In retaliation for U.S. depredations in Canada, particularly the burning of York, Ross ordered Washington's public buildings burned, including the Capitol and the president's mansion, but insisted that his men respect private property and punished soldiers who did not. His raid on the American capital concluded, Ross led his men back to the Patuxent.

Ross's soldiers next participated in the assault against the more strategically important target of Baltimore. While the Royal Navy attacked Fort McHenry at the entrance to Baltimore's inner harbor, Ross landed his men and began making for the city itself. Baltimore's defenses, however, were more formidable than those at Washington, and militia resistance to the British advance challenged Ross with a stiff fight. Eager to reach the city's main defenses as soon as possible, Ross rode ahead of his men to scout the situation, and an American sharpshooter mortally wounded him as he was returning to the main British column. With the bullet lodged in his chest, Ross died as his men tried to convey him back to the ships. The expedition stalled on both land and water, and the British abandoned the campaign against Baltimore.

Tecumseh (1768–1813)

This great Shawnee war leader had been tirelessly working to bring about the unity of Native Americans since early in the nineteenth century.

His efforts had gained impetus from the native spiritual movement started by his younger brother Tenskwatawa (known as Lalawethika before his religious conversion and called the Prophet by European Americans). The two brothers hoped to unite all Native Americans to prevent further U.S. expansion. The vast land cessions forced upon northwestern Indians by Indiana territorial governor William Henry Harrison especially disturbed Tecumseh. He and his brother gathered followers at Prophet's Town on Tippecanoe Creek.

After failing to persuade Harrison to rescind some earlier land sessions, Tecumseh redoubled his efforts to form an Indian confederation, traveling through the South in 1811 to recruit members from that region. Although he made some headway among the Red Stick faction of the Creek Indians, Tecumseh was mainly disappointed in this effort. Worse, he returned home in the fall of 1811 to learn that Harrison had destroyed Prophet's Town. Tecumseh turned to the British for aid, and, in the summer of 1812, he led warriors to join the British at Fort Malden to help defend Upper Canada against William Hull's invasion. Tecumseh's activities along American supply lines so unnerved Hull that he retreated to fortifications at Detroit, and British commander Isaac Brock's threat to allow his Indian allies free rein if the Americans did not capitulate caused Hull to surrender his army.

During the spring and summer of 1813, Tecumseh's followers were valuable allies to the British in forays out of Michigan deep into American territory. During the first British siege of Fort Meigs, Tecumseh commanded many of the operations around the fort, and when an American party was ambushed, he entered white folklore by preventing the massacre of American prisoners. By the end of summer, however, Tecumseh was disgusted with the British inability to oust Americans from what had been Indian lands. When the American naval victory on Lake Erie compelled British commander Henry Procter to withdraw into Upper Canada, Tecumseh's alienation was nearly complete. Only the fear that pursuing Americans under William Henry Harrison would destroy his warriors induced him to accompany the retreating British.

The march up the Thames River dispirited Tecumseh, for it featured a steady evaporation of his following as Indians abandoned the failed British. Near Moraviantown, Procter stopped to fight his pursuers in what would be the Battle of the Thames. Tecumseh and his warriors were some of the few who did not break and run. While trying to prevent the envelopment of Procter's right flank, Tecumseh was killed, reputedly by Richard Johnson of the Kentucky militia, a purported deed that would later boost the Kentuckian's political career.

James Wilkinson (1757–1825)

A veteran of the American Revolution, Wilkinson had been in the regular army since 1791 and had been the senior officer of that army from 1800 to 1812. When war erupted in June 1812, Wilkinson commanded U.S. troops at New Orleans. By the fall of 1812, there was some concern that the British might try to use Spanish possessions along the Gulf of Mexico as a base of operations against Louisiana. As a result, Wilkinson was authorized to seize Spanish Mobile to prevent it from falling into British hands. He did so in April 1813, even though the United States was not (and would not be) at war with Spain. Mobile was the only foreign territory acquired by the United States in the War of 1812.

Wilkinson's success at Mobile did nothing to repair his bad relationship with civilian officials in Louisiana. The government transferred him to the command of the Ninth Military District in the summer of 1813, a command that included much of the border with Canada along the Vermont, New York, and Pennsylvania frontiers. Under orders from Secretary of War John Armstrong to coordinate his activities with Major General Wade Hampton and launch an invasion of Canada, Wilkinson botched almost every aspect of the operation. Sallying forth from his headquarters at Sackets Harbor, he presided over considerable disorganization while feuding with Hampton, arguing with Armstrong, alienating his subordinates, and addling his senses with opiates.

Wilkinson's defenders would point out that he was quite ill (hence, the opiates) as his campaign inched toward the St. Lawrence River in October 1813. In addition, starting a campaign in the North so late in the year almost assured failure. The weather certainly contributed to his army's poor morale, and Wilkinson increasingly left command matters to others. He even delegated command of the force that was defeated by inferior British numbers at Crysler's Farm on 11 November. This poor showing confirmed that the expedition was unfit to meet its objective, and shortly afterward Wilkinson ordered the army into winter quarters. He then did little to see that his men were supplied with food and clothing during the hard winter.

The following spring when Wilkinson tried to revive the campaign with a much smaller army, he was repulsed by a force less than a tenth his size. The government promptly removed him from command, which as it happened was his last.

James Wilkinson was a self-serving officer whose past included vaguely unsavory and some blatantly traitorous acts—before the war, for instance, he had been in the pay of Spain. Always reluctant to give up his comfort for the rigors of the field, his performance in the war was marred by bad health, advancing age, and incompetence. Even a less ambitious campaign against Canada would not have prospered under such a flawed commander.

PRIMARY DOCUMENTS OF THE WAR OF 1812

The United States' Restrictive System

When the British and the French resorted to commercial warfare in 1807, it exacted a heavy toll on neutral shipping, especially that of the United States. The United States suffered a further humiliation in the summer of 1807 when the British ship *Leopard* fired on and boarded the USS *Chesapeake*. Although Americans wanted war, Jefferson judged that such a course would be a disastrous mistake for the unprepared republic. Instead, he used American commercial pressure to force the European antagonists to respect U.S. neutral rights. The result was the Embargo Act of 1807 that barred the export of American goods to foreign ports. The embargo not only failed to persuade England and France to repeal their restrictions, it also became infamous among the American people. On 1 March 1809, Congress repealed the Embargo Act with the passage of the Non-Intercourse Act. Non-intercourse, however, proved as unenforceable as the embargo, and the legislation was due to expire at the close of the congressional session. Consequently, Congress passed Macon's Bill No. 2 on 1 May 1810, repealing non-intercourse and reopening trade with both Great Britain and France. Under Macon's Bill, the United States pledged to suspend trade with one should the other revoke its restrictions. When Napoleon falsely claimed to withdraw his Berlin and Milan Decrees, Madison announced non-intercourse with Great Britain to become effective in February 1811. The ramifications were profound, for despite Napoleon's obvious insincerity, the United States had essentially joined his Continental System, the French plan to destroy English commerce.

Document 1
The Embargo Act, 22 December 1807

Be it enacted by the Senate and House of Representatives of the United States of America in Congress assembled, That an embargo be, and hereby is laid on all ships and vessels in the ports and places within the limits or jurisdiction of the United States, cleared or not cleared, bound to any foreign port or place; and that no clearance be furnished to any ship or vessels bound to such foreign port or place, except vessels under the immediate direction of the President of the United States: and that the President be authorized to give such instructions to the officers of the revenue, and of the navy and revenue cutters of the United States, as shall appear best adopted for carrying the same into full effect: *Provided*, that nothing herein contained shall be construed to prevent the departure of any foreign ship or vessel, either in ballast, or with the goods, wares and merchandise on board of such foreign ship or vessel, when notified of this act. . . .

APPROVED, December 22, 1807.

Source: Richard Peters, ed., *The Public Statutes at Large of the United States of America* (Boston: Charles C. Little and James Brown, 1845), 2: 451–53.

Document 2
The Non-Intercourse Act, 1 March 1809

An Act to interdict the commercial intercourse between the United States and Great Britain and France and their dependencies; and for other purposes.

Be it enacted by the Senate and House of Representatives of the United States of America in Congress assembled, That from and after the passing of this act, the entrance of the harbors and waters of the United States and of the territories thereof, be, and the same is hereby interdicted to all public ships and vessels belonging to Great Britain or France, excepting vessels are only which may be forced in by distress, of which are charged with actual or visit the government will also having no cargo nor merchant and on board. . . .

SEC. 11. *And be if further enacted*, That the President of the United States be, and he hereby is authorized, in case either France or Great Britain shall so revoke or modify her edicts, as that they shall cease to violate the neutral commerce of the United States, to declare the same by proclamation: after which the trade of the United States, suspended by this act, and by the [Embargo Act] and the several acts supplementary thereto, may be renewed with the nation so doing. . . .

SEC. 19. That this act shall continue and be in force until the end of the next session of Congress, and no longer; and that the act laying an embargo on all ships and vessels in the ports and harbors of the United States, and the several acts supplementary thereto, shall be, and the same are hereby repealed from and after the end of the next session of Congress.

APPROVED, March 1, 1809

Source: Richard Peters, ed., *The Public Statutes at Large of the United States of America* (Boston: Charles C. Little and James Brown, 1845), 2: 528–33.

Document 3
Macon's Bill No. 2, 1 May 1810

An Act concerning the commercial intercourse between the United States and Great Britain and France and their dependencies, and for other purposes.

Be it enacted . . .

Sec. 4. That in case either Great Britain or France shall, before the third day of March next, so revoke or modify her edicts as that they shall cease to violate the neutral commerce of the United States, which fact the President of the United States shall declare by proclamation, and if the other nation shall not within three months thereafter so revoke or modify her edicts in like manner, then the third, fourth, fifth, sixth, seventh, eighth, ninth, tenth, and eighteenth sections of the act, entitled "An act to interdict the commercial intercourse between the United States and Great Britain and France . . ." shall, from and after the expiration of three months from the date of the proclamation aforesaid, be revived and have full force and effect, so far as relates to the dominions, colonies, and dependencies, and to the articles the growth, produce or manufacture of the dominions, colonies and dependencies of the nation thus refusing or neglecting to revoke or modify her edicts in the manner aforesaid. And the restrictions imposed by this act shall, from the date of such proclamation, cease and be discontinued in relation to the nation revoking or modifying her decrees in the manner aforesaid.

Source: Richard Peters, ed., *The Public Statutes at Large of the United States of America* (Boston: Charles C. Little and James Brown, 1845), 2: 605–606.

The United States Declares War

In the face of British inflexibility, President James Madison had limited diplomatic options. The communication he sent to Congress on 1 June 1812 reflected his exasperation. Subsequently known as the "war message," it set into motion the congressional activity that culminated in the declaration of war later that month. The House of Representatives, where the War Hawks exerted considerable influence, voted immediately for war, but the Senate debated the issue for almost three weeks before deciding for war in an extremely close vote.

Document 4
Madison Makes the Case for War, 1 June 1812

WASHINGTON, *June 1, 1812.*
To the Senate and House of Representatives of the United States:

I communicate to Congress certain documents, being a continuation of those heretofore laid before them on the subject of our affairs with Great Britain.

Without going back beyond the renewal in 1803 of the war in which Great Britain is engaged, and omitting unrepaired wrongs of inferior magnitude, the conduct of her Government presents a series of acts hostile to the United States as an independent and neutral nation.

British cruisers have been in the continued practice of violating the American flag on the great highway of nations, and of seizing and carrying off persons sailing under it, not in the exercise of a belligerent right founded on the law of nations against an enemy, but of a municipal prerogative over British subjects. . . .

[T]housands of American citizens, under the safeguard of public law and of their national flag, have been torn from their country and from everything dear to them; have been dragged on board ships of war of a foreign nation and exposed, under the severities of their discipline, to be exiled to the most distant and deadly climes, to risk their lives in the battles of their oppressors, and to be the melancholy instruments of taking away those of their own brethren. . . .

British cruisers have been in the practice also of violating the rights and the peace of our coasts. They hover over and harass our entering and departing commerce. To the most insulting pretensions they have added the most lawless proceedings in our very harbors, and have wantonly spilt American blood within the sanctuary of our territorial jurisdiction. . . .

Under pretended blockades, without the presence of an adequate force and sometimes without the practicability of applying one, our commerce has been plundered in every sea, the great staples of our country have been cut off from their legitimate markets, and a destructive blow aimed at our agricultural and maritime interests. . . .

Not content with these occasional expedients for laying waste our neutral trade, the cabinet of Britain resorted at length to the sweeping system of blockades, under the name of orders in council, which has been molded and managed as might best suit its political views, its commercial jealousies, or the avidity of British cruisers. . . .

It has become, indeed, sufficiently certain that the commerce of the United States is to be sacrificed, not as interfering with the belligerent rights of Great Britain; not as supplying the wants of her enemies, which she herself supplies; but as interfering with the monopoly which she covets for her own commerce and navigation. She carries on a war against the lawful commerce of a friend that she may the better carry on a commerce with an enemy—a commerce polluted by the forgeries and perjuries which are for the most part the only passports by which it can succeed. . . .

In reviewing the conduct of Great Britain toward the United States our attention is necessarily drawn to the warfare just renewed by the savages on one of our extensive frontiers—a warfare which is known to spare neither age nor sex and to be distinguished by features peculiarly shocking to humanity. It is difficult to account for the activity and combinations which have for some time been developing themselves among tribes in constant intercourse with British traders and garrison without connecting their hostility with that influence and without recollecting the authenticated examples of such interpositions heretofore furnished by the officers and agents of that Government. Such is the spectacle of injuries and indignities which have been heaped on our country and such the crisis which its unexampled forbearance and conciliatory efforts have not been able to avert. . . .

Our moderation and conciliation have had no other effect than to encourage perseverance and to enlarge pretensions. We behold our seafaring citizens still the daily victims of lawless violence, committed on the great common and highway of nations, even within sight of the country which owes them protection. We behold our vessels, freighted with the products of our soil and industry, or returning with the honest proceeds of them, wrested from their lawful destinations, confiscated by prize courts no longer the organs of public law but the instruments of arbitrary edicts, and their unfortunate crews dispersed and lost, or forced or inveigled in British ports into British fleets, whilst arguments are employed in support of these aggressions which have no foundation but in a principle equally supporting a claim to regulate our external commerce in all cases whatsoever.

We behold, in fine, on the side of Great Britain a state of war against, the United States, and on the side of the United States a state of peace toward Great Britain.

Whether the United States shall continue passive under these progressive usurpations and these accumulating wrongs, or, opposing force to force in defense of their national rights, shall commit a just cause into the hands of the Almighty Disposer of Events, avoiding all connections which might entangle it in the contest or views of other powers, and preserving a constant readiness to concur in an honorable reestablishment of peace and friendship, is a solemn question which the Constitution wisely confides to the legislative department of the Government. In recommending it to their early deliberations I am happy in the assurance that the decision will be worthy the enlightened and patriotic councils of a virtuous, a free, and a powerful nation. . . .

JAMES MADISON.

Source: James D. Richardson, comp., *A Compilation of the Messages and Papers of the Presidents,* 20 vols. (New York: Bureau of National Literature, Inc., 1897) 2: 484–90.

Disaster in the Northwest

The 1812 American invasion of Canada led by William Hull not only failed, it ended in Hull's humiliating surrender of Detroit to an inferior British force. In addition to devastating American morale and confidence, the episode provoked a loud public criticism of the Madison administration, an example of which appears below. The New York *Evening Post*, from which this excerpt is taken, was founded in 1801 as New York City's Federalist paper at the urging of Alexander Hamilton. It remained Federalist during the War of 1812 and strongly opposed the war from its start to its finish.

Document 5
Hull's Surrender of Detroit Is Condemned

On the disgraceful and deplorable results of our first military efforts in Canada, we are not in a temper to say much. How much soever we deprecated this ruinous war at the outset; however satisfied we were that the whole plan of the campaign was miserably imbecile and must be utterly inefficient—yet such a catastrophe as is just announced was beyond our most gloomy apprehensions. Mr. Madison, Mr. Gallatin, Dr. Eustis, and Dr. Hamilton, it was evident, must be utterly unequal to cope with the experienced veteran British officers in Canada. And when, besides this disheartening fact, we beheld how small a force was relied upon, what could reasonable men feel but despair? With inferior numbers and inferior skill, the odds were fearful indeed.

Yet we did not expect so deep a stain upon our country's character. A nation, counting eight millions of souls, deliberating and planning for a whole winter and spring and part of a summer, the invasion and conquest of a neighboring province; at length making that invasion; and in one month its army retiring—captured—and captured almost without firing a gun! Miserably deficient in practical talent must that Administration be which formed the plan of that invasion; or the army which has thus surrendered must be a gang of more cowardly poltroons than ever disgraced a country. A parallel to this melancholy defeat is not to be found in all history. But we do not, we cannot brand our countrymen in General Hull's army with cowardice. We shall not till we are compelled. For when were Americans known to shrink from danger? When have they not been heroes? But the folly, the weakness, the utter incapacity of our Administration to conduct affairs of difficulty to a successful issue, has not only been the tedious theme of many an appeal to our fellow-citizens, but is felt in the privations and distresses of almost every man, woman, and child in this once happy and prosperous country. And he who can longer doubt that incapacity, would not believe though one should rise from the dead.

What! March an army into a country where there were not more than seven or eight hundred soldiers to oppose them, and not make the army large enough! March them from a country which is the granary of the world, and let them famish on the very frontiers for want of provisions! Issue a gasconading proclamation threatening to exterminate the enemy, and surrender your whole army to them! If there be judgment in this people, they will see the utter unfitness of our rulers for anything beyond management, intrigue, and electioneering. They have talents enough to inflame a misguided populace against their best friends; but they cannot protect the nation from insult and disgrace. They have talents enough to persecute the pupils and disciples of Washington, but not to meet the enemies whom they have called into the field. "Woe to the people whose King is a child!"

Source: New York *Evening Post*, 31 August 1812.

Washington Burns

The British captured Washington, D.C., on 24 August 1814 and burned its public buildings. During the night, as the city blazed, a violent storm broke over the scene, enhancing the nightmarish quality of the event for the Americans and providing the British with an appropriately flamboyant close to their successful raid. The following account by a British officer drips with condescension and sarcasm, especially relating to the activities of James Madison.

Document 6
George Robert Gleig Describes the Burning of Washington

But towards morning a violent storm of rain, accompanied with thunder and lightning, came on, which disturbed the rest of all those who were exposed to it. Yet in spite of the inconvenience arising from the shower, I can not say that I felt disposed to grumble at the interruption, for it appeared that what I had before considered as superlatively sublime, still wanted this to render it complete. The flashes of lightning vied in brilliancy with the flames which burst from the roofs of burning houses, whilst the thunder drowned . . . the noise of crumbling walls, and was only interrupted by the occasional roar of cannon, and of large depôts of gunpowder, as they one by one exploded.

I need scarcely observe, that the consternation of the inhabitants was complete, and that to them this was a night of terror. So confident had they been of the success of their troops, that few of them had dreamt of quitting their houses or abandoning the city; nor was it till the fugitives from the battle began to rush it, filling every place as they came with dismay, that the President himself thought of providing for his safety. That gentleman, as I was credibly informed, had gone forth in the morning with the army, and had continued among his troops till the British forces began to make their appearance. Whether the sight of his enemies cooled his courage or not I cannot say, but according to my informer, no sooner was the glittering of our arms discernible, than he began to discover that his presence was more wanted in the senate than in the field; and having ridden through the ranks, and exhorted every man to do his duty, he hurried back to his own house, that he might prepare a feast for the entertainment of his officers, when they should return victorious. For the truth of these details I will not be answerable; but this much I know, that the feast was actually prepared, though, instead of being devoured by American officers, it went to satisfy the less delicate appetites of a party of English soldiers. When the detachment sent out to destroy Mr. Maddison's house, entered his dining parlour, they found a dinner-table spread, and covers laid for forty guests. . . .

They sat down to it, therefore, not indeed in the most orderly manner, but with countenances which would not have disgraced a party of aldermen at a civic feast; and having satisfied their appetites with fewer complaints than would have probably escaped their rival *gourmands*, and partaken pretty freely of the wines, they finished by setting fire to the house which had so liberally entertained them.

I have said that to the inhabitants of Washington this was a night of terror and dismay. . . . The first impulse naturally tempted them to fly, and the streets were speedily crowded with soldiers and senators, men, women, and children, horses, carriages, and carts loaded with household furniture, all hastening towards a wooden bridge which crosses the Potomac. The confusion thus occasioned was terrible, and the crowd upon the bridge was such as to endanger its giving way. But Mr. Maddison, as is affirmed, having escaped among the first, was no sooner safe on the opposite bank of the river, than he gave orders that the bridge should be broken down; which being obeyed, the rest were obliged to return, and to trust to the clemency of the victors.

In this manner was the night passed by both parties; and at daybreak next morning the light brigade moved into the city, whilst the reserve fell back to a height about half a mile in the rear. Little, however, now remained to be done, because everything marked out for destruction was already consumed. Of the Senate-house, the President's palace, the barracks, the dockyard, &c., nothing could be seen, except heaps of smoking ruins; and even the bridge, a noble structure upward of a mile in length, was almost entirely demolished. There was, therefore, no farther occasion to scatter the troops, and they were accordingly kept together as much as possible on the Capitol Hill.

Source: George R. Gleig, *The Campaigns of the British Army at Washington and New Orleans in the Years 1814–1815* (London: John Murray, 1847), 71–73.

Federalists Oppose the War

Daniel Webster was destined to become one of the nation's most influential nationalists. In his youth, however, he espoused the sectionalism of his native New England. He opposed Republican policies before the war and Madison's methods of paying for and prosecuting it once it was under way. Elected to the House of Representatives from New Hampshire in the fall of 1812, Webster became a vocal opponent of the administration, voting against increased taxes, occasionally questioning the president's integrity and, after the capture of Washington, his courage. He particularly condemned conscription, and the bill calling for it drew his special ire. Beyond the central issue of the draft, Webster expanded on the meaning of dissent in a constitutional republic under crisis. It was a subject of considerable importance just then, for the Hartford Convention, which Webster supported, would gather that month to ventilate Federalist resentment over a variety of grievances. Federalists were to bear the taint of this apparently unpatriotic gesture at Hartford for what remained of their abbreviated existence and, afterward, Webster would occasionally have to endure the jabs of political enemies for the stands he had taken during the war.

Document 7
Daniel Webster on Conscription, 9 December 1814

It will be the solemn duty of the state governments to protect their own authority over their own militia, and to interpose between their citizens and arbitrary power. These are among the objects for which the state governments exist; and their highest obligations bind them to the preservation of their own rights and the liberties of their people.

I express these sentiments here, sir, because I shall express them to my constituents. Both they and myself live under a constitution which teaches us that "the doctrine of nonresistance against arbitrary power and oppression is absurd, slavish, and destructive of the good and happiness of mankind." With the same earnestness with which I now exhort you to forbear from these measures, I shall exhort them to exercise their unquestionable right of providing for the security of their own liberties.

In my opinion, sir, the sentiments of the free population of this country are greatly mistaken here. The nation is not yet in a temper to submit to conscription. The people have too fresh and strong a feeling of the blessings of civil liberty to be willing thus to surrender it. You may talk to them as much as you please of the victory and glory to be obtained in the enemy's provinces; they will hold those objects in light estimation if the means be a forced military service. You may sing to them the song of Canada conquest in all its variety, but they will not be charmed out of the remembrance of their substantial interests and true happiness. Similar pretenses, they know, are the grave in which the liberties of other nations have been buried, and they will take warning.

Laws, sir, of this nature can create nothing but opposition. If you scatter them abroad, like the fabled serpents' teeth, they will spring up into armed men. A military force cannot be raised in this manner but by the means of a military force. If administration has found that it cannot form an army without conscription, it will find, if it venture on these experiments, that it cannot enforce conscription without an army. The government was not constituted for such purposes. Framed in the spirit of liberty and in the love of peace, it has no powers which render it able to enforce such laws. The attempt, if we rashly make it, will fail; and having already thrown away our peace, we may thereby throw away our government.

Allusions have been made, sir, to the state of things in New England, and, as usual, she has been charged with an intention to dissolve the Union. The charge is unfounded. She is much too wise to entertain such purposes. She has had too much experience, and has too strong a recollection of the blessings which the Union is capable of producing under a just administration of government. It is her greatest fear that the course at present pursued will destroy it, by destroying every principle, every interest, every sentiment, and every feeling which have hitherto contributed to uphold it.

Those who cry out that the Union is in danger are themselves the authors of that danger. They put its existence to hazard by measures of violence which it is not capable of enduring. They talk of dangerous design against government when they are overthrowing the fabric from its foundations. They alone, sir, are friends to the union of the states who endeavor to maintain the principles of civil liberty in the country and to preserve the spirit in which the Union was framed.

Source: The Writings of and Speeches of Daniel Webster, Hitherto Uncollected, 18 vols. (Boston: Little, Brown, 1903): 2: 68–69.

Document 8
Resolutions of the Hartford Convention, 5 January 1815

Therefore, resolved: that it be and hereby is recommended to the legislatures of the several states represented in this Convention, to adopt all such measures as may be necessary effectually to protect the citizens of said states from the operation and effects of all acts which have been or may be passed by the Congress of the United States, which shall contain provisions, subjecting the militia or other citizens to forcible drafts, conscriptions, or impressments, not authorised by the constitution of the United States.

Resolved, that it be and hereby is recommended to the said Legislatures, to authorize an immediate and earnest application to be made to the government of the United States, requesting their consent to some arrangement, whereby the said states may, separately or in concert, be empowered to assume upon themselves the defence of their territory against the enemy; and a reasonable portion of the taxes, collected within said states, may be paid into the respective treasuries thereof, and appropriated to the payment of the balance due said states, and to the future defence of the same. The amount so paid into the said treasuries to be credited, and the disbursements made as aforesaid to be charged to the United States.

Resolved, that it be, and hereby is, recommended to the legislatures of the aforesaid states, to pass laws (where it has not already been done) authorizing the governors or commanders-in-chief of their militia to make detachments from the same, or to form voluntary corps, as shall be most convenient and conformable to their constitutions, and to cause the same to be well armed, equipped and disciplined, and held in readiness for service; and upon the request of the governor of either of the other states to employ the whole of such detachment or corps, as well as the regular forces of the state, or such part thereof as may be required and can be spared consistently with the safety of the state, in assisting the state, making such request to repel any invasion thereof which shall be made or attempted by the public enemy.

Resolved, that the following amendments of the constitution of the United States be recommended to the states represented as aforesaid, to be proposed by them for adoption by the state legislatures, and in such cases as may be deemed expedient by a convention chosen by the people of each state.

First. Representatives and direct taxes shall be apportioned among the several states which may be included within this Union, according to their respective numbers of free persons, including those bound to serve for a term of years, and excluding Indians not taxed, and all other persons.

Second. No new state shall be admitted into the Union by Congress, in virtue of the power granted by the constitution, without the concurrence of two thirds of both houses.

Third. Congress shall not have power to lay any embargo on the ships or vessels of the citizens of the United States, in the ports or harbours thereof, for more than sixty days.

Fourth. Congress shall not have power, without the concurrence of two thirds of both houses, to interdict the commercial intercourse between the United States and any foreign nation or the dependencies thereof.

Fifth. Congress shall not make or declare war, or authorize acts of hostility against any foreign nation, without the concurrence of two thirds of both houses, except such acts of hostility be in defence of the territories of the United States when actually invaded.

Sixth. No person who shall hereafter be naturalized, shall be eligible as a member of the senate or house of representatives of the United States, nor capable of holding any civil office under the authority of the United States.

Seventh. The same person shall not be elected president of the United States a second time; nor shall the President be elected from the same state two terms in succession.

Resolved, that if the application of these states to the government of the United States, recommended in a foregoing resolution, should be unsuccessful and peace should not be concluded, and the defence of these states should be neglected, as it has been since the commencement of the war, it will, in the opinion of this convention, be expedient for the legislatures of the several states to appoint delegates to another convention, to meet at Boston . . . with such powers and instructions as the exigency of a crisis so momentous may require.

Source: Theodore Dwight, *History of the Hartford Convention* (New York: N. & J. White, 1833), 375–79.

Victory at New Orleans

At the end of 1814, Andrew Jackson was in New Orleans to resist a large British invasion there. After almost a month of defensive preparations, the city was rendered virtually impregnable, as the British attack on 8 January 1815 was to show. The following is Jackson's account of the battle in a letter to Secretary of War James Monroe the day after it had occurred. Although Jackson promised to remain vigilant, the British would not attack at New Orleans again. The invasion force broke off the campaign and retreated from the environs of the city.

Document 9
Jackson Reports on the Battle of New Orleans

Camp, four miles below Orleans, 9th January, 1815.

Sir,

During the days of the 6th and 7th, the enemy had been actively employed in making preparations for an attack on my lines. With infinite labour they had succeeded on the night of the 7th in getting their boats across from the lake to the river, by widening and deepening the canal on which they had effected their disembarkation. It had not been in my power to impede these operations by a general attack—added to other reasons, the nature of the troops under my command, mostly militia; rendered it too hazardous to attempt extensive offensive movements in an open country, against a numerous and well-disciplined army. Although my forces, as to number, had been increased by the arrival of the Kentucky division, my strength had received very little addition; a small portion only of that detachment being provided with arms. Compelled thus to wait the attack of the enemy, I took every measure to repel it when it should be made, and to defeat the object he had in view. General Morgan with the Orleans contingent, the Louisiana militia, and a strong detachment of the Kentucky troops, occupied an intrenched camp on the opposite side of the river, protected by strong batteries on the bank, erected and superintended by commodore Patterson.

In *my* encampment every thing was ready for action, early on the morning of the 8th the enemy, after throwing a shower of bombs and congreve rockets, advanced their columns on my right and left, to storm my intrenchments. I cannot speak sufficiently in praise of the firmness and deliberation with which my whole line received their approach. MORE could not have been expected from veterans inured to war.—For an hour the fire of the small arms was as incessant and severe as can be imagined. The artillery, too, directed by officers who displayed equal skill and courage, did great execution. Yet the columns of the enemy continued to advance with a firmness which reflects upon them the greatest credit. Twice the column which approached me on my left, was repulsed by the troops of general Carroll, those of general Coffee and a division of the Kentucky militia, and twice they formed again and renewed the assault. At length, however, cut to pieces, they fled in confusion from the field, leaving it covered with their dead and wounded. The loss which the enemy sustained on this occasion, cannot be estimated at less than fifteen hundred in killed, wounded, and prisoners. Upwards of three hundred have already been delivered over for burial; and my men are still engaged in picking them up within my lines, and carrying them to the point where the enemy are to receive them. This is in addition to the dead and wounded whom the enemy have been enabled to carry from the field during and since the action, and to those who have since died of the wounds they received. We have taken about five hundred prisoners, upwards of three hundred of whom are wounded, and a great part of them mortally. My loss has not exceeded, and I believe has not amounted to ten killed and as many wounded. . . .

The enemy having concentrated his forces, may again attempt to drive me from my position by storm. Whenever he does, I have no doubt my men will act with their usual firmness, and sustain a character now become dear to them.

> I have the honour to be, &c.
> ANDREW JACKSON.

Source: Arsène Lacarrière Latour, *Historical Memoir of the War in West Florida and Louisiana in 1814–15, with an Atlas,* edited by Gene A. Smith (Gainesville: University Press of Florida, 1999), 237–39.

The End of the War

When Britain agreed to enter negotiations in early 1814, an American delegation met with its British counterpart that summer in Ghent. The treaty they produced was signed on Christmas Eve 1814 and was curiously devoid of the maritime issues that had caused the war. Instead, it restored the *status quo antebellum* (the situation as it existed before the war). Most important, the nations agreed to settle boundary disputes by joint commission, a practice that over the years would help sustain an Anglo-American peace through a variety of difficult controversies. The Senate unanimously ratified the treaty on 15 February 1815, and the exchange of ratifications officially ended the war at 11:00 P.M. on 17 February 1815.

Document 10
Treaty of Ghent, 24 December 1814

Treaty of Peace and Amity between His Britannic Majesty and the United States of America

His Britannic Majesty and the United States of America desirous of terminating the war which has unhappily subsisted between the two Countries, and of restoring upon principles of perfect reciprocity, Peace, Friendship, and good Understanding between them, have for that purpose appointed their respective Plenipotentiaries . . . who, after a reciprocal communication of their respective Full Powers, have agreed upon the following Articles.

ARTICLE THE FIRST. There shall be a firm and universal Peace between His Britannic Majesty and the United States. . . . All hostilities both by sea and land shall cease as soon as this Treaty shall have been ratified by both parties as hereinafter mentioned. All territory; places, and possessions whatsoever taken by either party from the other during the war, or which may be taken after the signing of this Treaty, excepting only the Islands hereinafter mentioned, shall be restored without delay. . . .

ARTICLE THE SECOND. Immediately after the ratifications of this Treaty by both parties as hereinafter mentioned, orders shall be sent to the Armies, Squadrons, Officers, Subjects, and Citizens of the two Powers to cease from all hostilities: and to prevent all causes of complaint which might arise on account of the prizes which may be taken at sea after . . . shall be restored on each side. . . .

ARTICLE THE THIRD. All Prisoners of war taken on either side as well by land as by sea shall be restored as soon as practicable after the Ratifications of this Treaty. . . .

ARTICLE THE FOURTH. [Regarding ownership of the Passamoquoddy Islands under the terms of the Peace of Paris of 1783] . . . In order . . . finally to decide upon these claims it is agreed that they shall be referred to two Commissioners to be appointed in the following manner: viz: One Commissioner shall be appointed by His Britannic Majesty and one by the President of the United States, by and with the advice and consent of the Senate thereof, and the said two commissioners so appointed shall be sworn impartially to examine and decide upon the said claims according to such evidence as shall be laid before them on the part of His Britannic Majesty and of the United States respectively. The said commissioners shall meet at St Andrews in the Province of New Brunswick, and shall have power to adjourn to such other place or places as they shall think fit. The said Commissioners shall by a declaration or report under their hands and seals decide to which of the two Contracting parties the several Islands aforesaid do respectively belong . . . and . . . both parties shall consider such decision as final and conclusive. It is further agreed that in the event of the two Commissioners differing upon all or any of the matters so referred to them . . . [they will refer the matter] to some friendly Sovereign or State . . . who shall be requested to decide on the differences. . . .

ARTICLE THE FIFTH. Whereas [the northeastern border between Canada and the United States] has [not] yet been ascertained . . . [and] has not yet been surveyed: it is agreed that for these several purposes two Commissioners shall be appointed, sworn, and authorized to act exactly in the manner directed with respect to those mentioned in the next preceding Article unless otherwise specified in the present Article. . . .

ARTICLE THE SIXTH. [Settlement of the Great Lakes boundary by joint commission under procedures similar to those outlined earlier.]

ARTICLE THE SEVENTH. [Settlement of the boundary from the Great Lakes to the Lake of the Woods by joint commission under procedures similar to those outlined earlier.]

ARTICLE THE EIGHTH. The several Boards of two Commissioners mentioned in the four preceding Articles shall respectively have power to appoint a Secretary, and to employ such Surveyors or other persons as they shall judge necessary. . . .

ARTICLE THE NINTH. The United States of America engage to put an end immediately after the Ratification of the present Treaty to hostilities with all the Tribes or Nations of Indians with whom they may be at war at the time of such Ratification, and forthwith to restore to such Tribes or Nations respectively all the possessions, rights, and privileges which they may have enjoyed or been entitled to in one thousand eight hundred and eleven previous to such hostilities. Provided always that such Tribes or Nations shall agree to desist from all hostilities against the United States of America, their Citizens, and Subjects upon the Ratification of the present Treaty being notified to such Tribes or Nations, and shall so desist accordingly. And His Britannic Majesty engages on his part to put an end immediately after the Ratification of the present Treaty to hostilities with all the Tribes or Nations of Indians with whom He may be at war at the time of such Ratification, and forthwith to restore to such Tribes or Nations respectively all the possessions, rights, and privileges, which they may have enjoyed or been entitled to in one thousand eight hundred and eleven previous to such hostilities. Provided always that such Tribes or Nations shall agree to desist from all hostilities against His Britannic Majesty and His Subjects upon the Ratification of the present Treaty being notified to such Tribes or Nations, and shall so desist accordingly.

ARTICLE THE TENTH. Whereas the Traffic in Slaves is irreconcilable with the principles of humanity and Justice, and whereas both His Majesty and the United States are desirous of continuing their efforts to promote its entire abolition, it is hereby agreed that both the contracting parties shall use their best endeavours to accomplish so desirable an object.

ARTICLE THE ELEVENTH. This Treaty when the same shall have been ratified on both sides without alteration by either of the contracting parties, and the Ratifications mutually exchanged, shall be binding on both parties, and the Ratifications shall be exchanged at Washington in the space of four months from this day or sooner if practicable.

In faith whereof, We the respective Plenipotentiaries have signed this Treaty, and have hereunto affixed our Seals. Done in triplicate at Ghent the twenty fourth day of December one thousand eight hundred and fourteen.

GAMBIER [Seal]

HENRY GOULBURN [Seal]

WILLIAM ADAMS [Seal]

JOHN QUINCY ADAMS [Seal]

J.A. BAYARD [Seal]

H. CLAY [Seal]

JON. RUSSEL [Seal]

ALBERT GALLATIN [Seal]

Source: Hunter Miller, ed., *Treaties and Other International Acts of the United States of America. Volume 2, Documents 1–40: 1776–1818* (Washington, D.C.: Government Printing Office, 1931), 574–582.

GLOSSARY OF SELECTED TERMS

Brig: A two-masted sailing warship, smaller than a **frigate** and larger than a **sloop**, that carried armament similar to a medium-sized sloop. See also **Rate**.

Brigade: A military unit consisting of two or more **regiments**.

Congreve Rocket: An explosive rocket developed by Sir William Congreve and used by the British during the War of 1812. Congreve Rockets were inaccurate but noisy and thus were more frightening than dangerous to an enemy; at Fort McHenry, they provided Francis Scott Key's "rocket's red glare."

Continental System: Napoleon Bonaparte's scheme to hurt British commerce by closing European markets to British goods.

Embargo: A ban on trade accomplished by the closing of ports to incoming and outgoing ships.

Federalists: One of the two major American political parties of the period. Federalists generally embraced commercial policies that inclined them toward Great Britain and philosophical positions that perceived the French Revolution as anarchistic; opponents of the **Republicans**.

Flank: (n.) The left or right side of an army or its position as deployed in the field. (v.) To gain the flank of an opposing army through maneuver and thereby attack with superior numbers.

Flotilla: A small fleet of ships.

Frigate: A medium-sized sailing warship, larger than a **brig** but smaller than a **ship of the line**. See also **Rate**.

Gunboat: Small, lightly armed vessel designed for coastal defense; a reflection of Republican frugality, gunboats composed the bulk of the U.S. Navy during the period.

Headman: Among Native Americans, the leader of a particular clan, faction, or place; preferred usage over the term "chief."

Impressment: During the Anglo-French wars, the British government's policy of compelling service in the Royal Navy by forced conscription.

Kedging: The practice of pulling a ship through the water by setting an anchor and hauling on its cable.

Letter of marque: A commission from a sovereign government authorizing a private vessel (a **privateer**) to act as a ship of war.

Militia: A military force composed of local citizens (a state in the United States; a province in Canada) called out (or mustered) during emergencies.

Minister: Diplomatic representative. Until the late nineteenth century, the United States did not appoint ambassadors to foreign capitals, believing the rank was a vestige of aristocracy.

Nativism: Among Native Americans, the manifestation of a spiritual revival during the late eighteenth and early nineteenth centuries that urged a return to traditional Indian religion and customs.

Orders in Council: British government edicts technically issued by the king on advice by his privy council, hence the name; orders in council carried the weight of law and required repeal by Parliament.

Paper Blockade: Shutting off ports by proclamation only and without possessing or employing the physical means to do so.

Privateer: A privately financed ship with authorization (a **letter of marque**) from a government to attack enemy shipping and keep captured property upon the judgment of a **prize court**.

Prize Court: A tribunal, usually situated in a **privateer**'s sponsoring country or those of its allies, empowered to determine the validity of captures and award proceeds accordingly.

Raid-in-force: A rapidly conducted attack by a relatively large military contingent, usually to destroy an objective rather than occupy territory.

Rate: The number of long-range cannon a warship carried; during the War of 1812, the actual number of guns aboard a ship usually exceeded its rate; for instance, the USS *Constitution*, rated at 44, actually carried 52 guns.

Regiment: A military unit consisting in the War of 1812 of ten companies, at full strength numbering 1,073 officers and men, and combining with other regiments to form a **brigade**.

Regular: A soldier in a standing military establishment, hence a professional in the "Regular Army;" a regular is distinct from a **volunteer**.

Ship of the line: The largest sailing man-of-war, carrying at least 74 guns, and by its size qualified to take a place in fleet deployment for battle (or "line of battle"). Only the Royal Navy employed ships of the line during the War of 1812.

Sloop: A singled-masted sailing warship. See also **Rate**.

Status quo antebellum: Literally "the situation before the war;" the phrase described the framework for the Treaty of Ghent that ended the War of 1812 by restoring all captured territory as a condition of peace.

Volunteer: A soldier whose decision to serve is a function of his own free will (in contrast to a conscript); a volunteer was usually in national service during the War of 1812 and is distinct from a **regular** soldier.

ANNOTATED BIBLIOGRAPHY

General Histories

Adams, Henry. *History of the United States during the Administrations of Jefferson and Madison*. 9 vols. New York: Charles Scribner's Sons, 1889–1891. Volumes 3 through 9 narrate the causes and conduct of the war from a political, military, and diplomatic perspective. Still an excellent analysis of the period.

Beirne, Francis F. *The War of 1812*. New York: E. P. Dutton, 1949. Based primarily on secondary sources, the book makes its main contribution in its discussion of the results as leading to greater British-American cooperation.

Caffrey, Kate. *The Twilight's Last Gleaming: Britain vs. America, 1812–1815*. New York: Stein and Day, 1977. Lively, popular account written from the British perspective.

Hammack, James W., Jr. *Kentucky and the Second American Revolution: The War of 1812*. Lexington: University of Kentucky Press, 1976. Details why Kentuckians were such enthusiastic supporters of the war, provided many soldiers for the conflict, but generally did not perform very well militarily.

Hickey, Donald R. *The War of 1812: A Forgotten Conflict*. Urbana: University of Illinois Press, 1989. The best comprehensive look at the war's causes, military events, domestic impact, and diplomacy in which author demonstrates that the United States failed to achieve any of its goals in the conflict.

Horsman, Reginald. *The Frontier in the Formative Years, 1783–1815*. New York: Holt, Rinehart, and Winston, 1970. An examination of the importance of the American frontier in precipitating the War of 1812 and that area's role in the conflict.

———. *The War of 1812*. New York: Alfred A. Knopf, 1969. A general account of the causes of the war as tied to the wars in Europe, the military conduct of the conflict, the political ramifications, and the diplomatic efforts that brought the war to its conclusion.

Lemmon, Sarah. *Frustrated Patriots: North Carolina and the War of 1812*. Chapel Hill: University of North Carolina Press, 1973. Examines the role of North Carolina in the war, how much support there was within the state, and the impact on the state's Federalists.

Mason, Philip P., ed. *After Tippecanoe: Some Aspects of the War of 1812*. East Lansing: Michigan State University Press, 1963. Six essays dealing with different aspects of the war presented at conferences in 1961 and 1962.

Sapio, Victor. *Pennsylvania and the War of 1812*. Lexington: University of Kentucky Press, 1970. The state had no real reason to support the war except its overwhelming Republicanism and anger over violations of American honor.

Sheppard, George. *Plunder, Profit and Paroles: A Social History of the War of 1812 in Upper Canada*. Montreal: McGill-Queen's University Press, 1994. Well-researched work that emphasizes tremendous divisions in Upper Canada before and after the war and attempts to demonstrate that the Canadian militia was not responsible for British victories.

Stagg, J.C.A. *Mr. Madison's War: Politics, Diplomacy, and Warfare in the Early American Republic, 1783–1830*. Princeton: Princeton University Press, 1983. Meticulously researched, standard work on the civil–military relations of the Early Republic.

Tucker, Glenn. *Poltroons and Patriots: A Popular Account of the War of 1812*. 2 vols. Indianapolis: Bobbs-Merrill Co., 1954. Detailed, primarily military history of the war.

Tucker, Glenn, and James Ripley Jacobs. *The War of 1812: A Compact History*. New York: Hawthorn Books, 1969. Good, short overview of the war.

Turner, Wesley B. *The War of 1812: The War that Both Sides Won*. Toronto: Dundurn Press, 1990. Brief history of the war that holds that both sides achieved something from the conflict—the United States an end to Indian threats in the Northwest and Southwest and the British because they would no longer be threatened with American attempts to conquer Canada.

Watts, Stephen. *Republic Reborn: War and the Making of Liberal America, 1790–1820*. Baltimore: Johns Hopkins University Press, 1990. Provocative look at how War of 1812 shaped American institutions.

White, Patrick C. T. *A Nation on Trial: The War of 1812*. New York: John Wiley and Sons, 1965. Sees the war as most valuable to the United States in that honor and nationalism were enhanced by the results.

Causes of the War

Brown, Roger H. *The Republic in Peril: 1812*. New York: W. W. Norton, 1971. Provides a provocative argument that the government went to war to save the republic from self-destruction.

Carr, Albert Z. *The Coming of War: An Account of the Remarkable Events Leading to the War of 1812*. Garden City, NY: Doubleday and Company, 1960. Sees the causes of the war stretching back to the post-Revolutionary War period and the failure of both countries to reach a reasonable accommodation.

Horsman, Reginald. *The Causes of the War of 1812*. Philadelphia: University of Pennsylvania Press, 1962. Sees the war largely stemming from anger over British violations of neutral shipping and the practice of impressment rather than the desire for territorial expansion.

Perkins, Bradford. *Prologue to War: England and the United States, 1805–1812*. Berkeley: University of California Press, 1963. Views both the United States with its stubborn attachment to neutral trading rights and the British indifference to American concerns as causing the war.

Perkins, Bradford, ed. *The Causes of the War of 1812: National Honor or National Interest?* New York: Holt, Rinehart and Winston, 1962; reprint edition, Malabar, Florida: R. E. Krieger, 1983. Essays by a variety of leading scholars on the various causes of the War of 1812.

Pratt, Julius. *Expansionists of 1812*. New York: Macmillan, 1925; reprint edition, Gloucester, MA: Peter Smith, 1957. Standard and original work on the view that the desire for western expansion and the annexation of Canada were the primary causes of the War of 1812.

Rutland, Robert A. *Madison's Alternatives: The Jeffersonian Republicans and the Coming of the War, 1805–1812*. Philadelphia: J.B. Lippincott, 1975. Through a narrative of the Republicans' reactions to international events, the author analyzes the possible approaches that could have been taken by James Madison.

Sears, Louis M. *Jefferson and the Embargo*. Durham, NC: Duke University Press, 1927. Attempt to demonstrate that the Embargo was not all bad for the country and that in some ways it improved some areas economically while doing some real harm to the British war effort in Europe.

Spivak, Burton. *Jefferson's English Crisis: Commerce, Embargo, and the Republican Revolution*. Charlottesville: University of Virginia Press, 1979. While dealing with the external problems of Great Britain's threat to United States neutral rights, Jefferson encouraged economic independence within the United States to ease dependence on foreign powers.

Tucker, Spencer C., and Frank T. Reuter. *Injured Honor: The Chesapeake-Leopard Affair, June 22, 1807*. Annapolis, MD: Naval Institute Press, 1996. A narrative of the events of the attack and, more important, its impact on American-British diplomacy and the U.S. Navy.

Zimmermann, James F. *Impressment of American Seamen*. New York: Columbia University Press, 1966. Demonstrates the importance of impressment to the American people and President Madison and why the practice was so harmful to American national honor.

Biographies

Ammon, Harry. *James Monroe: The Quest for National Identity*. New York: McGraw-Hill, 1971. Standard, definitive biography of James Monroe.

Bartlett, C. J. *Castlereagh*. New York: Scribner, 1966. Standard biography that naturally emphasizes Castlereagh's role in European diplomacy. Contains one lengthy chapter on Castlereagh's diplomacy during the War of 1812 and end of the Napoleonic Wars.

Billias, George Athan. *Elbridge Gerry: Founding Father and Republican Statesman*. New York: McGraw-Hill, 1976. Comprehensive biography that emphasizes Gerry's career in the Early Republic.

Bohner, Charles H. *John Pendleton Kennedy, Gentleman from Baltimore*. Baltimore: The Johns Hopkins University Press, 1969. Biography of a fascinating observer of the national scene.

Borden, Morton. *The Federalism of James A. Bayard*. New York: Columbia University Press, 1955. Ends with informative chapters detailing Bayard's attempts to prevent the war and his role on the peace commission at Ghent.

Brant, Irving. *James Madison*. 6 vols. Indianapolis: Bobbs-Merrill, 1941–1961. The definitive biography of James Madison. While generally positive, Brant did not believe that Madison had the temperament to deal with the ambitious men around him.

Cleeves, Freeman. *Old Tippecanoe: William Henry Harrison and His Time*. New York: Charles Scribner's Sons, 1939. Most of this biography is appropriate for this period since it deals with Harrison's life as governor of Indiana Territory and his military exploits during the War of 1812.

Coit, Margaret L. *John C. Calhoun: American Portrait*. New York: Houghton Mifflin, 1950. Positive, but overall very sound biography of Calhoun.

Cornog, Evan. *The Birth of Empire: DeWitt Clinton and the American Experience, 1769–1828*. New York: Oxford University Press, 1998. An excellent interweaving of the massive changes taking place in New York state and New York City with the life of this very influential man.

Crocker, Matthew H. *The Magic of Many: Josiah Quincy and the Rise of Mass Politics in Boston, 1800–1830*. Boston: University of Massachusetts Press, 1999. Excellent study of the role Josiah Quincy played in transforming Boston politics in the Early Republic.

Dillon, Richard. *We Have Met the Enemy: Oliver Hazard Perry, Wilderness Commodore*. New York: McGraw-Hill, 1978. Popular account that spends well over half the book examining Perry's role in the War of 1812.

Edmunds, R. David. *The Shawnee Prophet*. Lincoln: University of Nebraska Press, 1983. Well-researched biography that demonstrates that Tenskwatawa was as important as Tecumseh in the early movement for Indian unification in the northwest.

————. *Tecumseh and the Quest for Indian Leadership*. Boston: Little, Brown and Co., 1984. Excellent biography that emphasizes Tecumseh's failure to bring about Indian unity.

Eisenhower, John S. D. *Agent of Destiny: The Life and Times of General Winfield Scott*. New York: Free Press, 1997. Important study of Scott's role in national expansion.

Erney, Richard Alton. *The Public Life of Henry Dearborn*. New York: Arno Press, 1979. Straightforward account of Dearborn's career as secretary of war under Jefferson and his role as a general during the War of 1812.

Ewing, Frank E. *America's Forgotten Statesman, Albert Gallatin*. New York: Vantage Press, 1959. Straightforward biography that focuses on Gallatin's public life.

Footner, Hulbert. *Sailor of Fortune: The Life and Adventures of Commodore Barney, U.S.N.* New York: Harper, 1940. Best biography of Barney that successfully weaves his life into the politics and societies of his time.

Govan, Thomas Payne. *Nicholas Biddle, Nationalist and Public Banker, 1786–1844.* Chicago: University of Chicago Press, 1959. Contains short chapter on Biddle's activities during the war and his concerns with wartime finance.

Haeger, John D. *John Jacob Astor: Business and Finance in the Early Republic*. Detroit: Wayne State University Press, 1991. While using Astor's life as the framework, the author explains the importance of entrepreneurship in the early life of the nation.

Hatcher, William B. *Edward Livingston: Jeffersonian Republican and Jacksonian Democrat*. Baton Rouge: Louisiana State University Press, 1940. Informative chapter on Livingston's activities during the war, especially his role as advisor and confidant to Andrew Jackson during the New Orleans campaign.

Hatfield, Joseph T. *William Claiborne: Jeffersonian Centurion in the American Southwest*. Lafayette: University of Southwestern Louisiana, 1976. Standard biography of Louisiana's governor.

Horsman, Reginald. *Matthew Elliott: British Indian Agent*. Detroit: Wayne State University Press, 1964. A biography of Elliott that emphasizes Elliott's role in carrying out British Indian policy with Indians across the border in the United States.

Irvin, Ray W. *David D. Tompkins: Governor of New York and Vice President of the United States*. New York: New-York Historical Society, 1968. Contains strong section on Tompkins' term as governor of New York during the war.

Jacobs, James R. *Tarnished Warrior: Major-General James Wilkinson*. New York: Macmillan, 1938. Looks primarily at Wilkinson's career before the War of 1812.

James, Marquis. *The Raven: A Biography of Sam Houston*. Indianapolis: Bobbs-Merrill, 1953. Excellent biography of Houston that spends a considerable amount of time on his life on the frontier.

Johnson, Timothy D. _Winfield Scott: The Quest for Military Glory_. Lawrence: University Press of Kansas, 1998. The best analysis of Scott's military career with especially good treatment of Scott's early career during the War of 1812.

Ketcham, Ralph. _James Madison: A Biography_. Charlottesville: University Press of Virginia, 1971; reprint edition, 1992. Very positive biography that defends Madison's failures as a war president.

Knopf, Richard C. _Return Johnathan Meigs and the War of 1812_. Columbus, OH: Anthony Wayne Board, 1957. Focuses on Meigs' very active term as governor of Ohio.

Lewis, Charles L. _The Romantic Decatur_. Philadelphia: University of Pennsylvania Press, 1937. About one-third of the book details Decatur's activities during the war.

Long, David F. _Nothing Too Daring: A Biography of Commodore David Porter, 1780–1843_. Annapolis, MD: Naval Institute Press, 1970. Detailed sections on Porter's worldwide activities during the war.

Long, David F. _Sailor-Diplomat: A Biography of Commodore James Biddle, 1783–1848_. Boston: Northeastern University Press, 1983. Balanced look at Biddle's strengths and weaknesses as a commander and diplomat that also provides an informed look at the early nineteenth-century navy.

Madsen, Axel. _John Jacob Astor: America's First Multimillionaire_. New York: John Wiley and Sons, 2001. Excellent biography that successfully interweaves Astor's life with the monumental changes taking place in early nineteenth-century America.

Malone, Dumas. _Jefferson and His Time: The Sage of Monticello_. Boston: Little, Brown and Co., 1981. Laudatory, but by far the most comprehensive biography of Jefferson.

Maloney, Linda M. _The Captain from Connecticut: The Life and Naval Times of Isaac Hull_. Boston: Northeastern University Press, 1986. Comprehensive biography that contains detailed information on Hull's wartime activities.

Mayo, Bernard. _Henry Clay: Spokesman for the New West_. Boston: Houghton Mifflin, 1937. Comprehensive look at Clay's role in bringing about America's declaration of war.

McCaughey, Robert A. _Josiah Quincy, 1772–1864: The Last Federalist_. Cambridge: Harvard University Press, 1974. Insightful two chapters on Quincy's opposition to the war in Congress and at home in Massachusetts.

Meyer, Leland W. _Life and Times of Colonel Richard M. Johnson of Kentucky_. New York: Columbia University Press, 1932. Looks at Johnson's entire career with interesting section on his wartime activities.

Morison, Samuel Eliot. _The Life and Letters of Harrison Gray Otis, Federalist, 1765–1848_. 2 vols. Boston: Houghton Mifflin, 1913. Comprehensive look at Otis's long career with selected primary documents.

Morris, John D. *Sword of the Border: Major General Jacob Jennings Brown, 1775–1828*. Kent, OH: Kent State University Press, 2000. Best though not uncritical biography of one of the most important figures of the war and the most powerful general afterward.

Nagel, Paul C. *John Quincy Adams: A Public Life, A Private Life*. New York: Alfred A. Knopf, 1997. Very important biography that looks at Adams' personality as well as his monumental accomplishments.

Norton, Louis Arthur. *Joshua Barney: Hero of the Revolution and 1812*. Annapolis, MD: Naval Institute Press, 2000. Important biography of one of the few capable officers involved in the defense of Washington.

Pack, A. James. *The Man Who Burned the White House: Admiral Sir George Cockburn, 1772–1853*. Emsworth, UK: Mason, 1987. Provides detail on Cockburn's activities in the Chesapeake with an emphasis on the campaigns of the summer of 1814.

Pancake, John S. *Samuel Smith and the Politics of Business: 1752–1839*. Tuscaloosa: University of Alabama Press, 1972. Short biography, but contains details on Smith's political and military activities during the war.

Parton, James. *Life of Andrew Jackson*. 3 vols. New York: Mason Brothers, 1860. Old, but very well-researched biography that makes use of personal interviews with people who knew Old Hickory.

Pound, Merritt B. *Benjamin Hawkins: Indian Agent*. Athens: University of Georgia Press, 1951. Very positive biography of Hawkins with an emphasis on his life as U.S. agent to the Creek Indians.

Remini, Robert V. *Andrew Jackson and the Course of American Empire*. New York: Harper and Row, 1981. Laudatory, standard biography of Jackson from his early life through his military career.

Shalhope, Robert F. *John Taylor of Caroline: Pastoral Republican*. Columbia: University of South Carolina, 1980. An examination of Taylor's life with an emphasis on his political philosophy.

Silver, James W. *Edmund Pendleton Gaines: Frontier General*. Baton Rouge: Louisiana State University Press, 1949. Emphasizes Gaines' post–War of 1812 career, but contains valuable information on his wartime experiences.

Siry, Steven E. *DeWitt Clinton and the American Political Economy*. New York: Peter Lang, 1990. Examination of Clinton's entire career, including section on his actions as war mayor of New York City.

Skeen, C. Edward. *John Armstrong, Jr., 1758–1843: A Biography*. Syracuse, NY: Syracuse University Press, 1981. Analyzes Armstrong's failures as secretary of war during the War of 1812 as occurring not for lack of effort or good intentions but because he had too many problems to overcome in too short a time period.

Smith, Elbert B. *Magnificent Missourian: The Life of Thomas Hart Benton*. Philadelphia: J. B. Lippincott, 1958. Good comprehensive biography of Benton.

Smith, Gene A. *Thomas ap Catesby Jones: Commodore of Manifest Destiny*. Annapolis, MD: Naval Institute Press, 2000. Comprehensive biography of sailor who tried to defend Lake Borgne at New Orleans.

Stevens, William O. *An Affair of Honor: The Biography of Commodore James Barron, U.S.N.* Norfolk: Norfolk County Historical Society of Chesapeake, Virginia, in cooperation with the Earl Gregg Swem Library of the College of William and Mary, 1969. A solid study of this controversial and occasionally maligned naval officer.

Sugden, John. *Tecumseh, A Life*. New York: Henry Holt and Company, 1997. The definitive, best researched biography of Tecumseh.

Van Deusen, Glyndon G. *The Life of Henry Clay*. Boston: Little, Brown, 1937. A standard biography from one of the twentieth century's great American historians.

Vipperman, Carl J. *William Lowndes and the Transition of Southern Politics, 1782–1822*. Chapel Hill: University of North Carolina Press, 1989. A detailed look at the political maneuverings in the Early Republic.

Walters, James Raymond, Jr. *Alexander James Dallas: Lawyer, Politician, Financier, 1759–1817*. New York: Da Capo Press, 1969. Contains good section on Dallas's career as Madison's secretary of the Treasury.

Wiltse, Charles M. *John C. Calhoun: Nationalist, 1782–1828*. Indianapolis: Bobbs-Merrill, 1944. First part of multivolume work that emphasizes Calhoun's early political career.

Military Histories

Antal, Sandy. *A Wampum Denied: Procter's War of 1812*. Ottawa: Carleton University Press, 1997. Excellent, revisionist view of Henry Procter's military career during the war that demonstrates that he was largely a talented, successful officer.

Babcock, Louis L. *The War of 1812 on the Niagara Frontier*. Buffalo: Buffalo Historical Society, 1927. Details how the outnumbered British were able to repel American offensives because the British military leadership was allowed to fight the war without interference. Also contains primary documents from the war on the Niagara.

Barbuto, Richard V. *Niagara 1814: America Invades Canada*. Lawrence: University Press of Kansas, 2000. The best overview and analysis of this often overlooked but extremely important theater of the war.

Benn, Carl. *The Battle of York*. Belleville, Ontario: Mika Publishing, 1984. Short analysis with excellent illustrations and maps of the battle.

Berton, Pierre. *Flames Across the Border: The Canadian-American Tragedy, 1813–1814*. Boston: Little, Brown and Co., 1981. Berton believes that the American attack on York and subsequent fighting in Canada through 1814 forged a Canadian national identity.

———. *The Invasion of Canada, 1812–1813*. Boston: Little, Brown and Co., 1980. Berton believes that British preparations and Indian ties and American incompetence saved Upper Canada in the early months of the war.

Bird, Harrison. *War for the West, 1790–1813*. New York: Oxford University Press, 1971. A look at the American military's efforts to gain control of the Northwest from Harmar's expedition in 1790 through Harrison's defeat of the British and Tecumseh at the Battle of the Thames.

Bowler, Arthur, ed. *War Along the Niagara: Essays on the War of 1812 and Its Legacy*. Youngstown, NY: Old Fort Niagara Association, 1991. Useful essays on a variety of military topics about the Niagara frontier.

Brown, Wilburt S. *The Amphibious Campaign for West Florida and Louisiana, 1814–1815: A Critical Review of Strategy and Tactics at New Orleans*. Tuscaloosa: University of Alabama Press, 1969. Brown asserts that the British had all of the advantages going into the campaign and that Jackson and his men were largely responsible for their victory over the British.

Chartrand, René. *Uniforms and Equipment of the United States Forces in the War of 1812*. Youngstown, NY: Old Fort Niagara Association, 1992. Abundantly illustrated work that provides tremendous detail on uniforms and equipment of all American servicemen in the war.

Chartrand, René, and Gerry Embleton. *British Forces in North America, 1793–1815*. London: Osprey Publishing, 1998. Brief look with illustrations at uniforms and equipment of British soldiers during the war.

Coles, Harry L. *The War of 1812*. Chicago: University of Chicago Press, 1965. Although it contains some errors, particularly on the southern campaigns, it is still a good overview of the military events of the war.

Crackel, Theodore J. *Mr. Jefferson's Army: Political and Social Reform of the Military Establishment, 1801–1809*. New York: New York University Press, 1987. Excellent study of the impact of politics on the officer corps of the army in the Early Republic.

Elting, John R. *Amateurs to Arms! A Military History of the War of 1812*. Chapel Hill: Workman Publishing Company, 1991. Straightforward, though not terribly original, narrative of American problems in prosecuting a war for which it was not prepared.

Everest, Allan S. *The War of 1812 in the Champlain Valley*. Syracuse, NY: Syracuse University Press, 1981. Excellent look at the entire war effort along this traditional invasion route.

George, Christopher T. *Terror on the Chesapeake: The War of 1812 on the Bay*.

Shippensburg, PA: White Mane Publishing Company, 2000. An exciting overview focusing on Admiral Cockburn's destruction of bay towns that culminates in the repulse of the British at Baltimore.

Gilpin, Alec R. *General William Hull and the War on the Detroit in 1812*. Ann Arbor: University of Michigan, 1949. Attempts to spread the blame for the U.S. loss of Detroit between Hull, the militia, and a lack of direction from the Madison administration.

———. *The War of 1812 in the Old Northwest*. East Lansing: Michigan State University Press, 1958. A military account of the fight for control of the Northwest that holds that the results of the campaigns there destroyed Indian power and created a more settled situation on the U.S.–Canadian border.

Graves, Donald E. *Field of Glory: The Battle of Crysler's Field, 1813*. Toronto: Robin Brass Studio, 1999. Author sees this battle as the reason for the replacement of some of the army's top leadership.

———. *Red Coats & Grey Jackets: The Battle of Chippawa, 5 July 1814*. Toronto: Dundurn Press, 1994. Excellent account with excellent maps of this important battle on the Niagara frontier.

———. *Where Right and Glory Lead! The Battle of Lundy's Lane, 1814*. Toronto: Robin Brass Studio, 1997. Lively and easily understood analysis of the battle.

Gray, William Melville. *Soldiers of the King: The Upper Canadian Militia, 1812–1815*. Erin, Ontario: Boston Mills Press, 1995. Author attempts to demonstrate that Canadian militia played a decisive role in the war.

Hitsman, J. Mackay. *The Incredible War of 1812: A Military History*. Updated by Donald E. Graves. Toronto: University of Toronto Press 1972; reprint edition, Toronto: Robin Brass Studio, 1999. A Canadian view of the war that deals primarily with the combat on the U.S.–Canadian border.

Lord, Walter. *The Dawn's Early Light*. New York: W. W. Norton, 1972. Excellent narrative of the British Chesapeake campaign in the summer of 1814.

Lossing, Benson J. *Pictorial Field Book of the War of 1812*. New York: Harper, 1868; reprint edition, Temecula, California: Reprint Services Corporation, 2000. Provides illustrations, maps, and documents from the war.

Mahon, John K. *The War of 1812*. Gainesville: University Presses of Florida, 1972. Straightforward analysis of the lack of coordination and misuse of militia in the military campaigns of the War of 1812.

Muller, Charles G. *The Darkest Day: 1814, the Washington-Baltimore Campaign*. Philadelphia: Lippincott, 1963. Covers primarily the battle of Bladensburg and the subsequent burning of the public buildings in Washington.

Nelson, Larry L. *Men of Patriotism, Courage, and Enterprise: Fort Meigs in the War of 1812*. Canton, OH: Daring Books, 1986; reprint edition, Bowie, MD:

Heritage Books, 1998. An excellent account of the sieges of Fort Meigs in the spring and summer of 1813.

Owsley, Frank Lawrence, Jr. *Struggle for the Gulf Borderlands: The Creek War and the Battle of New Orleans, 1812–1815.* Gainesville: University Presses of Florida, 1981. Well-researched, straightforward account of the military events of the Creek War and its relationship to the New Orleans campaign.

Patrick, Rembert W. *Florida Fiasco: Rampant Rebels on the Georgia-Florida Border, 1810–1815.* Athens: University of Georgia Press, 1954. A fairly comprehensive study of the international relations concerning Florida and the so-called Patriots' War of 1812.

Pitch, Anthony S. *The Burning of Washington: The British Invasion of 1814.* Annapolis, MD: Naval Institute Press, 1998. Exhaustive account of Washington campaign.

Quimby, Robert S. *The U. S. Army in the War of 1812: An Operational and Command Study.* 2 vols. East Lansing: Michigan State University Press, 1997. An extremely detailed account and analysis of successes and failures of the U.S. Army during the war with an emphasis on a few representative campaigns.

Reilly, Robin. *The British at the Gates: The New Orleans Campaign.* New York: G. P. Putnam's Sons, 1974. Reilly sees the results of the battle as the beginning of a better relationship between the United States and Great Britain.

Remini, Robert V. *The Battle of New Orleans.* New York: Viking, 1999. Not terribly original account of the battle that sees this action as one of the most important in U.S. history.

Skaggs, David Curtis, and Larry L. Nelson. *The Sixty Years' War for the Great Lakes, 1754–1814.* East Lansing: Michigan State University Press, 2001. Collection of conference presentations that covers the international struggle for control of the Great Lakes from the French and Indian War through the War of 1812.

Skeen, C. Edward. *Citizen Soldiers in the War of 1812.* Lexington: University Press of Kentucky, 1999. Very well-researched study of the effectiveness and lack thereof of militias during the war and the reasons for the problems.

Skelton, William B. *An American Profession of Arms: The Army Officer Corps, 1784–1861.* Lawrence: University Press of Kansas, 1993. Contains excellent analysis of the impact of the war on the development of the officer corps.

Stanley, George F. G. *The War of 1812: Land Operations.* Canadian War Museum Historical Publication 18. Toronto: Macmillan, 1983. Written primarily from Canadian point of view giving a good amount of detail on actions along the Canadian–U.S. border.

Sutherland, Stuart. *His Majesty's Gentlemen: A Directory of British Regular Army Officers of the War of 1812.* Toronto: Iser Publications, 2000. Biographies of British officers in Canada with interpretive essays by the author on the British army officers in the war.

Turner, Wesley B. *British Generals in the War of 1812: High Command in the Canadas*. Montreal: McGill-Queens University Press, 1999. Analysis of military competence of Isaac Brock, George Prevost, Roger Hale Sheaffe, Francis de Rottenburg, and Gordon Drummond.

Whitehorne, Joseph A., and Carleton Jones. *The Battle for Baltimore: 1814*. Baltimore: The Nautical and Aviation Publishing Company of America, 1993. Well-researched argument that the British never viewed the Chesapeake as an important theater of the war.

Whitehorne, Joseph A. *While Washington Burned: The Battle for Fort Erie, 1814*. Baltimore: The Nautical and Aviation Publishing Company of America, 1992. Good narrative of the American efforts during the summer of 1814 to hold Fort Erie with interesting analysis of archaeology done at the fort.

Wilder, Patrick. *The Battle of Sacket's Harbor*. Baltimore: Nautical and Aviation Book Company, 1994. Very well-researched look at this pivotal battle for control of part of Lake Ontario.

Zaslow, Morris, ed. *The Defended Border. Upper Canada and the War of 1812*. Toronto: Macmillan, 1964. A collection of twenty-six essays on many of the military aspects of the war on the U.S.–Canadian border.

Naval Histories

Altoff, Gerard T. *Deep Water Sailors, Shallow Water Soldiers: Manning the United States Fleet on Lake Erie, 1813*. Put-in-Bay, OH: Perry Group, 1993. Description of the men who served under Perry in the Battle of Lake Erie.

Crisman, Kevin James. *The Eagle, An American Brig on Lake Champlain during the War of 1812*. Annapolis, MD: Naval Institute Press, 1987. An examination of the actions of the *Eagle* during the Battle of Plattsburgh.

DeKay, James Tertius. *The Battle of Stonington: Torpedoes, Submarines, and Rockets in the War of 1812*. Annapolis, MD: Naval Institute Press, 1990. Only book-length study of inspiring story of American resistance to the British on the New England coast.

Dudley, William S., ed. *The Naval War of 1812; A Documentary History*. 2 vols. Washington, D.C.: Department of the Navy, 1985–1992. Excellent collection of primary sources that is projected to be four volumes when completed.

Dudley, William S. *The Navy Department in the War of 1812*. Gainesville: University Presses of Florida, 1973. Interesting look at government bureaucracy and its impact on a combat arm.

Duffy, Stephen W. H. *Captain Blakeley and the* Wasp: *The Cruise of 1814*. Annapolis, MD: Naval Institute Press, 2000. Well-written account of the *Wasp's* incredible success and mysterious disappearance.

Dye, Ira. *The Fatal Cruise of the* Argus: *Two Captains in the War of 1812*. Annapolis, MD: Naval Institute Press, 1994. A dual biography of American William Henry Allen and British captain John Fordyce Maples and the naval events that brought them together in the War of 1812.

Forester, C. S. *The Age of Fighting Sail: The Story of the Naval War of 1812*. Garden City, NY: Doubleday, 1956. Exciting narrative of how the infant U.S. Navy dealt with the most powerful navy in the world.

Fowler, William M., Jr. *Jack Tars & Commodores: The American Navy, 1783–1815*. Boston: Houghton Mifflin, 1984. Good overview of the developing American navy.

Gardner, Robert, editor. *The Naval War of 1812*. Annapolis, MD: Naval Institute Press, 1999. Provides interesting revisions very much slanted to the British side.

Kert, Faye Margaret. *Prize and Prejudice: Privateering and Naval Prizes in Atlantic Canada in the War of 1812*. St. Johns, Newfoundland: International Maritime Economic History Association, 1997. Demonstrates that Canadian privateering during the war helped the economy of eastern Canada.

Langley, Harold D. *A History of Medicine in the Early U.S. Navy*. Baltimore: Johns Hopkins University Press, 1995. Traces progress of navy's attempts to modernize medical treatment for seamen.

Mahan, Alfred Thayer. *Sea Power in its Relation to the War of 1812*. 2 vols. Boston: Little, Brown and Co., 1919; reprint ed., Westport, CT: Greenwood Press, 1968. Unromantic view of the inferiority of the U.S. Navy compared to the British Navy during the war.

Malcomson, Robert, and Thomas Malcomson. HMS Detroit: *The Battle of Lake Erie*. Annapolis, MD: Naval Institute Press, 1990. Heavily illustrated, balanced account of the battle that gives good deal of attention to the British side of the battle.

Malcomson, Robert. *Lords of the Lake: The Naval War on Lake Ontario, 1812–1814*. Annapolis, MD: Naval Institute, 1999. Well-researched account of the longest naval struggle of the war.

Martin, Tyrone G. *A Most Fortunate Ship: A Narrative History of Old Ironsides*. Annapolis, MD: Naval Institute Press, 1997. An excellent study by the captain of the vessel during its bicentennial that recounts the history of the ship and the U.S. Navy during the ship's long service.

McKee, Christopher. *A Gentlemanly and Honorable Profession: The Creation of the U.S. Naval Officer Corps, 1794–1815*. Annapolis, MD: Naval Institute Press, 1991. A social history of the early officer corps that focuses on those young officers who would later be the leaders of the mid-nineteenth-century navy.

Muller, Charles G. *The Proudest Day: Macdonough on Lake Champlain*. New York: John Day, 1960. Argues that Macdonough's victory was one of the most important in the war.

Roosevelt, Theodore. *The Naval War of 1812*. New York: G. P. Putnam's Sons, 1882. Still the best overall naval history of the war.

Skaggs, David Curtis, and Gerald T. Altoff. *A Signal Victory: The Lake Erie Campaign, 1812–1813*. Annapolis, MD: Naval Institute Press, 1997. Good overview of British and American preparation for and conduct of the naval campaign that gave the U.S. control of Lake Erie.

Tucker, Spencer C. *Arming the Fleet: U.S. Navy Ordnance in the Muzzle-Loading Era*. Annapolis, MD: Naval Institute Press, 1989. Important sections on naval ordnance during the war.

———. *The Jeffersonian Gunboat Navy*. Columbia: University of South Carolina Press, 1993. An examination of the military value of gunboats in the early nineteenth century that argues that gunboats were useful in the War of 1812.

Welsh, William J., and David C. Skaggs, eds. *War on the Great Lakes: Essays Commemorating the 175th Anniversary of the Battle of Lake Erie*. Kent, OH: Kent State University Press, 1991. An overview and ten essays that examine various aspects of the battle of Lake Erie from the combat to the impact on Native Americans in the region.

Diplomacy

Bemis, Samuel Flagg. *John Quincy Adams and the Foundations of American Foreign Policy*. New York: Alfred A. Knopf, 1969. Contains two very informative chapters on Adams's wartime diplomacy.

Bolkhovitinov, Nikolai N. *The Beginnings of Russian-American Relations, 1775–1815*. Cambridge: Harvard University Press, 1975. Last section analyzes Russia's role in and reasons for bringing about the negotiations that ended the war.

Egan, Clifford L. *Neither Peace nor War: Franco-American Relations, 1803–1812*. Baton Rouge: Louisiana State University Press, 1983. Insightful study of the importance of Franco-American relations in understanding growing tensions between the United States and Great Britain.

Engelman, Fred L. *The Peace of Christmas Eve*. London: Hart-Davis, 1960. A full account of the negotiations in Ghent with special insight into the personalities of the negotiators.

Perkins, Bradford. *Castlereagh and Adams: England and the United States, 1812–1823*. Berkeley: University of California Press, 1964. A focus on these two men in an analysis of U.S.–British diplomacy during the War of 1812 and its aftermath.

Russell, Greg. *John Quincy Adams and the Public Virtue of Diplomacy*. Columbia: University of Missouri Press, 1995. Original analysis of how Adams' personal philosophies shaped his approach to foreign policy.

Native Americans

Allen, Robert S. *His Majesty's Indian Allies: British Indian Policy in the Defence of Canada, 1774–1815*. Toronto and Oxford: Dundurn Press, 1992. Sees Indians as essential for Canadian defense during the war.

Benn, Carl. *The Iroquois in the War of 1812*. Toronto: University of Toronto Press, 1998. Important study that through impeccable research demonstrates the key roles played by the Iroquois on the Niagara frontier.

Braund, Kathryn E. Holland. *Deerskins and Duffels: The Creek Indian Trade with Anglo America, 1685–1815*. Lincoln: University of Nebraska Press, 1993. By far the most compelling study of the impact of European trade on native culture.

Calloway, Colin G. *Crown and Calumet: British-Indian Relations, 1783–1815*. Norman: University of Oklahoma Press, 1987. A laudable attempt to treat the Indian side of British-Indian relations.

Dowd, Gregory Evans. *A Spirited Resistance: The North American Indian Struggle for Unity, 1745–1815*. Baltimore: The Johns Hopkins University Press, 1992. Successfully demonstrates that Native-American spiritualism and the desire for unity were outgrowths of religious leaders' response to American expansion.

Halbert, H. S., and T. H. Ball. *The Creek War of 1813 and 1814*. Chicago: Donohue and Henneberry, 1895; reprint ed., Tuscaloosa: University of Alabama Press, 1995. Standard narrative of the war. Somewhat ahead of its time in that the authors attempted to provide the Indian side of the war.

Green, Michael D. *The Politics of Indian Removal: Creek Government and Society in Crisis*. Lincoln: University of Nebraska Press, 1982. An attempt to explain the impetus for removal in political terms and to analyze the Creek political turmoil that resulted.

Griffith, Benjamin W., Jr. *McIntosh and Weatherford, Creek Indian Leaders*. Tuscaloosa: University of Alabama Press, 1988. Uneven parallel biography of two warriors on opposite sides of the Creek War.

Heidler, David S., and Jeanne T. Heidler. *Old Hickory's War: Andrew Jackson and the Quest for Empire*. Mechanicsburg, PA: Stackpole Books, 1996. Provides background for Jackson's invasion of Florida in 1818 through an examination of the Creek War and its impact on Creek society.

Henri, Florette. *The Southern Indians and Benjamin Hawkins, 1796–1816*. Norman: University of Oklahoma Press, 1986. Admiring treatment of Hawkins' attempts to acculturate Creek society.

Holland, James W. *Andrew Jackson and the Creek War: Victory at the Horseshoe*. Tuscaloosa: University of Alabama Press, 1969. An examination of Jackson's decisive role in the destruction of the Creeks.

Martin, Joel W. *Sacred Revolt: The Muscogees' Struggle for a New World*. Boston: Beacon Press, 1991. Martin interprets the Creek War in almost purely religious terms.

Sugden, John. *Tecumseh's Last Stand*. Norman: University of Oklahoma Press, 1985. Revisionist account of Tecumseh's last campaign that casts Henry Procter in a more favorable light than most previous treatments.

White, Richard. *The Middle Ground: Indians, Empires, and Republics in the Great Lakes Region, 1650–1815*. New York: Cambridge University Press, 1991. White views the place of Indians in the Old Northwest as pivotal to the balance of power in the region.

Wright, J. Leitch, Jr. *Creeks and Seminoles: The Destruction and Regeneration of the Muscogulge People*. Lincoln: University of Nebraska Press, 1986. An ethnographic study that tries to explain the various origins and history of these people.

African Americans

Altoff, Gerard T. *Amongst My Best Men: African-Americans and the War of 1812*. Put-in-Bay, OH: Perry Group, 1996. Argues that by the end of the war, African Americans were an important component of all aspects of the American war effort.

Bolster, W. Jeffrey. *Black Jacks: African American Seamen in the Age of Sail*. Cambridge: Harvard University Press, 1996. Excellent study of the essential importance of African Americans in the merchant and U.S. navies from the mid-eighteenth century through the Civil War.

Foner, Jack D. *Blacks and the Military in American History: A New Perspective*. New York: Praeger, 1974. Revisionist look at the contributions of African Americans to American military developments.

Wilson, Joseph T. *The Black Phalanx: African American Soldiers in the War of Independence, the War of 1812, and the Civil War*. New York: Da Capo Press, 1994. Reprint of the classic 1887 edition that was the first effort to recount important contributions of African Americans to the American military.

Diaries, Letters, Memoirs

Adams, Henry, ed. *The Writings of Albert Gallatin*. 3 vols. Philadelphia: J. B. Lippincott, 1879. Volume 1 contains Gallatin's letters during the war.

Adams, John Quincy. *Memoirs of John Quincy Adams: Comprising Portions of His Diary from 1795 to 1848*. Edited by Worthington Chauncey Ford. 12 vols. Philadelphia: J. B. Lippincott, 1874–1877. Intimate look at Adams's views on the negotiations in Ghent.

Armstrong, John. *Notices of the War of 1812*. New York: Whiley and Putnam, 1840. A collection of documents from the war with which Armstrong tried to settle some of the disputes of the war.

Gleig, G.R. *The Campaigns of the British Army at Washington and New Orleans, in the Years 1814–1815*. London: John Murrary, 1847.

Graves, Donald E. *Merry Hearts Make Light Days: The War of 1812 Journal of Lieutenant John Le Couteur, 104th Foot*. Ottawa, Canada: Carleton University Press, 1993. Enlightening journal of the war on the Niagara frontier from the perspective of a young British officer.

Hopkins, James F., et al., eds. *The Papers of Henry Clay*. 11 vols. Lexington: University of Kentucky Press, 1959–1992. Comprehensive set of papers. Volumes 1 and 2 are most appropriate for this period.

Knopf, Richard C., ed. *Document Transcriptions of the War of 1812 in the Old Northwest*. 10 vols. Columbus: Ohio Historical Society, 1956–1962. Series of documents including military reports from William Henry Harrison, contemporary newspaper accounts, and War Department correspondence.

Latour, Arsène Lacarrière. *Historical Memoir of the War in West Florida and Louisiana in 1814–1815*. Expanded edition edited by Gene A. Smith. 1816; reprint ed., Gainesville: The Historic New Orleans Collection and University Press of Florida, 1999. Valuable memoir from Andrew Jackson's engineer concerning the defenses of New Orleans.

Madison, Dolley. *Memoirs and Letters of Dolley Madison, Wife of James Madison, President of the United States*. Boston: Houghton Mifflin, 1888. Reminiscences and some of Mrs. Madison's personal papers.

Madison, James. *The Papers of James Madison: Presidential Series*. Vol. 3. Edited by J.C.A. Stagg, Jeanne Kerr Cross, and Susan Holbrook Perdue. Charlottesville: University Press of Virginia, 1996. Good collection of Madison's wartime papers.

Martin, Tyrone G., ed. *The USS* Constitution's *Finest Fight, 1815: The Journal of Acting Chaplain Assheton Humpheys, US Navy*. Baltimore: Nautical and Aviation Publishing Company, 2000. Important journal of the *Constitution's* daring run through the Atlantic Ocean in the early months of 1815.

Moser, Harold, et al., eds. *The Papers of Andrew Jackson*. 5 vols. Knoxville: University of Tennessee Press, 1996. Volumes two and three contain Jackson's wartime papers.

Politics during the War

Banner, James M., Jr. *To the Hartford Convention: The Federalists and the Origins of Party Politics in Massachusetts, 1789–1815.* New York: Alfred A. Knopf, 1970. Demonstrates through a history of the Federalists in Massachusetts how that state's party led the movement to meet at Hartford in 1814.

Broussard, James H. *The Southern Federalists, 1800–1816.* Baton Rouge: Louisiana State University Press, 1978. An analysis of the continuing strength and loyalty of southern Federalists through the War of 1812.

Fischer, David Hackett. *The Revolution of American Conservatism: The Federalist Party in the Era of Jeffersonian Democracy.* New York: Harper and Row, 1965. A topical analysis that provides insight into the impact of the war on the Federalists.

Hatzenbuehler, Ronald L. *Congress Declares War: Rhetoric, Leadership, and Partisanship in the Early Republic.* Kent, OH: Kent State University Press, 1983. A detailed examination of the impact of party and individuals on Congress's decision to declare war.

Kerber, Linda K. *Federalists in Dissent: Imagery and Ideology in Jeffersonian America.* Ithaca, NY: Cornell University Press, 1980. An examination of the decline of the Federalist Party.

Smelser, Marshall. *The Democratic Republic, 1801–1815.* New York: Harper and Row, 1968. Comprehensive examination of the period with emphasis on political developments.

Reference Works

Collins, Gilbert. *Guidebook to the Historic Sites of the War of 1812.* Toronto: Dundurn Press, 1998. Comprehensive look at primarily sites of most of the battles of the war.

Fredriksen, John C., comp. *Free Trade and Sailors' Rights: A Bibliography of the War of 1812.* Westport, CT: Greenwood Press, 1985. Comprehensive bibliography of monographs, journal articles, and primary accounts.

Fredriksen, John C. *Officers of the War of 1812 with Portraits and Anecdotes.* Lewiston, NY: Edwin Mellan Press, 1989. Short biographies of many of the officers who served in the war.

———. *War of 1812 Eyewitness Accounts: An Annotated Bibliography.* Westport, CT: Greenwood Press, 1997. Comprehensive examination of firsthand accounts of the war covering military, naval, political, and social aspects of the war.

Heidler, David S., and Jeanne T. Heidler, eds. *Encyclopedia of the War of 1812.* Santa Barbara, CA: ABC-Clio, 1997. The only comprehensive reference source covering the military, political, social, and diplomatic aspects of the war.

Rutland, Robert A., ed. *James Madison and the American Nation, 1751–1836: An Encyclopedia*. New York: Simon and Schuster, 1994. A large part of this encyclopedia deals with the war.

Smith, Dwight L. *The War of 1812: An Annotated Bibliography*. New York: Garland Publishing, 1985. Excellent list of sources arranged by category, including brief descriptions of each source.

Films

1812: The Forgotten War. Oakville, Ontario: Little Brick Schoolhouse, 1995. Ninety-minute examination of the war with reenactments of battles. Excellent for classroom use.

Battles That Changed the World—Battle of New Orleans. St. Laurent, Quebec: Madacy Entertainment Group, 1997. Part of a series that includes good overview and reenactors demonstrating parts of the battle.

Canada: A People's History. Made by Mark Starowicz. Toronto: CBC/Radio Canada, 2000–2002. Epic history of the country. Episode Five covers the War of 1812.

The Final Invasion: The War of 1812 & The Battle of Plattsburgh. Made by Bruce Carlin and David Fitz-Enz. Plattsburgh, NY: Cannonade Filmworks, 1999. Approximately one-hour video that contains interviews with experts, animation of battles, and onsite footage.

War of 1812. Made by Arnie Gelbart. Montreal: Galafilm, 1999. Four-part (sixty minutes each) Canadian documentary done in English and French that covers the entire war.

Web sites

http://www.militaryheritage.com/1812.htm   Largely a commercial site, but contains valuable book reviews, chronology of the war, articles, and battle maps.

http://www.members.tripod.com/~war1812/   Good overviews of major events of the war including such items as uniforms, Native-American involvement and some primary sources.

http://www.multied.com/1812/   Commercial site part of History Central's American Wars series. Contains short descriptions and contemporary battle maps.

http://www.alpha.binatech.on.ca/~bhmchin/   Official site for Battle of Stoney Creek Battlefield House Museum. Contains detailed account of battle with pictures and maps.

http://www.history.navy.mil/wars/war1812/1815list.htm   Official Naval Historical Center site that lists navy and marine officers who served in the war by date of commission.

http://www.hillsdale.edu/dept/History/Documents/War/FR1812.htm   Good collection of primary documents on most of the important events of the war.

http://www.yale.edu/lawweb/avalon/diplomacy/britian/br1814m.htm   Part of Avalon Project of the Yale Law School. Contains diplomatic and political documents related to the war.

http://www.nps.gov/pevi/   National Park Service site on Oliver Hazard Perry's victory on Lake Erie.

http://www.ohiokids.org/ohc/history/h_indian/events/btippeca.htm   Ohio History Central site on battle of Tippecanoe with links to related material.

INDEX

About the Authors

DAVID S. HEIDLER, author of *Pulling the Temple Down: The Fire-eaters and the Destruction of the Union*, lives in Colorado Springs, Colorado.

JEANNE T. HEIDLER is Professor of History at the United States Air Force Academy and, along with her husband David, is co-author/editor of *Old Hickory's War: Andrew Jackson and the Quest for Empire*, *The Encyclopedia of the War of 1812*, and the award-winning *The Encyclopedia of the American Civil War, a Social, Political, and Military History*.